8.00

TEXAS LEGACY FROM THE GULF

A Report on Sixteenth Century
Shipwreck Materials
Recovered from the Texas Tidelands

TEXAS LEGACY FROM THE GULF

A Report on Sixteenth Century
Shipwreck Materials
Recovered from the Texas Tidelands

By Dorris L. Olds

Miscellaneous Papers Number 5, Texas Memorial Museum
Publication Number 2, Texas Antiquities Committee
A Joint Publication, 1976

CONTENTS

PREFACE
ix

HISTORY OF RECOVERY AND DELIVERY TO TARL
1

INVENTORY AND PRESERVATION
8

ARCHEOLOGICAL EVIDENCE FOR DATING THE WRECKAGE
14

NAVIGATIONAL APPARATUS
22

SHIP'S GEAR, FITTINGS, AND EQUIPMENT
43

ARMAMENT AND WEAPONS
62

CARGO
100

SHIPBOARD LIVING
136

SUMMARY
151

APPENDIX – TABLES 1–7
159

BIBLIOGRAPHY
183

ILLUSTRATIONS

1. Treasure ships area, Gulf of Mexico. 2
2. Padre Island coast and location of shipwreck 3
3. ACF of Texas Archeological Research Laboratory 6
4. Processing activities at ACF. .10
5. Processing sequence of encrustation 11
6. Three navigational astrolabes. 16
7. Artist's drawing of astrolabe in use 17
8. Determining latitude by mid-day sun 25
9. Cast brass navigational astrolabe 26
10. Scale drawing, details of calibration 27
11. Astrolabe No. 1449, details .28
12. Cast brass navigational astrolabe 29
13. Scale drawing and calibration details, Astrolabe 1446. .36
14. Calibration marks on Astrolabe No. 1446 37
15. Cast brass navigational astrolabe 38
16. Scale drawing and calibration details, Astrolabe 1448. .39
17. Lead sounding weights 40
18. Rudder gudgeon and pintle 44
19. Heavy copper sleeve bearing .45
20. Anchor fluke fragment 46
21. Largest chain in collection. 47
22. Chains for standing rigging 48
23. Complete chain with ring and pin 49
24. Wrought iron fastenings for the ship 51
25. Assortment of tools. 53
26. Small lead objects 56
27. Portion of lead ingot 57
28. Piece of lead sheathing 59
29. *Bombardeta* No. 1475-1a 64
30. *Bombardeta* No. 1476-1a 65
31. *Bombardeta* No. 1477-1a 66
32. X-ray photographs of *bombardeta* construction 68
33. Artist's drawing of *bombardeta* lashed to stock. 68
34. Wrought iron breechblocks for *bombardetas* 70
35. Necks of hooped-barrel breechblocks 74
36. *Verso* No. 328. 76
37. *Verso* No. 330. 77
38. *Verso* No. 1457-1a 78
39. *Verso* No. 1458-1a 80

40. *Verso* No. 1611 82
41. Beer stein-shaped breechblocks 84
42. Projectiles 85
43. Small hunting crossbows 90
44. Crossbow No. 1510 .92, 93
45. X-ray photograph of trigger section, Crossbow 1510 . . .94
46. Crossbow and cocking device, goat's foot lever 97
47. Fragment of sword or knife blade 99
48. Fragments of brass chain mail 101
49. Sampling of treasure cargo 104, 105
50. Carlos and Johanna silver coin 107
51. Santo Domingo 4-reales coin 108
52. Hand hammering dies (Nesmith) 110
53. Mint during Maximilian I reign (Weisskunig) 111
54. Examples of Early Series C&J silver coins 112
55. Examples of Early Series C&J silver coins 113
56. Examples of Early Series C&J silver coins 114
57. Examples of Early Series C&J silver coins 115
58. Examples of Late Series C&J silver coins 116
59. Examples of Late Series C&J silver coins 116
60. Examples of Late Series C&J silver coins 117
61. Early Series 4-*maravedíes* copper coin 117
62. Gold ingot 120
63. Silver disks 122
64. Drawings of stamped marks on silver disks 124
65. Drawings of stamped marks on silver disks 126
66. Stamped marks on Silver Disk No. 1417 135
67. Early Style Olive Jar (Goggin) 137
68. Mouth details of jars (Goggin) 138
69. Sketch of rim sherd 139
70. Partially reconstructed rim fragment 140
71. Two pewter plates 141
72. Encrusted serving spoon bowl 143
73. Cylinders identified as candle prickets 144
74. Gold crucifix 145
75. Small silver thimble 147
76. Miscellaneous materials .149

PREFACE

Preparation of this report has been made possible by the contributions of many people to whom I am deeply indebted. Of primary importance has been the encouragement and support given by Dr. Dee Ann Story, Executive-Director of the Texas Archeological Research Laboratory (TARL), and the teamwork and cooperation provided by the staff of TARL's Antiquities Conservation Facility. All have brought their special talents, insights, good sense, and enthusiasm to help solve the various problems that have been encountered. What one person might not understand, two or three together sometimes could figure out. My particular thanks go to Dr. D. L. Hamilton, Conservator of the Antiquities Facility, who generously and brilliantly assisted with much of the artifact analysis and supervised the many details of putting the final product together. He analyzed the weapons and armament, determining what they were made of and how they were constructed. Charles Locke drafted the line and scale drawings, and Pauline Zocller assembled the plates for the figures. Peter Farmer made most of the photographs. Dr. Story and Dr. W. W. Newcomb read several sections of the report, offering valuable suggestions, and in addition to his other major contributions, Dr. Hamilton painstakingly went over the entire manuscript. I am grateful to them all. Responsibility for any errors in description and interpretation, though, are mine alone.

My sincere thanks go to Richard Belding, who translated an entire chapter of Vigon's Spanish language treatise on Spanish artillery, and Dr. Earl Ingerson, who provided information on the sixteenth century mines of New Spain. Clyde Hubbard, noted numismatist, and Dr. Henry Grunthal of the American Numismatic Society were most helpful on coins and silver, and Mr. and Mrs. Roderick Webster of the Adler Planetarium contributed their knowledge of astrolabes. Sr. Antonio Barrios Pavia of Madrid supplied copies of cannon illustrations from the Museo de Ejército in Madrid.

It is a pleasure to acknowledge the kindness of publishers who allowed us to reproduce illustrations from the following sources:

1) Fig. 25, G, from *The Lore of Ships,* by Tre Tryckare. Holt, Rinehart, & Winston, Inc., 1963.

2) Fig. 52, from *The Coinage of the First Mint of the Americas at Mexico City 1536-1572,* by Robert I. Nesmith. The American Numismatic Society, Numismatic Notes and Monographs 131, 1955.

3) Fig. 53, The Austrian National Library (Osterreis-chische Nationalbibliothec), Vienna, Austria.

4) Figs. 67 and 68 (lower), from "The Spanish Olive Jar," *Spanish Selected Writings,* by John M. Goggin. University of Miami Press, 1964.

Finally, I extend my sincere thanks to the editors, Curtis D. Tunnell and Willena C. Adams, whose hard work and experienced skill have put the report in readable form.

Dorris L. Olds
Texas Memorial Museum
Texas Archeological Research Laboratory

HISTORY OF RECOVERY AND DELIVERY TO TARL

A favorite pastime of vacationers, beachcombers, and treasure hunters exploring along the Texas Gulf coast shores is the exciting search for old Spanish coins and other relics of shipwrecks or even of pirate activities, that might be discovered on Padre and Mustang Islands. Often the search is rewarded, for a number of ships have been sunk in the Gulf during the past four and a half centuries, and many objects from the wrecks have washed up on the shore. Also, hurricanes have exposed artifacts that were long hidden in the dunes. Hurricane Carla, which hit Padre Island with tremendous force in September, 1961, changed the configuration of the beaches, tore down dunes, and uncovered numerous treasures (Mahan 1967), to the everlasting delight of searchers.

The largest and most destructive treasure hunting enterprise was carried out by a group from Gary, Indiana, between September and December, 1967. Organized under the name Platoro, Ltd., Inc., they began recovery of sunken wreckage located in about 20 feet of water north of the Mansfield Cut near Port Mansfield, Texas (Figs. 1, 2). The collection was first identified and reported in press accounts as Spanish ship wreckage from a 1553 silver fleet, but underwater excavations conducted in 1972 and 1973 by the Texas Antiquities Committee (TAC), and extensive research in the Spanish Archives may prove the wreckage came from a 1554 fleet disaster. In any case, whichever year can be documented as accurate, this is probably the earliest such material ever recovered from the waters of the Western Hemisphere. The Platoro crew continued diving and recovery operations, interrupted only by Hurricane Beulah in October, 1967, until a temporary court order issued December 13, 1968 by Judge Paul Martineau of the Twenty-eighth Judicial District Court, Kenedy County, Texas, enjoined the corporation from further activity at the site. Texas citizens had raised the question of ownership of the "Spanish Galleon Treasure" since it had been recovered from state tidelands.

Meanwhile, the collection had been removed by Platoro to Gary, Indiana, where processing of the artifacts was begun. Arrangements were made between the Texas Land Commissioner, Jerry Sadler, and Platoro, that pending the court's decision concerning ownership, the collection was to be given into the custody of Sadler's office in Austin, Texas. Sadler's published report on the affair, *Treasure Tempest in Texas* (1967: 15) says that part of the collection was de-

1

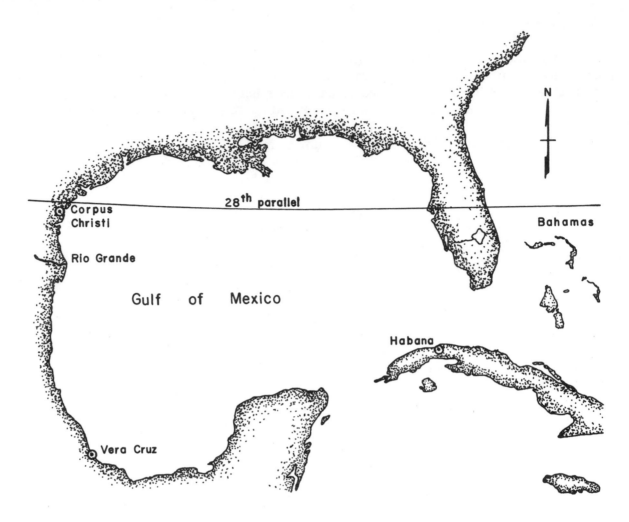

N

28th parallel

Corpus
Christi

Rio Grande

Gulf   of   Mexico

Bahamas

Habana

Vera Cruz

Fig. 1.—The Gulf of Mexico. Treasure ships left New Spain from the Port of Vera Cruz, sailed north along the Gulf coast to about the twenty-eighth parallel, then turned east and put into Havana for a stopover before crossing the Atlantic to Seville.

livered to his office in December, 1968 and another part in June, 1969. The court, in the interim, had appointed a special committee to make an inventory of the collection for the state, giving it authority to preserve the objects under its jurisdiction. The committee consisted of Joe M. Kilgore, Don Cavness, and W. W. Newcomb, all of Austin.

In August, 1969 the State Archeologist, Curtis Tunnell, and two members of the Department of Public Safety, traveled to Gary and brought back to Austin the third portion of the collection, placing it in the care of committee member Dr. Newcomb, Director of the Texas Memorial Museum.

A State Antiquities Code, passed earlier by the Texas Legislature, went into effect in September, 1969. The code provided for the creation of an antiquities committee which, among other duties, would control and supervise the salvage or excavation of prehistoric and historic sites and artifacts from state lands, including pre-twentieth century shipwrecks found on the tidelands. Although an antiquities code had been proposed for some time, its passage at this time was directly related to the controversy surrounding Platoro, Ltd., Inc. vs. the State of Texas.

Following the recommendation of the Inventory Committee, Judge Martineau, on September 24, 1969, directed that the collection be placed in the temporary custody of the Texas Archcological Research Laboratory (known as TARL) at Balcones Research Center, The University of Texas at Austin. The mandate stated that the laboratory was thereby:

authorized, empowered, and directed to do all things necessary to restore and process all artifacts which may require treatment and said Research Laboratory is further authorized and empowered to fully study, describe, photograph and analyze all said artifacts with a view to a full preservation of all the data which may be accumulated as concerns such artifacts.

On October 14, 1969 part of the collection, mainly small objects of gold and silver, was delivered to TARL. Except for a quantity of ballast stones left at the Texas Memorial Museum for storage (later delivered to TARL) the remainder of the collection was taken to the laboratory on October 15. Upon receipt, the more valuable items were immediately placed in a secure vault, and materials requiring immersion for their preservation were placed in a special corrosion-inhibiting solution in large wooden vats and other watertight containers. The ballast stones and other stable remains were stored on open shelves. Debris saved from Platoro's earlier processing was left in the metal containers in which it was delivered.

A small separate collection was delivered to the laboratory in March, 1972. These materials had been recovered by the Institute for Underwater Research (IUR), a non-profit organization located at Southern Methodist University, Dallas. It conducted a survey of a portion of the Texas Gulf coast during the summer of 1971 and brought up a few arti-

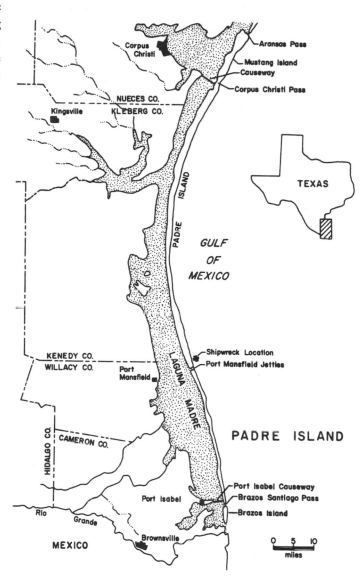

Fig. 2.—Padre Island and the southern tip of Texas along the Gulf coast. Location of the shipwreck is approximate. Hatchured rectangle on small insert at right indicates the area of Texas shown on the larger map section.

facts from one of the wreck sites. Most of the specimens from the IUR had been stored since recovery at the office of the Texas Historical Survey Committee (now called the Texas Historical Commission) in Austin, although a few of the artifacts were sent to SMU for cleaning and processing by their archeological laboratories. The 1971 collection made by the institute was probably from the site excavated by the Antiquities Committee in 1972 and 1973. This site is designated 41 KN 10 UW in TARL files. All materials from this site will be described in a forthcoming TAC report on underwater investigations along the Gulf Coast.

When the antiquities recovered by Platoro were first received, TARL had no precise information on where the wreck site was located, so specimens were catalogued using 41 Ti 1, indicating Tidelands Site No. 1, and an inventory was begun immediately. The Texas Antiquities Committee has now located three wreck sites, probably from a single fleet, and, based on documents recently studied in Spanish archives, believes that the wreckage worked by Platoro was from the *Santa Maria de Iciar* (or *Yciar*). This shipwreck site, recorded in TARL's files as 41 WY 3 UW, has been located off the shore of Willacy County.

The recovered portion of the ship's cargo appears to have been composed of silver coins from the Mexico City mint and silver bullion in the shape of crude disks that range from a few inches to nearly two feet in diameter. A single gold ingot is all that remains of whatever gold bullion was aboard. Ship's fittings, equipment and gear, navigational instruments and aids, weapons and armament, items necessary for ordinary living aboard ship, and a few personal belongings make up the bulk of the assemblage. Assignment of artifacts to these categories was necessarily arbitrary, and it is recognized that some specimens might well have been put in other classes. Aside from the cargo, most of the artifacts are of metal, largely iron, but other materials include wood, bone, ceramics, stone, hemp cordage and rope, five tiny scraps of cloth, and a few examples of natural organic materials. A detailed inventory and description of the antiquities recovered by Platoro will be discussed in subsequent chapters, and data on individual spikes, nails, pins, small lead objects, breechblocks and breech wedges for guns, ammunition, and pieces of silver bullion are given in tabular form.

When the antiquities recovered by Platoro were delivered to TARL it became obvious immediately that to house them adequately, safeguard, and process them, one of the first requirements would be space. Along with that primary need would be specialized equipment and a number of supplies, especially chemical and photographic. In January, 1970 the University of Texas Board of Regents was asked for funds to build and equip a suitable facility. The funds were granted and construction of a building began in the summer of 1971. This building, called the Antiquities Conservation Facility of TARL, was completed and in operation by October.

Equipping the laboratory included installation of a de-ionized water supply for use in processing, and facilities for compressed air, gas, and electricity. Numerous power sources were required for electrolytic cleaning as well as fume hoods necessary for removing caustic vapors resulting from the cleaning process. A safety shower in case of chemical accident was obligatory. A well equipped darkroom and studio had to be provided. Power tools, scales, stoves, chains, fork lift, hoist, vats, microscope, typewriter, and many other pieces of apparatus were needed. Additional funds for such materials were furnished by the University Office of Organized Research, and funds for laboratory assistants and expendable supplies were provided by TAC, with supplementary assistance by the Texas Memorial Museum and the State Archeologist's office.

But monetary backing was not the only help TARL received from the university. It called upon the university's extensive resources for advice in planning and equipping the new facility and in setting up equipment and procedures for processing the collection. This support came from members of the faculty and staff of a number of departments and laboratories, who freely and enthusiastically gave of their expert knowledge and experience. Contacts with specialists from all over the United States and Europe brought invaluable assistance. We especially acknowledge with deep gratitude the advice and guidance provided by Worth Carlin of PPG Industries, Corpus Christi, Texas, in working out modern procedures in electrolytic cleaning. His wide knowledge and expertise in electrochemistry enabled laboratory personnel to make important advances in this technique, contributing immeasurably to the success of the project.

During the first year of operations the Texas Highway Department loaned TARL the services of its radiographic technician, the late Don Wood, who, as his time permitted, made radiographs of some of the large encrusted objects. Later, use was made of a large industrial X-ray machine already installed at the Balcones Research Center.

The collection has been kept under adequate security conditions at all times, thanks largely to the Balcones Research

Fig. 3.—The Antiquities Conservation Facility of the Texas Archeological Research Laboratory. Exterior of building from northwest (top). Views of the interior (lower), showing work areas and some of the equipment for processing.

Center Administration, although provision has not yet been made for ideal controlled temperature and humidity conditions needed for long-term safety. The collection's permanent housing should make provision for continuous observation of the specimens, particularly in the case of ferrous and cuprous objects. Evidences of beginning corrosion should be treated immediately if the collection is to be preserved for future generations.

Because the Platoro group's goal was the recovery of treasure, the range of materials probably is biased in favor of what might prove to be monetarily valuable. Apparently little or no effort was made to map the site or record information that would preserve the orientation, association, or location of the various objects before they were disturbed. Hence, much priceless information has been lost forever, reducing the historic and scientific value of this distinctive assemblage. With only a few pages of Platoro's dive records accompanying the collection, there is no certainty of the number of wrecks actually involved in its operations, although, for the sake of simplicity, this report will refer to the antiquities recovered as one unit.

INVENTORY AND PRESERVATION

As a first step in carrying out the directive from Judge Martineau, TARL made a complete inventory of the collection. This included a preliminary identification of each item, if possible, although, often, objects could be recorded only as amorphous encrustations that might or might not contain embedded artifacts. Most metal articles that have been immersed for a long period in sea water accumulate a coating of concrete-like calcium carbonate made up of sand, shell, coral, and other substances. Some encrustations contain an agglomeration of things that may include not only diverse metals but a variety of other materials as well. Platoro had partially or completely removed the encrustation from many of the artifacts before TARL received them, and in some instances may have carried out other treatments whose nature is unknown to TARL.

An individual TARL specimen number was assigned to each discrete item and cross-referenced to the inventory numbers previously designated by Platoro if these were still attached or could be identified. Some Platoro number tags had come off the objects to which they had originally been fastened and these could not always be matched. Where the Platoro inventory indicated more than one specimen in a lot or group, all the items recorded under the same designation by Platoro were catalogued by TARL together as a lot unit, with separate sub-numbers assigned to the individual articles within it. In this way, if the Platoro categories had any significance, the relationship between them would be preserved. The same system was also used in cataloguing the separate specimens later as they were extracted from their concretions. For example, Platoro Lot OL 82, a large concretion, was assigned TARL Lot 41 Ti 1-210. After processing, it was found to contain 12 different specimens, so the set was catalogued 41 Ti 1-210-1 through 210-12. Among them, one object broken in two pieces was recorded as a single unit; three existed as molds from which cast replicas were made of two; and a bit of encrustation containing nothing was recorded and then discarded. After all the inventoried specimens and concretions had been processed and identified if possible, the cans of residue from Platoro's preliminary cleaning activities were searched and the contents carefully examined for additional items of possible interest. A number were found, including impressions of markings and letters from coins and other devices that were visible in some of the concretion fragments.

All catalogued specimens were photographed before any

treatment was begun, and, if appropriate, during and after processing as well. Color slides were made in many instances. In addition, to assist in the location and identification of objects that might be camouflaged and sealed in an encrustation, and often to check the condition of metal pieces, hundreds of radiographs and X-rays were made. Another technique employed in identifying disintegrated artifacts consisted of preparing castings of impressions in order to make replicas of missing objects. In this way it was possible to make copies of several unusual artifacts that otherwise would never have been recognized. Casts also were made of several actual specimens to be used for display. Complete records of TARL's cleaning and processing procedures were kept for every artifact that required treatment.

Various materials react in different ways to salt water immersion, but almost all need attention of some sort after removal from a sea environment, especially after hundreds of years under water. Bacterial, electrochemical, and mechanical forces combine to attack the remains of a shipwreck, according to Dr. Hamilton (Hamilton 1976). He explains that deterioration of metal in the sea results from the electrochemical cells that are formed between metals of different electrode potential in the presence of an electrolyte—in this case sea water. The galvanic current thus set up will accelerate the corrosion process of a metal such as iron, with a high electrode potential, if it is in the presence of a "nobler" metal like silver. The action, however, will usually provide cathodic protection for the silver and thus tend to preserve it. For this reason a silver coin resting next to a piece of iron theoretically will be protected by the iron, which itself may corrode. Likewise, copper will usually be protected by iron, but will disintegrate next to silver. TARL has, however, found mystifying exceptions to the rule. Sometimes two silver coins on one piece of iron vary widely in their condition, perhaps because different parts of the two metals are reacting in different ways to electrolysis and the local environment. During recent research in conservation, Hamilton observed that the presence of wood in direct association with most metals has an adverse effect on the latter. This led him to recognize that as the wood decays it consumes oxygen, thus creating an anaerobic environment favorable for the sulfate-reducing bacteria to thrive. The result is that hydrogen sulfide is formed as a metabolic by-product that reacts with the metals and accelerates the corrosion process.

Iron and silver, in particular, have an electronic attraction for calcareous materials that combine around them; often

A

Fig. 4.—Processing activities at ACF.

(A) Large encrusted object being lifted from vat containing others awaiting cleaning.

B

(B) Technician Jack Ward places small encrusted object in position for X-ray.

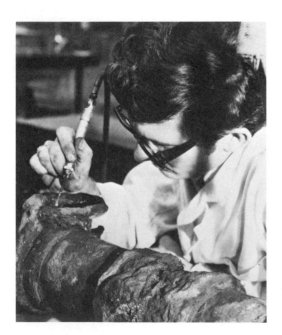

C

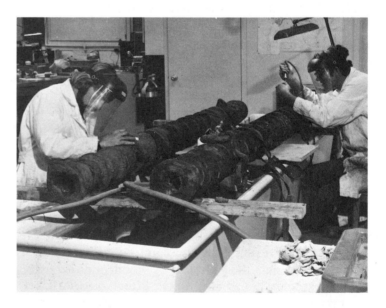

D

(C) Conservator Dr. D. L. Hamilton cleans surface of hooped-barrel gun using an air tool for delicate work around handle.

(D) Steve Rogers and Dr. Hamilton removing encrustation from around rings of partially cleaned hooped-barrel guns.

this coating completely disguises the contents so the resulting concretion resembles nothing but an indeterminate blob without distinguishing features. The encrustation probably helps to inhibit further corrosion after it forms, but almost always some corrosion would have taken place beforehand, and the sulfate-reducing bacteria continue to act in the anaerobic atmosphere thus sealed inside. Gold is quite inert in sea water and does not corrode but may be scratched by other objects or even nibbled upon by fish (Peterson 1969: 63). Lead is almost inert although it may develop an encrustation or film on the surface, but like other metals is sus-

Fig. 5.—(A) Large encrustation no. 210 before processing.

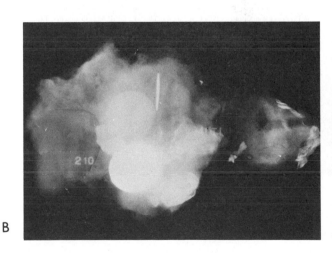

(B) X-ray photograph of the encrustation.

(C) Using the X-ray for a guide, Barto Arnold carefully proceeds to extract the objects, using a hammer to break the calcium carbonate encrustation from the artifacts.

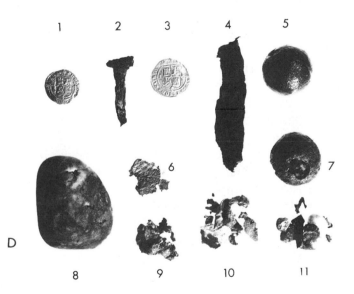

(D) The objects found in the conglomerate or casts made from molds within it where the iron specimens had corroded:

1. Two-reales silver coin
2. Latex cast of nail fragment
3. Four-reales silver coin
4. Latex cast of iron strap fragment
5. Cast iron cannon ball
6. Small stone, possibly part of ballast
7. Lead scrap
8. Lead cannonball
9. Lead scrap
10. Lead scrap
11. Lead scrap and pebbles encrusted together

11

ceptible to the sulfate-reducing bacteria. The harmful corrosive chloride compounds in most metals, especially iron and cupreous objects, must be completely removed or the specimens will continue to corrode after recovery and eventually be destroyed by exposure to the atmosphere.

Various salts (especially sodium chloride) enter other materials too, but usually can be removed more easily than from metal; normally long and repeated washing will take care of it. Ordinarily glass, ceramics, and stone are fairly well preserved but may have some surface erosion or calcareous deposit. Organic materials such as bone, leather, textiles, or cordage may survive under some conditions. Wood is often found in fragile condition, with the greatest damage coming from the devastating teredo or shipworm *(Teredo navalis),* which was the source of tremendous damage to wooden ships. This was the reason the Spaniards, by the 1520s, were taking the precaution of sheathing the keel or bottom of some of their ships in thin lead (Waters 1958: 92, ftn. 1; Potter 1960: 78). Of course, the lead set up an electrolytic action with the iron nails with which it was fastened, and although this went unrecognized scientifically, the nails oxidized and fell out.

It will be recognized, then, that the cleaning and preservation of the very large iron objects and the diversity of materials represented by the entire collection from this ancient shipwreck presented great problems that required specialized knowledge, techniques, and equipment. Although a number of methods have been developed for cleaning and preserving metal, not all are completely successful. The few laboratories that have had experience or been concerned with processing large metal specimens such as naval guns and anchors continue to experiment and exchange information with one another in order to develop the best and most economical techniques. Metal cleaning methods may require mechanical, electrolytic, electrochemical, chemical, or diffusion techniques, or a combination of them. Much innovative work has been done recently in Europe in the salvaging of ancient wooden ships, and such experiments continue. Other complex conservation problems include choosing a suitable final preservative for wood and metal, and the provision of proper storage conditions both before and after treatment. It must always be recognized that an object once treated may in time need further attention and frequent checking, for no process can be guaranteed to hold up forever. Although an effective conservation program is notably time-consuming and expensive, it is fully as important to the preservation of these precious fragments of history as is their recovery from the sea. Those left without treatment will soon be lost permanently. A detailed account of conservation methods used by TARL's Antiquities Conservation Facility is given in "Electrolytic Cleaning and Artifacts Recovered from the Sea" (Hamilton 1973) and *Conservation of Metal Objects from Underwater Sites: A Study in Methods* (Hamilton 1976).

ARCHEOLOGICAL EVIDENCE FOR
DATING THE WRECKAGE

The shipwreck materials recovered by Platoro were first believed to have come from a ship involved in a 1553 disaster. This attribution was based on Carlos Castañeda's *Our Catholic Heritage in Texas,* Vol. I, Ch. V, entitled, "The Dominican Martyrs of Texas 1553-1554" (Castañeda 1936: 14 -156). W. W. Newcomb narrated the stirring and tragic story of these shipwreck victims in *The Mustang* ("Yo ho ho and..........................." Newcomb 1969: 1-5), basing his account on a pamphlet, "Spanish Documents Concerning the 1553 Flota of New Spain by Padilla, Barcia, and Torquemada," conversations with its compiler, Ford Green, and on Chapter V of Castañeda's *Our Catholic Heritage in Texas,* Vol. I (Castañeda 1936). Briefly, Newcomb's version relates that a fleet of 20 vessels set forth in the spring of 1553 from Vera Cruz in Mexico, the port from which all treasure ships departed, bound for Spain with some 1,000 passengers and crew aboard. The ships were laden with silver, gold, and other valuables. On reaching port at Havana, the fleet took on supplies, discharged merchandise, and made ready for the voyage across the ocean. Three ships acting as an advance force left a few days ahead of the others and did reach Spain, but when the rest of the fleet started out through the treacherous Bahama channel, they were caught in swift currents and bad weather and were driven back into the Gulf. Two of these ships, in badly battered condition, managed to reach Europe eventually, and a third returned to Vera Cruz. The remaining 14 vessels of the fleet were lost somewhere in the Gulf, with several said to have been wrecked off lower Padre Island. Although 300 survivors came ashore, it was only a few weeks before Indian attacks, hunger, and fatigue brought death to all but two of the ill-fated travelers as they tried to make their way back to New Spain (Mexico). One, Fray Marcos de Mena, severely wounded and left for dying, was able to reach Tampico with the help of friendly Indians, where he recounted the pathetic story of his compatriots' loss. The other, Francisco Vasquez, escaped from the Indians and remained on Padre Island for nearly a year until a salvage party of Spaniards arrived from New Spain under a Captain Angel de Villafana intent on locating the wrecks and recovering the sunken treasure. They rescued Vasquez and claimed that they retrieved much gold and silver.

The Castañeda account may be a confused and inaccurate version of what actually happened. The State Antiquities

Committee, in a recent underwater survey of the Gulf tidelands, located other wrecks from various time periods and recovered data and artifacts from a Spanish ship that appears to have been a contemporary of the vessel worked by Platoro, perhaps from the same fleet. The committee commissioned an intensive search of the archives of Seville, Spain, in an effort to document identification of Spanish ships recorded as having been lost near this part of Padre Island and the dates upon which they went down. This brought to light records of a fleet of four ships that foundered near Padre in 1554, and their treasure was said to have been salvaged under the direction of Captain Angel de Villafana. It is not at all certain whether the two accounts relate to the same tragedy, or whether there was a single disaster and two salvage projects, or two wrecks and two recovery episodes. The archival search is expected to establish the true story, and results will be published by the Antiquities Committee in a report on underwater excavations carried out under its direction.

It should be noted that other wrecks occurred about this time. *The Treasure Diver's Guide* (Potter 1960) describes a battle that took place in the Gulf in 1552 between the *Capitana,* an escort vessel, and unidentified pirates. The *Capitana* was said to be carrying some 30 tons of gold and silver. Without giving his sources, the author says, "From recorded descriptions of the battle it seems likely that it took place not far from Padre Island, and this treasure ship sank somewhere off its shore" (Potter 1960: 184). In addition, Potter lists the *Santa Maria de Guadalupe,* a merchant ship, as having sunk in the Gulf in 1564. Her registry silver was transferred to other ships of the fleet, but the contraband was not saved. Although her position was not recorded, Potter says that she, too, may lie off Padre Island.

From the nature of the artifacts recovered by Platoro, and the location of the wreck in what were considered exclusive Spanish waters until the eighteenth century, the identification of the wreckage as Spanish is certain. Those materials that can be attributed to a definite time period all point to the mid-sixteenth century. Only a few articles in the collection are known or suspected to be of foreign origin and some are easily explained. Two pewter plates give evidence of trade with England, normal practice at that time; and two of the guns may well have been made in the Netherlands or somewhere in the European area that was a part of Charles V's empire. The two astrolabes that are believed to be Portuguese, however, give rise to some questions as to what they

Fig. 6.—*Three cast brass navigational astrolabes. The two above are dated 1550; the one below, 1545.*

were doing on a Spanish ship. So far as can be determined from the objects in the collection, the shipwreck from which they came occurred at some time between 1550 and 1570, or very soon thereafter.

A brief recapitulation of the historical period sets the stage for the presentation of the materials recovered. This mid-century span of two decades was a time of many political and technological changes in Europe. These changes followed the Reformation, when Spain was reacting with brutal force to new religious ideas, when England under Henry VIII had separated from Rome and set up her own independent church, and when France, though Catholic, was the enemy of both Spain and England. Charles I (Carlos I) of Spain was the most powerful monarch in the world as the period began—ruler of the Holy Roman Empire under the title Charles V, and the first of the Hapsburgs to occupy the Spanish throne. In 1550 his empire included the Netherlands and most of Italy in addition to the vast lands to which Spain laid claim in the New World. His half-brother, Ferdinand, ruled the German states and Austria. In 1556 Charles abdicated the Spanish throne in favor of his son, Philip II, and Philip ruled the great Spanish Empire until his own death in 1598.

England's king in 1550 was the child Edward VI, son of Henry VIII and Jane Seymour; by 1553 he was dead and Mary Tudor, unhappy daughter of the Spanish Catherine of Aragon, became queen. The next year, 1554, Mary and Prince Philip of Spain were married and a period of friendly relations between England and Spain continued. Queen Mary, encouraged by Charles V and Philip, even attempted to restore Catholicism in England. Spain and England remained at peace for a time after the ascension of Elizabeth I in 1559, for Philip, upon the death of Mary, sought to add the English throne to his sphere of influence by marriage with Elizabeth. Henry II, arch rival of both Spanish and English rulers, reigned in France from 1547 to 1559, to be succeeded by Francis II. It was this Francis who had been married the previous year at the age of 16, to young Mary, Queen of Scots. Charles IX assumed the French throne when Francis II died in 1560, and ruled until 1574.

The great early Spanish and Portuguese voyages of exploration had made possible the establishment of European settlements in the New World, and Spain, at least, was profiting hugely from the wealth of her colonies. Ocean trade was brisk, with many ships sailing each year. Aside from shipwreck, French pirates presented the most pressing danger in the Atlantic, so that vessels always had to go armed. Shipments of treasure to Spain, especially the valuable silver cargoes, were increasing yearly, reaching their peak in the latter part of the century. During the last years of Charles V's reign, systems were being established for sending the merchant ships out in convoy under heavily armed escorts, but at this earlier time small groups of armed vessels could, with special permission, still travel together without this protection.

By 1562, the famous semi-annual silver fleets, *flotas* comprising 50 or 60 ships, were making the round-trip on more or less regular schedules, attended by two or more fighting galleons and often by small swift vessels called *pataches*. This arrangement proved so satisfactory that it lasted well into the eighteenth century. No one could foresee then that the vast riches pouring into Spain would in time cause disastrous inflation over all of Europe and would eventually bring about the fall of the Spanish Empire. As Spain came to rely on the treasure from the Indies to buy the agricultural and manufacturing products of other nations, she neglected her own resources. Philip II, always in debt to the great banking houses of Europe, as was his father, and fighting ever more costly wars financed by the silver and gold from the Indies, impoverished his land by his use of these riches and in the end contributed to the destruction of the empire (Haring 1964: 177-179).

Constant warfare in Europe inspired many innovations in armaments and weapons. The arquebus (a heavy matchlock or wheellock gun) was in common use, but in the early 1550s portable hand guns were just being developed for use on land and sea. The large, awkward musket of the time was still too unwieldy to be fired without support. Cast iron guns were being made in England, although they were necessarily small, for casting heavy cannons in iron was not practical. Most of the large guns and the cannons were of "brass"—probably some sort of brass-bronze alloy—or of wrought iron like the ones in the Texas collection. As hand weapons were improved and made smaller they replaced the ancient crossbows as protective weapons, although crossbows continued to be employed for hunting well into the eighteenth century. According to Spanish Crown regulations, from 1522, the amount and kinds of armament to be carried aboard ships were specifically decreed. Defenses were to be augmented by a netting that could be pulled over the decks to intercept mis-

Fig. 7.—*The ship's navigator might have held the astrolabe in this fashion to determine the sun's altitude at noon, focusing its rays through two peepholes on the vanes of the sighting device. At the end of the movable arm a pointer indicates the degree of altitude on a calibrated scale engraved around the upper half of the instrument.*

siles that might be dropped, and waistcloths were to be provided to prevent enemy boarding.

Navigation was accomplished by dead reckoning and the use of such early instruments as compasses, mariners' astrolabes, quadrants, and cross-staffs, along with detailed navigational charts, to determine latitude. The only time-keeping device was the hourglass, turned every half-hour. Speed was reckoned in terms of how long it took the ship to pass a wooden chip tied to a line and thrown out ahead.

TARL has actual dates of manufacture of all three navigational astrolabes in the Texas Gulf collection. Two are stamped 1550, one very clearly, the other barely visible; and we believe that the third is dated 1545; on it, the numeral 5 at the right end of the date is incomplete, but the remnant of the figure looks like the top bar of the Spanish 5 and unlike any other number. The astrolabes could have been in use for a number of years after they were stamped, so the 1550 date can establish only an earliest possible year for the shipwreck.

All but one of the Carlos and Johanna silver coins in the collection were struck at the Mexico City mint and represent examples of coinage covering the period from the founding of the mint in 1536 until 1570 when the assayer Luis Rodrigues, whose initial was L, is known to have died. But because about 90 percent of the coins in this collection were assayed by Luis, the span of his term of office would be significant in assigning a narrower time span for the wreck if the situation were not so confused. He may have assumed the office of assayer about 1553, or as late as 1556, although no documents have been discovered that would prove either date. To add to the problem, the date when Philip II introduced a new coin design is also in question and remains a matter of conjecture and argument among coin experts. Some say the new design must have been introduced soon after 1556 when Charles abdicated the Spanish throne in favor of Philip, but others are convinced that the old Carlos and Johanna pattern was used until 1572. These questions will be discussed in more detail in the section devoted to coins. The one coin that was foreign to Mexico City was of the same time period as that of the pre-1545 Early Series coins from that mint but came from Santo Domingo.

The English-made articles mentioned earlier are two pewter plates that bear touchmarks showing the crowned Tudor Rose accompanied by the initials RV. The English were noted for their fine pewter, and the rose mark with an open crown above was characteristic of the London pewterers of the sixteenth century. Although the flat rose was commonly used in Europe later to indicate quality, the placement of the letters on either side of the rose indicates English manufacture. At one time these marks could have been traced to the individual artisan, for the stamp with his initials would have been recorded in the pewterers' guildhall, but unfortunately the records of the earliest London marks were destroyed in the great fire of 1666. No English records survive illustrating pewterers' marks before 1635. Nevertheless, the Tudor Rose accompanied by initials was rarely used after 1564, according to Howard H. Cotterell in *Old Pewter: Its Makers and Marks* (1963: 25), and the fact that it appears on the plates in the collection tends to confirm a pre-1564 dating for them.

There is a tantalizing possibility that the silver bullion could some day give evidence for a more specific date—either before or after 1556—if metallurgical studies could determine whether or not the silver had been amalgamated with mercury. This technique, called the "patio process," was introduced into Mexico early in 1556 and could give a good cutoff date, at least. It was the introduction of this new process, credited to Bartolomé de Medina, a Spaniard, and his German colleague, and said to have been developed in the Pachuca mines (Prieto 1973: 78), that made possible the tremendous increase in silver production during the latter half of the sixteenth century. Medina actually published his findings on December 29, 1554, according to Alan Probert (1969: 90), but, in keeping with the custom of the times, he used the date December 29, 1555 as it was after Christmas. A patent was issued to Medina on July 10, 1556, Probert says, to run for eight years. From this time on, the new technique spread rapidly. Stamped marks appearing on disks and other pieces of silver offer still other promising but unresolved clues. The one most frequently used on this silver, bearing elements of the coin design (and in one variation featuring a profile head that greatly resembles Charles V), may have been related to the official *Casa de Contratación* (the House of Trade, a government agency in control of overseas trading practices); but if so, it probably had as long a life as the *Casa* was active, which could be 200 years or so. Two marks specify certain mines or mining districts: TASCO (often spelled TAXCO) and GUACHINANGO (alternate spelling HUACHINANGO), where silver mining had been flourishing for some time. Another two may represent the cockle or scallop shell, symbol of St. James, patron saint of Spain; if this is true, the stamp is probably another official mark. As for the remainder, it can only be assumed that they were the marks of individual assayers or owners, or special tax stamps that will be discussed in more detail later. All the marks must have been registered officially somewhere, but most will have to be left unidentified for the present.

Cast into one end of a heavy lead bar or ingot is a large round mark of another kind, possibly a shipping or owner's mark, but it has yet to be identified.

The quantity of lead sheeting scraps pierced with square nail holes definitely suggests the kind of protective sheathing that might have been nailed to the outside of the ship's keel or bottom to discourage shipworms from attacking the wood. It this is correct it would help to confirm the case for a Spanish ship of the sixteenth century.

Small and eroded as they are, even the pottery fragments fit properly into the time period named. Most of them appear to be sherds from Spanish olive jars of the Early Period that John M. Goggin names and describes in "The Spanish Olive Jar" (1964: 263), a type and style of vessel that he believes was probably manufactured in Spain during the first three-quarters of the sixteenth century.

The weapons and armament are appropriate to the suspected time period too, although they might have come from any of the European countries; marks on two of the guns suggest a central or northern European origin. Countries not only traded such implements with one another when at peace but also captured and used an enemy's equipment when at war. All the guns that were recovered were wrought iron breechloaders, but they were of two different types—swivel guns, known as *versos,* and hooped-barrel guns, *bombardetas.* By the latter part of the sixteenth century, cast iron or brass swivel guns were replacing the old wrought iron ones, although the design remained about the same. The hooped-barrel guns were obsolescent by mid-century, but they were used for some time afterward. Mendel Peterson (1972: 257) says that this heavier armament was replaced by cast iron muzzle-loading pieces in the last decades of the sixteenth century. Robert Marx presents evidence from the letters of a royal official that in 1590 the Spanish cargo ship *San Francisco* was still carrying almost useless old rusty iron cannon to the New World (Marx 1968: 64). Stone cannon balls, too, bespeak old fashioned but still usable weapons, as do the lead-covered iron cannon balls. Peterson considered them, along with hooped-barrel guns, as good evidence in dating a wreck found off the Bahamas. He believes the ship probably sank in the first half of the sixteenth century, certainly no later than 1580 (Peterson 1972: 256). If identification of the ship were based only on the type of armament recovered, it would have to be assumed it was a cargo vessel armed only for defense, for a fighting galleon would have had more up-to-date armament.

The crossbows are not military weapons at all, but seem to be the sporting type used for hunting small game; they are not especially helpful for dating because they were used for this purpose well into the eighteenth century. The goat's foot lever used for cocking them was around almost as long.

Arquebuses or muskets probably were carried on the ship, but the only evidence of weapons of this kind consists of two very small lead balls that might be ammunition for muskets; they could perhaps be identified as case shot with about as much justification. Tiny, fragmentary rings of brass chain mail were fittingly present, but the same kind of mail was made and in use from medieval days into the seventeenth century.

Ballast stones definitely indicate a pre-nineteenth century date and lend weight to a Spanish origin for the ship, without giving actual proof of it. In general, historians agree that the Spaniards tended to use cobblestones for ballast, while the English weighted their ships with sand or a coarse gravel called shingle. But it must be recognized that the ship's master had to use whatever was available for this purpose when and where he needed it.

Other artifacts in the collection are consistent with a mid-sixteenth century attribution but are not restricted to that period; ships' fittings, equipment, and tools did not change much from the fifteenth century to the nineteenth. Into this everyday category fall the wrought iron tools, chains, spikes, nails, and pins, the pieces of rope and scraps of sailcloth, and the sounding leads and fishing weights that were to be found on every vessel. Fragments of animal bones, too, should be included, suggesting that live animals were being carried along for fresh meat, another example of evidence that could be expected but is not conclusive.

It can be said then, with assurance, that the archeological

evidence identifies the wreckage as belonging to a Spanish cargo ship that came to grief one tragic day between 1550 at the earliest, and 1570 at the latest. Documentary evidence soon may be able to tell the exact day and year.

NAVIGATIONAL APPARATUS

Because of their contribution to our scanty knowledge of early navigational instruments, and their rarity, the most historically valuable items of equipment from the ship are the three cast brass wheel-type navigational astrolabes (Figs. 6, 7, 9–16). Probably no more than three dozen of this type survive, including several recently recovered from Spanish Armada ships that foundered off the coast of England, and one found in Florida waters. These forerunners of the modern sextant were used to determine the altitude of the sun at mid-day, or, less frequently, the altitude of a suitable star. From these observations, and the tables of solar or stellar declinations furnished by the land astronomers, navigators could calculate the latitude of their ships. David Waters, in his publication *The Sea-or Mariner's Astrolabe* (1966: 177) tells us that from about 1485 to 1635 they were among the most popular navigational instruments.

Essentially, the mariner's astrolabe of the mid-sixteenth century was a brass or bronze wheel divided by spokes into four open quadrants and calibrated in degrees around the periphery of one or more of the quarters. At the top was a suspension ring ("thumb-ring") secured to the instrument by a shackle. An alidade or sight rule, with index pointers at the ends, was mounted at the center in such a way that it could be swiveled through 360 degrees. This movable arm had two opposing upright vanes or pinnules on either side which were pierced by one or more sight-holes. For sighting a star, one could hold the instrument up, and by looking through the two aligned sight-holes, determine the altitude as indicated by the pointer at the degree marked on the rim. But this would be a difficult, eye-searing procedure in making solar observations. Instead, the astrolabe would be held by its suspension ring at waist level or below, or possibly hung from a stationary upright, and the sun's rays focused through the two holes onto the deck, after which the indicated degree could be noted. On a ship in motion it must have been necessary to take a number of readings as mid-day approached and receded in order to determine the point of greatest altitude, for they had no clocks or other accurate timekeeping devices. One could suppose that it might sometimes take two or more men to complete the operation—one to hold the instrument, one to steady it, and another to record the observations. Imagine, if you can, trying to be sure of the precise angle on a heaving deck with a gale blowing! An error of one degree could mean a difference of 60 or 70 miles.

Sea-astrolabes were modified versions of the ancient and elaborate land astrolabes by which astronomers and astrologers had studied the stars and told fortunes for hundreds of years. They were only developed for use at sea in the late fifteenth century when Portuguese navigators began to explore south and westward along the African coast into the Atlantic. Until then the quadrant had been adequate for observations of the North Star and its guards in the northern hemisphere, but south of the equator Polaris disappeared below the horizon and new methods of determining latitude were required. For stellar observations north of the equator the quadrant was easier to use than the astrolabe, though, and it continued as a useful piece of navigational equipment even after the navigational astrolabe became common.

Evidently an evolution toward the simpler instrument began when navigators first took land or planispheric astrolabes to sea and found them to be impractical and unwieldy on an unsteady deck. Early accounts relate that they had to take their observations from land, but at that time they were usually sailing fairly close to land and this was no great hardship. These early, solid disk-like instruments were modified in time to make them more suitable for use aboard ship. The sections between the arms were cut out to decrease wind resistance, and the top or bottom section was frequently made heavier than the others to give better balance and stability. Instead of being placed near the ends of the alidades as before, the pinnules were moved in closer to the center to make alignment of the holes, and thus the sighting, easier. Some of the first sea-astrolabes were made of wood and were quite large. Waters (1966: 9) notes that Vasco da Gama's wooden one was 24 inches in diameter—so large that he had to go ashore to use it; he did, however, have smaller brass ones with him as well. Eventually the metal instruments replaced the wooden ones since the added weight was a desired feature, and the most popular size became six to ten inches in diameter.

Among the other noted explorers who were known to have carried astrolabes with them on their voyages were Bartholomew Diaz in 1487-88 and the pilot of Cabral's fleet in 1500. Columbus is said to have had one with him on his return trip from the New World in 1492 but was unable to use it for solar observations. Marcel Destombes (1969: 44-45) relates that Magellan's 1519 expense report shows he was equipped for navigation with one planisphere, 21 wooden quadrants, one astrolabe of hardwood, and six metal astrolabes with alidades, along with a supply of compasses and magnetic needles.

Waters discovered the earliest illustration of a sea-astrolabe on a world chart of 1525, but this device appears to have consisted of a flat, solid, calibrated metal disk furnished with an alidade (Waters 1966: 13). The earliest illustration of how such an instrument was actually used appears in the Portuguese cosmographer Pedro Medina's *Regimiento de Navegacion,* first published in 1552 and reproduced by Waters (1966: 12). The navigator is shown holding the instrument by the thumb-ring, just below his waist, while he focuses the sun's rays through the sight-holes. Derek J. Price (1957a: 608-609) undoubtedly alludes to this modified cast-wheel type of astrolabe when he dates its invention at about 1535, saying that earlier mentions probably refer to the use of astronomical astrolabes at sea. The oldest known cast-wheel astrolabe, dated 1540, once was housed in the collections of the of the National Museum in Palermo, Sicily, but has not been seen since World War II.

Destombes examined a 1938 photograph of the 1540 Palermo instrument and identified it as Portuguese from a stamped mark on the surface—a device consisting of five small circles arranged in the form of a cross (Destombes 1969: 48-49):

$$\begin{matrix} & \circ & \\ \circ & \circ & \circ \\ & \circ & \end{matrix}$$

The same mark appears on a Portuguese navigational chart of about 1550, unsigned but undoubtedly made by Lopo Homem, official cosmographer of Portugal. It appears also on the "Dundee" astrolabe, dated 1555, illustrated in the catalogue of an exhibition at the Royal Scottish Museum (Anderson 1972: 10-11). On this basis Destombes attributes the manufacture of both instruments to Lopo Homem.

The Palermo instrument was calibrated for meridional, or horizonal, readings; that is, it was graduated from 0° at the sides to 90° at the summit. The zenith system, on the other hand, has the 90° marks at the sides and 0° at the top. According to Waters (1966: 11), meridional calibration was first employed because navigation was originally based on observations needed to find the linear distance from a known port, and also because stellar observations preceded solar ones—the latitude of the place of observation was the same as the altitude of the Pole Star. As the navigators were already familiar with this system it was natural to extend it to solar readings when sea voyages began to take them far from their customary routes, and the need arose to get their bearings under different and unfamiliar circumstances. The necessary calculations from the sun's altitude were complicated, however, and when the Portuguese realized that they could be simplified by just taking the sun's zenith distance instead of the meridional altitude they changed their method of calibration accordingly. The more conservative Spaniards continued to use the meridional system as before. Tables of declination were given for periods projected many years in advance, arranged by months according to the signs of the Zodiac. Waters (1958: Plates XIII, XIV, and XV) illustrates some of these tables and the accompanying instructions on how to use them. Figure 8 illustrates how the calculations were made and quotes Admiral Morison's explanation of how to figure the latitude from his book, *The European Discovery of America: The Northern Voyages.*

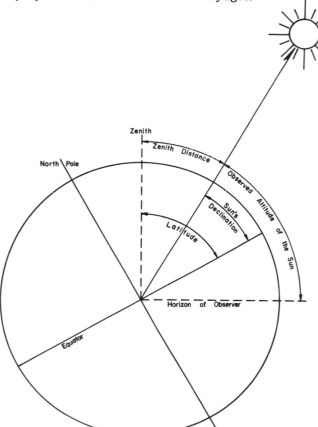

Fig. 8.—How to determine latitude from observation of the sun at noon. Samuel E. Morison explains the procedure this way:

You took the altitude of the sun in degrees, since the astrolabe of that era registered nothing less, subtracted this altitude from 90°, the result being the zenith distance. You then applied the sun's declination, plus or minus according to the season and hemisphere, and correct latitude should result. (Morison, 1971: 151-152)

Fig. 9.—Cast brass navigational astrolabe, wheel-type with base ballast (no. 1449). The instrument is complete with its alidade (the sighting device) and hanging ring. It is believed to be dated 1545.

The three astrolabes in the Texas Gulf collection had been superficially cleaned by Platoro. When received at the laboratory no encrustation adhered to the surfaces, but small patches of corrosion remained, with less on No. 1448 than on the others. Calibration, dates, and other marks can be made out on all the instruments, mostly crisp and clear on No. 1446, but very indistinct on No. 1449 and even more difficult to see on No. 1448; on it, in fact, the surface appears smooth, with just hints of markings, but under the right lighting conditions, and by examining faint spots under the microscope, vestiges of the marks can be discerned. Unfortunately, they are just shallow depressions and cannot be reproduced in a photograph (Figs. 9, 12, 15). All were graduated in the horizontal or meridional fashion, but styles were a little different in each instance as the scale drawings in Figures 10, 13, and 16 will show. Tick marks for the individual degrees surround the edge of the rim, the 5° segments are indicated just inside them, and the 10° sections appear next toward the center on the wheel. Each set of calibrations is delineated by engraved circles that surround the rim. The stamp for the digit 5 must have been particularly sharp, for that number is more easily recognized than any of the others. Among the cleaning debris left by Platoro are small pieces of encrustation that were broken off no. 1446; this was obvious because the exact markings, in reverse, can be seen readily on the inside of the fragments. No debris was found that could be related to either of the other astrolabes, and we do not know whether or not they were encrusted when brought up from the Gulf. Neither do we know whether the surfaces were damaged by undersea corrosion or by poor cleaning techniques.

All three astrolabes underwent qualitative analysis by Mr. Ralph Henry and Mr. Andrzej H. Pradzynski of the Nuclear Reactor Testing Laboratory of The University of Texas at Austin and were found to be made of alloys consisting mostly of copper with elements of zinc and lead in the order of magnitude of a few percentage points or less. Astrolabe No. 1449 may contain some very small trace of tin, but the data for tin are questionable. The two others are very much alike in the amount of lead they contain, but the zinc is about 40% higher in No. 1448 than in No. 1446. Plenderleith and Werner (1971: 192) say that there is evidence the early metal-

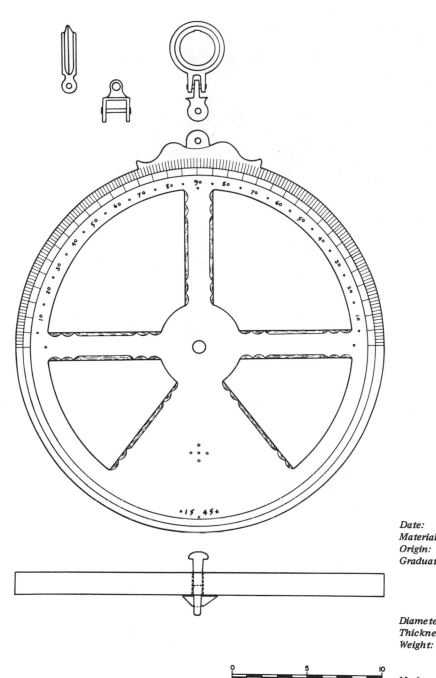

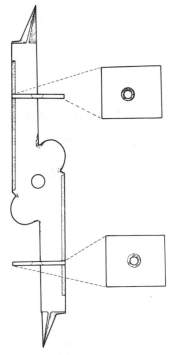

Fig. 10.—Scale drawing showing details of calibration and other marks that have been discerned or are indicated on Astrolabe No. 1449. The complete wheel as it most likely looked when new. Assignment of Portuguese origin is based on the five-circle mark of the Portuguese government.

Date:	1545
Material:	cast brass
Origin:	Portuguese
Graduation:	meridional, calibrated clockwise from the left side in 10° intervals, with the 5° segments indicated by lines and the 1° marks along the edge of the rim
Diameter:	245 mm., horizontal measurement
Thickness:	15 mm. top to bottom
Weight:	3968.725 g. with alidade and pin; 3613.6 g. without them
Marks:	★ 15 ★ 4 ★ [5] ° °°° °
Alidade (bent):	240 mm. long, sight-holes centered in vanes, punched inward from outer side, each 5 mm. in diameter
Pin secured:	by wedge and slot
Ballast:	bottom, triangular
Suspension ring & shackle	intact, brass

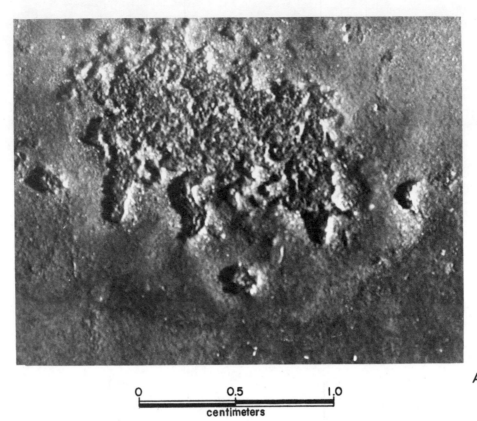

A

0   0.5   1.0
centimeters

Fig. 11.—(A) Astrolabe No. 1449, enlargement of date markings. (B) Details
of calibration in upper left quadrant.

B

0   1   2   3
CM

Fig. 12.—Cast brass navigational astrolabe, wheel-type with base ballast (no. 1446). The instrument is dated 1550. The alidade is missing, but the shackle and bail on the upper right may be the hanging pieces for the astrolabe (nos. 1447-1, 2).

lurgists did not always distinguish tin from lead; in using a preponderance of lead instead of tin they would make a less serviceable object than they intended.

These astrolabes can be classified according to the system organized by David Waters as "Type I (a): wheel type with base ballast" (Waters 1966: 26). Although they are calibrated for meridional readings in the Spanish fashion, they appear to fall within a transition period when such instruments could have been either Spanish or Portuguese. Destombes's research led him to conclude (1969: 51-52) that the Portuguese began to engrave their instruments sometime between 1540 (the date of the Palermo astrolabe, which was Portuguese) and 1555, when the Portuguese instrument calibrated for zenith readings was made. At the time he wrote, the 1555 instrument was the oldest one known to be surviving.

Judging only from their calibration, then, the examples in this collection could have been made in either country, but since they were found in the Gulf of Mexico, well out of Portuguese territory, the likelihood on first examination was considerably stronger for Spanish origin. But other factors must be taken into consideration.

The size of these astrolabes brings up an interesting point. Waters (1966: 26) says "The various descriptions which have come down to us of Spanish sea-astrolabes all describe them as being small instruments," and he quotes a Thomas Blundeville (1966: 21), who wrote in 1594 that the Spaniards usually made their astrolabes narrow and heavy—not much over five inches broad and weighing at least four pounds. The three that are described here, measuring 225, 227, and 245 mm. (ca. 8-7/8, 8-15/16, and 9-5/8 inches), more nearly resemble the width of the Portuguese ones from the sixteenth century as identified and described by Destombes (1969: 41), which range from 166 mm. to 324 mm. The three Spanish ones from this period that he records measure only 166 mm., 178 mm., and 198 mm. Still another example, identified as probably Spanish, was undated but thought to have been made about 1600; it was 184 mm. in diameter (Destombes 1969: 43). Of course, the very scarcity of sixteenth century sea-astrolabes from any source makes a judgment based on size very tenuous, and size may not be significant at all for these unusually early examples.

It is curious, though, that Astrolabe No. 1446, although retaining numerous clear markings, bears no recognizable official stamp. Since early in the sixteenth century it had been required in Spain that navigational instruments were to be brought before the pilot major for examination and approval. This regulation was reiterated in a royal *cédula* of March 9, 1545 in which it was required that all instruments must be inspected before they could be taken to sea. If approved, they would be stamped with the mark of the *Casa de Contratación,* but if rejected they would be broken up and melted. The 1563 Spanish astrolabe that Destombes writes about in detail in his 1969 paper, "Un astrolabe nautique de la Casa de Contratación (Séville, 1563)," was not discovered until 1969, but evidently it had been in the collections of the French *Conservatoire National des Arts et Metiers* since early in the nineteenth century. Among other marks, this astrolabe bears a stamp of the Pillars of Hercules, which the author believes must represent the official stamp mentioned in the *cédula*. It has been identified as the mark of the *Casa de Contratación* because it appears with several other stamps on the title page of an official compendium on the art of navigation published by the *Casa* in 1588, written by the Spanish cosmographer Zamorano (Destombes 1969: 61-63). The Pillars stamp, and one featuring the symbol of St. James, a scallop shell, helped to identify the *Casa* instrument with certainty as Spanish. Variations of the Pillars stamp appear on a number of the silver disks in the collection, as well as on the coins, and can only represent official marks of some kind. Marks identified as possible scallop shells also are found, although they have more than the seven scallops of the shell mark described by Destombes. Astrolabe No. 1446, under discussion, has no official mark that we recognize, but it does have a tiny triangular figure composed of 10 dots centered above the date. The dots are more clearly visible under magnification and a good cross-light (Fig. 14B). It has not been identified yet but might be the mark of the fabricator. The numerous Spanish rules and regulations were often circumvented, as Destombes cites in the instance of a lawsuit brought against the captain of a ship in 1561 whose pilot had used an unmarked astrolabe (Destombes 1969: 56). The calibration marks on the upper right quadrant of No. 1446 appear to have been engraved in reverse: that is, reading down from the top they appear as 90-08-07-06 and so on down to the zero. Destombes says this may be a mistake, serving no particular purpose. Since the other markings and graduations are accurately drawn and precisely located, allowing an observation to one-half a degree, he considers this a very good instrument, noting the resemblance of the figure 8 between this and the 1563 instrument that he studied. Could it be that the pilot thought it accurate enough, even with this unusual feature, that he took a chance on taking it along on the voyage without the official inspection and stamp? Bribery, fraud, and official "winking of the eye" at irregularities were not uncommon, and no doubt many instruments escaped proper inspection. The 1545 astrolabe (No. 1449) probably was made before the official stamp regulation was put into effect, but if the regulations had been followed, this 1550 one should bear it.

Who might have made these mariner's astrolabes? If a Spaniard was the manufacturer, it might have been either one of the royal cosmographers or possibly someone among the craftsmen who were eligible to make them. Destombes (1969: 54) lists Alonso de Chaves, Diego Gutierrez, Pedro

Mexia, and Alonso de Santa Cruz as official cosmographers for the *Casa* who were working during the years 1537 – 1551 when these instruments probably were made. Documents indicate that at any one time several men might have been on the job. As for Portugal, there seems to have been only one, Lopo Homem, whom Destombes identified as the maker of the 1540 Palermo astrolabe (1969: 59). He notes, though, that there were other official cosmographers who worked before 1600, also using the five-circle official Portuguese stamp, and who have not yet been identified. It would be interesting to know who made these fascinating instruments, and whether some day new technical knowledge might enable us to raise elusive marks that could reveal added information about them without damaging their surfaces.

Beyond the unique importance of these instruments because of their great age, and whether they are of Spanish or Portuguese origin, is the fact that they were made during a period of major controversy involving members of the Spanish pilot major's and the cosmographer major's offices in the *Casa de Contratación*. One of the duties of the pilot major *(piloto mayor)* and the official cosmographers of Spain, in addition to checking the instruments, was to see that navigators had up-to-date charts showing the sun's declination for finding the latitude of the ship at sea. In addition, the pilot major was responsible for the training of navigators and chart makers, so it can be seen that he held a very responsible position.

Ursula Lamb (1969: 40-57) recounts in detail the causes, arguments, and results of a lawsuit that took place in Spain between 1544 and 1546 and had a significant influence on the future of scientific thought. On one side were lined up the well-established pilot major, Sebastian Cabot, and licensed cosmographer Diego Gutierrez; opposing them were the cosmographer major, Alonso de Chaves, and the recently appointed licensed cosmographer Pedro de Medina. The quarrel arose over allegations made by Medina, an experienced and well educated cosmographer, that the instruments made by the Gutierrez family (father and three sons) had long enjoyed a profitable monopoly in the cosmographic industry, with the Gutierrez family manufacturing, and even buying, instruments that Cabot approved as a matter of course. Medina's criticism threatened this abuse of privilege, and the defendants proceeded to denounce him in court for his own work, which they had taken pains to obstruct. Chaves, as cosmographer major, agreed with Medina that the danger to seamen from faulty charts and instruments made it imperative that accurate information be available to pilots and navigators and not be kept secret.

Both sides brought their most persuasive arguments to bear, but Cabot and Gutierrez built their case on power and greed, while Chaves and his colleagues took a more scientific approach, saying that "interference with the God-given and reasonable design of the universe and the arbitrary doctoring of instruments, was, among other things, immoral and unorthodox" (Lamb 1969: 56). In the end, Lamb concludes, "The achievement of the Maestro Medina and his party was to win support for the idea that science is a search for truth and not for justice, and that a court of law is not the proper agency for the control of science." This controversy cannot but help add a special measure of concern as to which, if any, of the contending parties might have made the presumably Spanish astrolabe, No. 1446.

Astrolabe No. 1449, the largest and heaviest in the Texas Gulf collection, is complete with all its parts intact and in place (Figs. 9, 10, 11). It is in very good condition except that much of the detail in the markings has been almost obliterated; remaining ones are indistinct, although under strong lighting they can be seen. The arms of the alidade are bent upward slightly, and the tips of the pointers are twisted, but the piece does not appear to be damaged otherwise. The lower spoke expands from immediately below the center circle to form a wide arc at the base and provide extra weight for bottom ballast.

Dim vestiges of calibration numbers appear as depressions, but they are sufficiently clear to be distinguishable. The degrees are numbered to be read clockwise from the left side through the upper left and right quadrants, $0° - 90° - 0°$, terminating at the right horizontal spoke , in the meridional fashion. Some of the numbers are almost obliterated, but the pattern is quite evident. Midway between each $10°$ marking is a small circle indicating the $5°$ divisions, but there are no stamped figure 5s such as appear on the other two astrolabes. On the perimeter, each degree mark is engraved, with the $10°$ and $5°$ lines extending across the band formed by two engraved lines making concentric circles around the rim. Fig. 11B illustrates details of the calibration in the left quadrant where they are a little clearer than in the right, and Figure 10 is a scale drawing of the astrolabe as we believe it was originally marked.

A few small, corroded patches of the original surface can be seen here and there, and in one of them, centered in the lower part of the basal triangle, is located what remains of the date (Fig. 11A). We are convinced the date is 1545. The digits look like this:

$$154'$$

and are spaced like those of the 1550 date on No. 1446—that is, with a slightly greater space between the two central figures. It appears that the small remnant of the fourth digit of the date is the top of another 5 [*/*   ]. Below this remnant is a small depression that must be the remainder of the figure. If the date is 1545, then this is the oldest surviving dated mariner's astrolabe, so far as we know. A small mark resembling a star appears to the left and right of the date and just below the space between the second and third numbers. Traces of another stamped or punched figure can barely be discerned, but it appears to be an equal-armed cross made of five circles:

This is a significant symbol, for it was an identical mark that enabled Destombes to identify the 1540 Palermo astrolabe as Portuguese. It appeared on an anonymous, undated manuscript chart in the collections of the National Library in Lisbon (Destombes 1969: 42; A-1, A-2 and ftnts. 1, 2). Destombes ascribes the mark to Lopo Homem, master of nautical instruments and cartography for Portugal from 1517 to 1564, supported by documents that authenticate his findings. It is illustrated by Waters (1966: 24, Fig. 5). From this stamp, then, we infer that No. 1449 is of Portuguese manufacture. What was it doing on a Spanish ship? Was it brought on board surreptitiously by a Portuguese pilot?

Before discovering this mark on the astrolabe, we sent photographs of the three instruments to M. Destombes, who took time to study them and send us his comments (personal communication, 1975). At that time he thought they were probably Spanish, although he agreed, from suggestions we had made concerning the size and the lack of Spanish stamps, that there was a small possibility of a Portuguese origin. He wrote, "I think this possibility is slight, only for the reason that the Portuguese were very much in need of pilots as proved by the intensive process of formation of qualified pilots initiated by Pero Nuñez in Lisbon." But finding the cross-circles stamp sheds new light on the subject.

It is interesting that the sight-holes on the alidade are so much larger than those on Astrolabe No. 1448, and, unlike the latter, they are equal to each other in size and of the same diameter inside and outside; they were evidently perforated from the outside. The holes are placed very near to, but not quite at, the center of the vane. Their large size makes one wonder whether this instrument was either designed primarily for sighting the Pole Star instead of the sun, or whether it illustrates an experimental period during which the navigators were still trying to develop the most convenient and efficient design for shooting both the Pole Star and the sun.

Astrolabe No. 1446 is of cast brass in the usual wheel form, with four spokes dividing it into equal segments (Figs. 12, 13, 14). Beginning at the halfway point between the top and the bottom of the lower spoke, it widens to form a short, solid triangle with an arc of about 40° at the rim. The added weight, along with a gradual thickening of the body from top to bottom, provided bottom ballast for better control. All edges of the wheel, the spokes, and the central hub have been beveled, forming a small ridge where the edges meet. The alidade is missing and the swivel pin that would have fastened it is sheared off on each side just about flush with the body of the instrument.

Graduation marks are engraved precisely and most of them can easily be seen in the photograph. It appears that in preparation for marking the degrees, a small dot was first placed where each mark was to begin. Figure 14A shows details of the calibration. The date 1550, with a small dot on either side, is stamped or punched in the center of the basal triangle, about 10 mm. inward from the innermost peripheral double circle engraved on the instrument. Centered above the date, about 7.5 mm., is a tiny triangular grouping of ten dots:

The apex of this mark is in alignment with the apexes of the three-dot arrangements on the vertical spoke. This can be seen clearly in a photographic enlargement (Fig. 14B). The triangular motif of three dots is repeated a number of times on the spokes, appearing at the inner and outer ends, dividing the astrolabe into four 90° quadrants. Although once present, a companion mark is obscured at the left end of the horizontal spoke by a small patch of corrosion at the appropriate spot on the surface. The apexes of the triangles face toward each other on each spoke. Double dots can be seen at the lower left edge of the solid basal triangle, and single dots are found on either side of the outer ends of the spokes where they meet the wheel rim and at the edges of the orna-

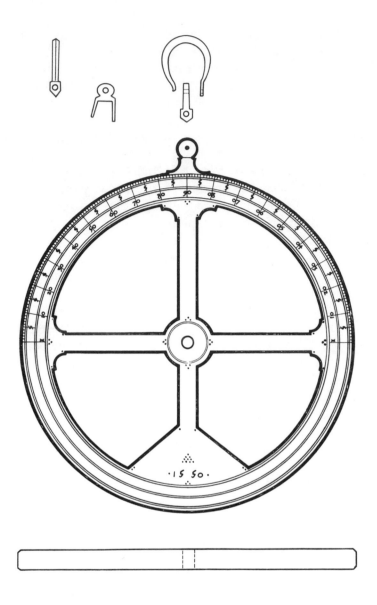

Fig. 13.—Scale drawing and details of calibration and other marks that have been found or are assumed to be present on Astrolabe No. 1446 and a separate ring and shackle (no. 1447-1, 2) that may belong to this instrument. The complete wheel as it most likely appeared when new, although the small 10-dot triangle appearing above the date can be seen only by magnification.

Date:	*1550*
Material:	*cast brass*
Origin:	*probably Spanish*
Graduation:	*meridional (0° − 90° − 0°); note numbers placed in reverse in upper right segment.*
Diameter:	*225 mm., horizontal measurement*
Thickness:	*top, 13 mm; side, 14 mm; base, 16 mm.*
Weight:	*2090.5 g.*
Marks:	
Alidade:	*missing*
Suspension ring & shackle:	*uncertain, but those shown above may belong to this instrument; they are of brass.*

mental curves with which they terminate. The front side of the hub is outlined by a double circle just inside the rim, and the only visible mark on the back of the instrument is a double circle surrounding the hub about three mm. inside the outer edge.

On the crown piece at the summit is a small, circular knob, with flat faces, that was cast in one piece with the body of the wheel. A tiny pin, complete with head, is still in place in the small central hole, at the point where the shackle would have been secured.

A

B

Fig. 14.—(A) Calibration marks on Astrolabe No. 1446. In right quadrant the numbers read 08, 07, 06, and so on down to the
zero point on the right spoke of the wheel.
(B) Basal section showing date and triangular designs composed of dot arrangements. Triangle above the date may be
maker's stamp.

0   5   10
centimeters

Fig. 15.—Cast brass navigational astrolabe, wheel-type with base ballast (no. 1448). The instrument is complete with its alidade but lacks a hanging ring.

The alidade is entirely missing and the suspension ring and shackle were not in place on the instrument when it was received. But a brass shackle (no. 1447-1) fits the crown nicely, and a brass bail (no. 1447-2) was wrapped with the shackle and catalogued by Platoro with the same number. These pieces are illustrated in Figures 12 and 13. It would be interesting to know whether these accessories were originally found in association with the astrolabe or with each other. Mr. and Mrs. Roderick Webster of the Adler Planetarium in Chicago are of the opinion that the shackle probably should be associated with this astrolabe, but the bail is not typical of an astrolabe suspension ring and therefore presumably should not be considered as belonging with it (Webster 1971). There are some special aspects of the piece, however, and they are noted here because they may hint that the bail might be a part of the assemblage. In the first place, the six-sided construction of the bail arms closely corresponds with that of the astrolabe body itself, suggesting that it might have been designed to go with the instrument. The style of the unbroken end of both shackle and bail is similar—something like a wide, pointed spade—and the metal of the two pieces looks very much alike under the microscope. All this, while not specific, adds a little weight to the speculation that they may belong together. The design of the suspension device may not serve to discount it completely, for if the bail were made to be secured by a pin through the top of the shackle the assemblage would be not unlike that of a mariner's astrolabe in the Oxford Museum of the History of Science, The University of Oxford. This instrument, illustrated on page 17 of a catalogue from an exhibition at the Royal Scottish Museum, Edinburgh (Anderson 1972), is presumed to be of Spanish origin, and was recovered from the harbor of Vera Cruz, Mexico. We offer the possibility, then, that the bail as well as the shackle belong to the Texas Gulf astrolabe, but without additional information about the circumstances under which they were found there is no way to prove it.

This astrolabe, with its good, clear markings, should have borne an official stamp if it was Spanish, but if there is one it has not been recognized as such, unless the 10-dot triangle can be so identified. On the other hand, it might have been smuggled aboard, never being subjected to inspection by Spanish officials.

Whatever its history, even lacking the alidade, it is a

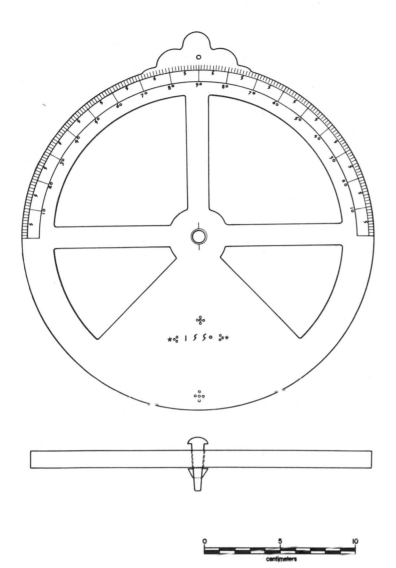

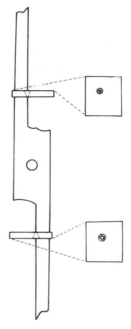

Fig. 16.—Scale drawing and details of calibration and other marks that have been found or are indicated on Astrolabe No. 1448. The drawing shows the complete wheel as it probably appeared when new, although most of the marks cannot be seen in a photograph because they appear only as depressions on the surface.

Date:	1550
Material:	cast brass
Origin:	Portuguese
Graduation:	meridional $(0° - 90° - 0°)$
Diameter:	227 mm., horizontal meas.
Thickness:	12 mm. top; 10-11 mm. base
Weight:	2066 g. with alidade & pin; 1976 g. without them.
Marks:	
Alidade:	arm length 205 mm.; conical sight-holes 5 mm. diam. on outside. On inside, 1 perforation is 0.75 mm., the other, 1.75 mm.
Secured by:	wedge and slot
Suspension device:	missing

handsome instrument in excellent condition. Its 1550 date, five years later than no. 1449, ranks it as one of the three oldest instruments of this type known.

The third astrolabe, no. 1448 (Figs. 15, 16), still has its sighting device, but the calibration and other markings are almost entirely obliterated, although under strong light it is possible to make them out. It is calibrated for meridional reading. The date 1550 can be found in the basal triangle, with a three-dot triangle to the left and another to the right, both with the apex pointing outward. Opposite the apex dot of each triangle is a mark that appears to be a star, a flower, or similar form. Above the date is the Portuguese five-circle cross figure similar to the one on no. 1449. At the hub, a short straight line above and below is directly aligned with the 90° mark at the top of the wheel; it runs through the cen-

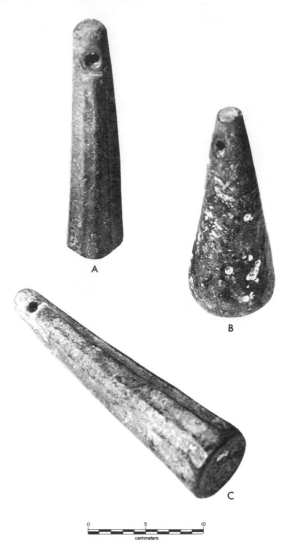

Fig. 17.—Lead sounding weights. nos. 1509 (A) and 1637 (C) evidently were cast in a similar type of mold. Lighter in weight than the third one, they were intended for use in shallower water. The heavy cone-shaped weight, no. 1636 (B), without facets, may have been a "dipsie" lead for soundings from about 100 to 200 fathoms. Its base was concave to enable the navigator to "arm" it with paraffin, tallow, or some other sticky substance in order to pick up a sample of the sea's bottom.

ter of the cross-arm stamp and between the numbers of the date. Details of calibration are shown in Figure 16, but unfortunately they do not show on the photographs. From the Portuguese stamp, it is assumed that this astrolabe also originated in that country.

The alidade is intact but the arms are bent, one upward and one downward, and one of the vanes is very tenuously attached. The sight-holes are placed somewhat off-center in the vanes, a little to the right and above the centers, and one is larger than the other. Both are conical in shape, the larger diameter to the outside. This may have made it easier for the navigator to catch the sun's rays and focus them through the two small, inner openings. The small pin for securing the shackle of the missing suspension ring at the crown is still in place.

Destombes remarked in his letter that it was strange that this instrument was slightly thinner at the bottom than at the top and believes that the anomaly might be a result of corrosion, in which case it might originally have been the same thickness throughout. This was the case with no. 1449. The alidade, with its conical sight-holes, is of the same design as the Spanish astrolabe of 1563, previously discussed.

From what we now know, it seems likely that two of the astrolabes are Portuguese, and the other Spanish.

Whether the navigator used the meridional or zenith method of finding the latitude, he needed another rule in addition to his Tables of Declination for sun and stars that would relate the change of latitude to the distance sailed. E. G. R. Taylor (1957b: 548) says that the Portuguese seem to have been the first to develop these, using a measure of about 70 miles to a degree. The earliest surviving printed manual for navigation was dated 1509, the Portuguese *Regimento do astrolabio e do quadrante,* mentioned previously, but there were probably manuscript editions that preceded it (Taylor 1957b: 547-548). Rules were laid out in this *regimento* for finding the latitude by sun and stars, from Cap Finisterre to the equator, and for "raising a degree." It was only a few years later that the latitudes were extended as far as the Indies. If all went well and the navigator and master brought the ship within sight of their destination, there were still problems to be faced.

Lead Sounding Weights

For the final, crucial approach to shore the navigator had lead sounding weights to help guide him in to a safe landing.

There are three of these weights in the collection (Fig. 17), representing typical examples of the most ancient kinds of navigational aids ever used. Still carried on ships today, sounding weights are made in the old-time conical form, traditional through the ages, often with a concavity in the bottom for "arming the lead." This was done by filling the shallow depression with paraffin, tallow, or even grease, in order to bring up a sample of the sea floor; whether it was sand, gravel, shell, or mud would provide a valuable clue for the navigator. On an oozy sea-bed, flannel smeared with a little tallow would be wrapped around the base to gather the specimen. These simple devices have been the safeguards of seamen for thousands of years, telling them how deep the water was, when they were approaching a shore, and what dangerous obstacles they might expect. Taylor (1957a: 36) has found that they were mentioned by the Greek historian Herodotus when he wrote about the geography of Egypt some 500 years before Christ, and she believes that they probably were used by the seafaring Phoenicians, and long before that by the Cretans.

The largest and heaviest weight, known as the "dipsic" lead, was used for deep sea soundings. The weight of this was usually given as 14 pounds, and it was furnished with a long line for taking soundings from about 100 to 200 fathoms. The fathom was a unit of measure first based upon the length of a man's outstretched arms, now established at six feet. The line was marked by leather or cloth at 10-foot intervals, beginning at 20 fathoms. In shoal water, less than 20 fathoms, a seven-pound weight was used, and the marks were placed closer together. The heaviest of the sounding weights in the Texas Gulf collection may have been a dipsie lead, but, judging from their weights, the other two probably were used for the middle depths.

The heaviest one, no. 1636 (Fig. 17B), weighs 6104 grams (about 13 lbs., 8 oz.). It is a simple cone that tapers from a basal diameter of 8.4 cm. to 2.3 cm. at the top. The suspension hole for the line is 1.0 cm. in diameter and starts about 2.2 cm. from the tip. The bottom of the weight is shallowly concave. Probably the surface was once smooth, but it is uneven and rough now, although there are no meaningful marks on it. If it was made in a mold, the mold marks are not evident. Aside from a few barnacles still adhering, along with small patches of surface corrosion, it may not look much different from what it did when the ship went down.

The second weight, no. 1637 (Fig. 17C), is of a different

style, still conical in shape but longer and slimmer, with a faceted surface, and evidently cast in a mold. Ten facets begin at the base, but four on each side terminate below the top where the two opposing sides were flattened to receive the suspension hole. The top is a sort of rounded oval that measures 2.2 cm. x 3.1 cm. The hole, 1.2 cm. in diameter, begins 2.7 cm. below the top. The facets that run the entire length of the weight meet in a slight, smoothed ridge at the summit. The specimen is 28 cm. long and weighs 5145 grams (about 11 lbs., 5 oz.). Its slightly concave base is 6.3 cm. wide. When the weight is standing on a flat surface, the upper part appears to be leaning over a little to the side. The faceted edges are no longer sharp, probably battered and smoothed from long use, and there are iron oxide stains and a few barnacles on the surface, but otherwise it is in good condition.

The third, no. 1509 (Fig. 17A), is made in exactly the same faceted style described above, and it leans to the side also, but it is smaller and the bottom is almost flat. A grid of small squares has been scratched across the bottom surface, but so shallowly that it appears to have been done with the tip of a knife. If the intention was to roughen the surface it could not have helped much. This lead is 24 cm. long and weighs 3880 grams (about 8 lbs., 7 oz.). It tapers from a 6 cm. width at the base to the rounded oval top. Again, the facets are battered and worn, and there are iron stains and some corrosion patches on the surface.

By dead reckoning, that is, by laying down a compass course and estimated distance on a chart, and estimating the speed of the ship, or by celestial navigation, using the sun and stars to find their way, navigators guided their ships across the sea. Their aids were simple and not very accurate: mathematical tables, maps, and charts (crude as they were), compass and dividers, and sand glasses for telling time. For celestial navigation there was the quadrant (and possibly the cross-staff, a wooden staff with three of four movable cross-pieces that came into use about the middle of the sixteenth century) for nocturnal readings and the astrolabe for finding the altitude of the sun or stars. For the final approach to shore, the lead sounding weights helped bring the ships safely in. Of these various navigational devices that might have survived from the ship, we have only the three astrolabes and three sounding weights.

SHIP'S GEAR, FITTINGS, AND EQUIPMENT

Perhaps the most significant recovered items of the ship's gear, in terms of indicating something about its construction and possibly its size, are the gudgeon and rudder pin, or pintle, which comprise parts of the steering mechanism. A ship's gudgeon is defined as a metal socket with straps on either side for attachment to the sternpost (Fig. 18). The pintle would have been inserted vertically through the centered socket, the combination of pieces forming part of the vessel's steering assemblage. A set of gudgeons would have been fastened vertically, one above the other on the stern, with a separate pintle for each gudgeon. Because the arms of the gudgeon extend almost horizontally from the socket instead of forming an angle with it, the piece appears to be most likely one of the top gudgeons of the set and probably indicates a flat stern.

Constructed of wrought iron, this gudgeon consists of a 7–10 cm. wide strap wrapped about three-quarters of the way around the socket, extending in straps of equal length on either side. The straps terminate in vertical rectangular elements. There are three holes for fastening the gudgeon to the stern along each strap and five holes on each vertical section. The entire piece weighed 1338.1 kg. (about 29.5 lbs.) after cleaning. Scale drawings are shown in Figure 18.

The rudder pintle (no. 1584) would also have had straps, more or less parallel to each other but making a narrow angle on either side of the shaft when complete; but as only a portion of one strap remains, the object is now roughly L-shaped (Fig. 18). The pintle shaft is 34.0 cm. long, and the incomplete strap section is 10.5 cm. long and 6.4 cm. high. The shaft tapers in thickness to 1.8 cm. at the lower end.

Copper Sleeve Bearing

This device (no. 1498) consists of a 9-cm. square block with a circular hole through the center; two dovetailed keys, extending from opposite sides, probably secured it in a wooden rigging block. Metallurgical analysis reveals that it consists almost entirely of copper with a very low percentage of lead alloy. Top and side views of the bearing are illustrated in Figure 19A and B, with a hypothetical placement in a wooden block shown by line drawing, 19C. The object has been tentatively identified by Carl Clausen (personal communication) as part of the heavy assemblage necessary for lifting a yard, possibly the mainsail yard. The keys of the bearing are flush

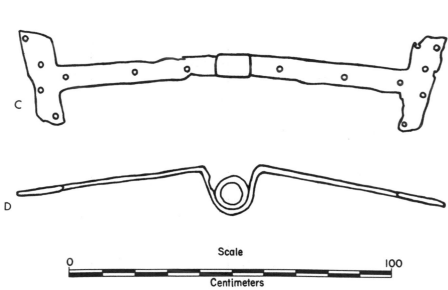

Fig. 18.—Complete rudder gudgeon (no. 1303) and fragmentary pin or pintle (no. 1584). (A) Rudder pintle lacking side straps, set above the gudgeon socket where it might have fit. (B) Rudder gudgeon. The wide angle formed by the straps indicates it came from a flat section of the stern, possibly near the top. (C, D) Scale drawings of the gudgeon, shown from top and side. (E) Artist's representation of how the gudgeon might have been placed on the stern. (F) Illustration of pintles in place on the rudder, one for each gudgeon.

Scale

0   100

Centimeters

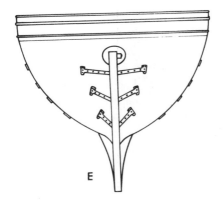

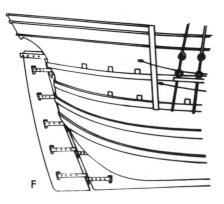

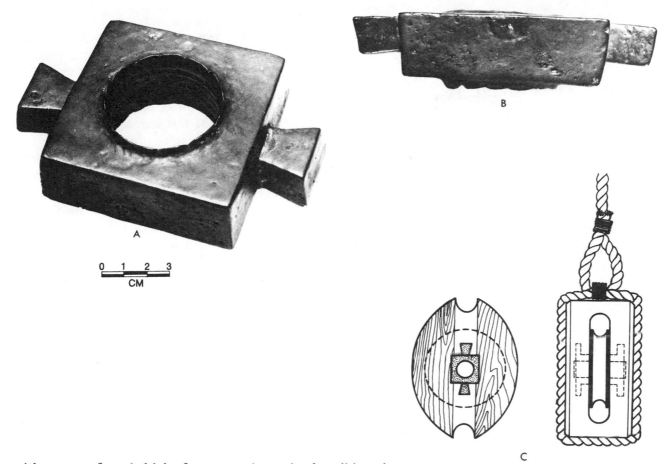

Fig. 19.—Heavy copper sleeve bearing (no. 1498), keyed to be set in wood. (A) Upper surface; (B) Side view; note that keys extend only half-way through the block; (C) Artist's reconstruction of possible placement in wooden block, shown in front and side view.

with one surface (which, for convenience in describing the piece, we are calling the upper surface), but extend only half-way down through the body. Both keys and cylindrical interior are slightly beveled from the upper face to the lower. Circular grooves are visible on the inside around the aperture but give no evidence of machine tooling. The upper edge of the hole seems to have been roughened by wear, while heat generated by friction and pressure has caused the metal of the lower rim to flare outward. Diameter of the aperture increases from 5.0 cm. on the upper face to 5.4 cm. on the lower. Measuring inward from their outer ends, the keys differ slightly in width, but both are 2.5 cm. long. One is 3.5 cm. across the top and 2.8 cm. across the bottom, and the other measures 3.4 cm. and 3.0 cm. respectively. The bearing weighs 1938.4 g. (more than 4 lbs., 4 oz.) and is in excellent condition.

Anchor Fluke Fragment

Only a remnant of the anchor is present, representing

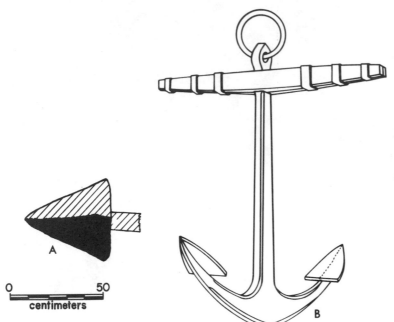

Fig. 20.—Anchor fluke fragment (no. 1481). (A) Photograph shows actual fragment, about half of the fluke, and the line drawing indicates shape of the missing half. (B) Drawing of a typical anchor of the period, wrought iron with wooden stock at right angles to the shank and triangular flukes at the ends of the arm.

about half of an anchor fluke (no. 1581), and like most of the ship's fittings and equipment is made of wrought iron. It is illustrated in Figure 20, along with a line drawing to indicate the appearance of the complete fluke and a sketch of a typical anchor of the period. Spanish anchors were notorious for their thin metal and consequent fragility, says J. W. van Nouheys (1951: 44). To be "as meagre as a Spanish anchor" was said to be a common Dutch expression. This half of the fluke is triangular, with straight sides measuring 44.5 x 47.0 x 22.0 cm., and maximum thickness of 2.2 cm. It weighs 6.615 kg.

Chains

Several wrought iron chains, or pieces of them, in varying condition and different somewhat in size and design, were evidently intended for diverse purposes.

The largest chain (no. 319) has been identified as possibly a main brace for the mainmast (Fig. 21). It consists of two sets of three links attached to a large yoke-like loop. This large loop is 39 cm. across its widest part and 80 cm. long, with metal thickness of 5 cm. The links vary in length from 48 to 60 cm.; they are pinched together near the center, no doubt to impede motion and reduce wear and tear, and the last link on each chain is bowed outward. The object is complete and in excellent condition.

Three chains are part of the assemblages for deadeyes, important elements of the standing rigging. The wooden deadeye, which would have fit inside the binding, would have been pierced with three holes to receive the lanyards, or ropes, for setting up shrouds and stays.

One chain of this type (no. 323-1) has a single set of links, two complete and one partial, suspended from the binding, or strop, which went around the deadeye, illustrated in Figure 22B). This binding is 37 cm. long and 14 cm. wide at its maximum, and the metal is 1.7 cm. thick. The two complete links are 24 and 23 cm. long, but the incomplete one was originally about 33.5 cm. As in the case of the very large chain described above, these links are also pinched together in the center.

The second deadeye chain set (no. 315-1, 2, 3) was broken apart, but the components were reassembled for the photograph, Figure 22A. It has a single set of three links that had been attached to the strop. Suspended from the last link was an eye-pin along which were fitted four iron washers that still slide along the shaft. Clausen (personal communication) suggests that the pin might have been improperly constructed and the washers were added to make it fit properly in place. The pin is 49 cm. long, with a diameter of 2.5 cm., and at its distal end is a slot for insertion of a fastening peg. This assemblage was found intact within its encrustation, but the iron was in such poor condition that the center link broke off in handling, and the pieces are now separated from one another.

The third set of this type (no. 314-1a, b, and 3) was once composed of two links, with the strop at one end and an eye-pin or bolt at the other. The pin is incomplete at 60 cm. long; its oval eye measures 3.4 x 4.0 cm. in a 6.8 cm. wide head. Attached to the pin was a broken chain link which, when complete, was probably about 26 cm. long. The strop is 41 cm. long and 19 cm. across its greatest width. This loop, like the other, is pinched inward, in this instance at a point below its center, narrowing to a width of 7 cm. where the first link would have been attached. One of the links, broken in two pieces, had been about 28 cm. long and 1.5 cm. thick. It is not illustrated, but the assemblage is like those shown in Figure 22A.

Quite a different type of chain (no. 1580) is complete with a circular ring at one end, an eyed pin at the other, and nine links joining them (Fig. 23). It may have been a preserver or safety chain to keep the rudder in tow if it became unshipped. The inside diameter of the ring is 11.3 cm., but the outside diameter is somewhat irregular because the metal thickness varies; it averages about 2 cm. Maximum outside diameter is 15.6 cm. The links range in length from 18.0 to 24.5 cm., and the inside widths vary from 2.4 cm. to 3.7 cm. Metal thickness averages about 2.0 cm. The pin is 46 cm. long, tapering to a blunt point from a diameter of 2.5 cm. near the eye.

Three other segments of chains or chain assemblages, also not illustrated, are similar to those already described. The first consists of a small chain link that was attached to a pin when they were encrusted together, but have been separated in cleaning (no. 1305). The pin, with a heart-shaped eye, is nearly complete at 60 cm. in length, lacking probably about 1 cm. at the tip. This end appears to have been slotted for a fastening key. The shank of the pin tapers from 7 cm. in thickness at the eye to about 2 cm. at the broken end. Two

Fig. 21.—Largest chain in the collection (no. 319). It was probably a main brace, strong enough to have secured the mainmast. Links are pinched together to keep them from sliding, and the terminal links are bowed outward.

47

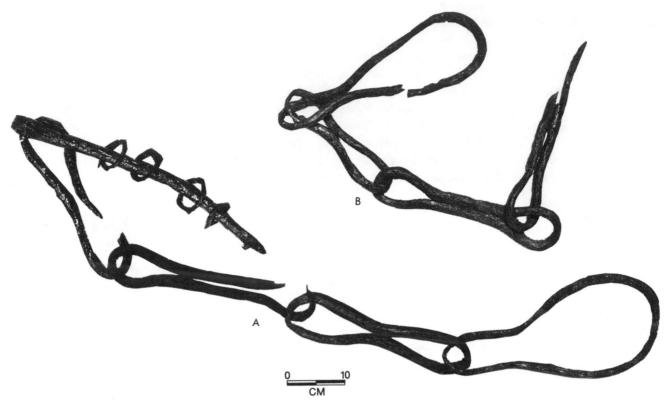

Fig. 22.—Chains for the standing rigging, part of the assemblages for the deadeyes. (A) Chain No. 315-1, 2, 3 was reassembled from the broken parts of the original chain. (B) No. 323-1 is intact but probably incomplete since the pin is missing.

additional chain link fragments, not associated with any of the other chains, are similar in general shape and size to the large ones already pictured in Figures 22 and 23 and are not illustrated.

Fasteners: Wrought Iron Spikes, Pins, Nails

Sixty-two of these hardware items are in the collection, including the four eye-pins already described as parts of chain assemblages, and one object cast from a fragmentary mold. All are listed by catalogue number in Table 1, with measurements and other details given. Figure 24 illustrates the size range. Many are in such badly corroded condition, or so incomplete, that it is impossible to tell much about them, but most are sufficiently intact that they can be arranged generally in order according to what we suspect they might have been used for. The 10 with square or rectangular shanks we are calling spikes or nails; the smaller ones were possibly intended for deck planks, and others for general planking spikes. Spike shanks or nails averaged about 1.3 cm. in width, measured just under the head at the widest part, and the measurable heads averaged about 2.4 cm. in diameter.

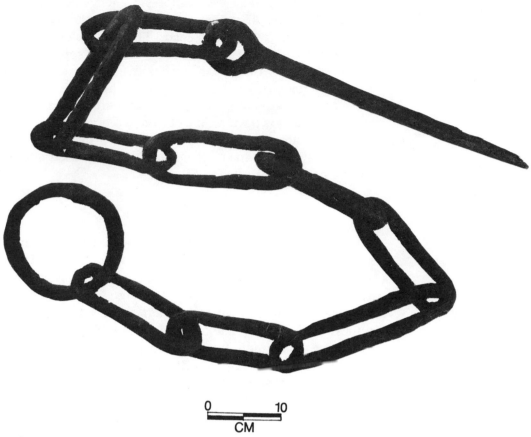

0 _____ 10
CM

Seven specimens are large, round-shanked through-pins that indicate their usage by the hole or slot at the distal end through which a small pin, wedge, or key would have been inserted as a fastening. The longest ones may have penetrated all the way through the hull and been secured on the inside of the ship. The through-pins averaged about 43.4 cm. in length, 3.7 cm. in diameter, and had circular heads 6.5 cm. across.

Other examples also have round shanks and circular heads but lack the hole or slot for a fastening device. Some may be pins with the slotted end broken off, and some may be spikes with the pointed distal end missing. We have simply called them broken or incomplete spikes or pins. They average a little smaller than the through-pins, 34.2 cm. long, 2.6 cm. in diameter, with heads about 5.3 cm. wide. The cast example is one of these, but represents only the head end of a round-shanked piece that may have been used for planking (no. C217a).

Some of the remaining pieces in this hardware category, with incomplete lengths, no doubt would fit well enough into one or another of these three categories, but others are

Fig. 23.—Complete chain with ring and pin, possibly a safety chain to keep the rudder in tow if it became unshipped.

so badly corroded that we cannot even tell whether their shanks were round or square; and many, whether complete or incomplete, have lost their heads. This may have occurred frequently because the heads were separately applied, in a wrap-around or "fillet-weld" technique, and broke off easily from the shank; others may never have had heads at all. Figure 24 is a good illustration of the wrap-around head construction that is obvious in a corroded piece (no. 1528-1). In Table 1, those specimens that have been mentioned before as elements of chain assemblages are identified as well as those that are illustrated in Figure 24.

Tools

The ship would have needed certain skilled tradesmen aboard—a carpenter, a caulker, and a cooper. As J. H. Parry (1969: 71) outlines their duties, the carpenter *(carpintero)* was responsible for repairing and looking after the hull and spars, the caulker (known as the *califate*) saw to the water-tightness of the vessel, caulking and paying of the seams, and maintaining the pump, and the cooper *(tonelero)* looked after the casks and barrels with their precious supplies of food, water, and wine. Morison (1962: 147), however, says the carpenter was also responsible for the caulking of decks and on topsides of the ship. These tradesmen could repair and improvise and even manufacture new fittings when it was necessary.

Few workmen's tools have survived, but at least two ot them seem to have belonged to the carpenter's kit. First, there is a large sledge hammer (no. 110-1) with heavily battered ends that prove what hard usage it had. It was constructed of three layered strips of iron wrought together in a fagoted or piled weld—a laminated structure of iron and steel—to fashion the solid heavy piece (Hodges 1964: 88). It probably once weighed about 9.5 kg. (about 20 lbs.), because even after its prolonged immersion in the sea it still weighed about 8.8 kg. after the encrustation was removed and before any processing took place. It is 26 cm. long, 8 cm. wide, and 6.5 cm. thick. Diameter of the hole for a wooden handle is 3.5 cm. A few scraps of wood (no. 110-2), discovered inside the hole, are all that remain of the handle. Figure 25H—J shows the hammer as it appeared still encrusted, then broken out of the encrustation, and after it was processed.

An ordinary hammer head, also of wrought iron, was so fragmentary that its particular type could not be identified

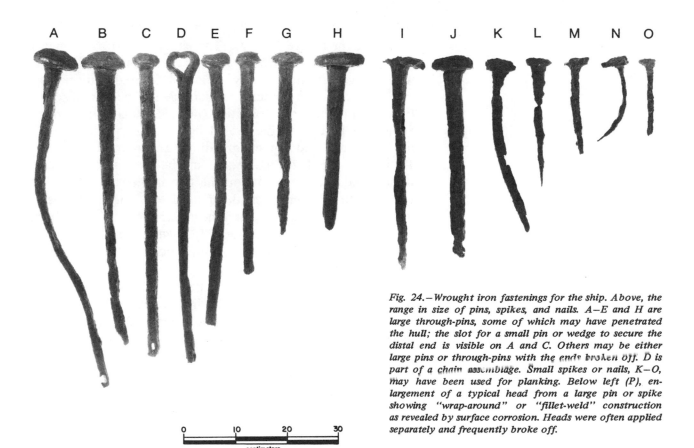

Fig. 24.—Wrought iron fastenings for the ship. Above, the range in size of pins, spikes, and nails. A–E and H are large through-pins, some of which may have penetrated the hull; the slot for a small pin or wedge to secure the distal end is visible on A and C. Others may be either large pins or through-pins with the ends broken off. D is part of a chain assemblage. Small spikes or nails, K–O, may have been used for planking. Below left (P), enlargement of a typical head from a large pin or spike showing "wrap-around" or "fillet-weld" construction as revealed by surface corrosion. Heads were often applied separately and frequently broke off.

P

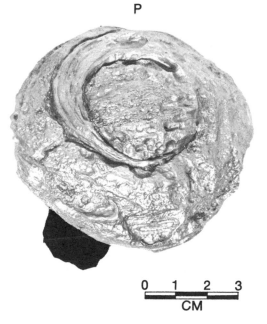

since only about a fourth of the socket was left (no. 1508). Judging from the remnant of the head that extended beyond the socket hole, it could either have been a claw hammer or double-polled type designed for pounding with either end (Fig. 25C).

Next were two unusual, seemingly highly specialized tools, wrought iron like the others, whose function is uncertain (nos. 69 and 1304). They were made just about alike with long shanks that terminate at one end in a curved, somewhat L-shaped head and at the other in a short, two-pronged fork that turns slightly upward. The area back of and just below the curved head is flattened out and wider than the remainder of the shank. The metal is corroded so the surfaces are damaged, but the outer edge of the heads are sharp, curving downward to what was probably a blunt point at the end; the inner edge of the curve is narrow, but flat. They bear a tenuous resemblance to a carpenter's tool that Tryckare describes as a "Rave hook or ripping iron for cleaning or caulking from the seams." (illustrated in his book *The Lore of Ships,* 1963: 35, No. 40). The two curious tools and a reproduction of Tryckare's line drawing of the rave hook are illustrated in Figure 25D—G. The shank of no. 69 appears now to be round in cross-section, but the encrustation that was removed from it clearly indicated from the impression in the matrix that its shank had originally been octagonal. From its present poor condition, however, this characteristic could not have been discovered had the encrustation itself not been at hand for examination. The second tool, no. 1304, is not as badly corroded, and its shaft seems to have been round. Measurements on the two implements are: (69) total length 43.0 cm.; length of head 9.0 cm., incomplete; width of flat section behind head 3.35 cm. (1304) total length 43.0 cm.; length of head 12.0 cm.; width of flat section behind head 4.0 cm.; maximum thickness (back of head) 2.0 cm., tapering to 1.25 cm. just above the prongs. Were these caulking tools for the carpenter (the kind that Trycare illustrated), used perhaps for light work on deck, digging out the oakum with the sharp point and edge, pulling out nails and spikes with the prongs, and pounding new caulking in with the flattened section? The function of the two curious tools remains a puzzle, but it still seems possible they might have been used for deck work.

Another special purpose tool (no. C324-1), shown in Figure 25B, is represented only by the latex cast that was made from a mold left in the encrustation when the iron object became completely oxidized. The reconstruction proved that this was once a ladle with a long, curved handle and a rounded trianguloid head. Most likely it was employed for melting lead, for we know that a great deal of lead was used on the ship. A similar implement is illustrated by R. J. Forbes (1956: 66, Fig. 34) from a woodcut published in an old German book dating about 1480. This shows the equipment used for one of the stages in smelting argentiferous copper to which lead or lead compounds had been added to extract the silver. Identification as a lead-working tool therefore seems to be reasonable. We believe the cast is a fairly accurate replica of the original object. If so, its total length was about 64.2 cm. The shallow bowl or scoop was 9.0 cm. wide at the sharp outer edge and tapered to about 1.75 mm. at the handle where it was only 5 mm. thick.

The only other recognizable tool is a sandstone hone, which, of course, could have been used by anyone who needed to sharpen a knife (no. 1611). It was rounded at the narrow end and ovate-rectangular at the wider end, generally circular in cross-section. The piece was broken in two parts when it was received but has been glued together. It was

Fig. 25.—Assortment of tools. (A) Broken sandstone hone, no. 1610. (B) Latex cast of oxidized wrought iron ladle that might have been used for lead-working processes, no. C324-1. (C) Fragmentary wrought iron tools for unknown purpose. Left, no. 69; right, 1304. Surfaces are eroded now, but the outer tip of the curved heads was pointed and the outside edge was sharp; inside edge was wider and flat. Back of the heads and just below them, the shank becomes flat and widened, as is shown in F. No. 69's shank was originally octagonal, that of 1304 was round. The tools bear some resemblance to the one shown in G. (F) View of 1304 from the back to show widening and thickening of the shanks behind the head. (G) Reproduction of tool illustrated by Tre Tryckare in The Lore of Ships and identified as a carpenter's rave hook or caulking tool for cleaning out old caulking (Tryckare 1963:35, no. 40). Reproduced by permission. (H) Encrustation no. 110 before processing, contents completely unknown. (I) Encrustation partially removed reveals wrought iron sledge hammer, no. 110-1. (J) The sledge hammer after being processed; weight 8.8 kg., probable weight when in use, 9.5 kg. (about 20 lbs.). A few fragments of wood remaining inside the socket hole were remnants of handle 110-2, not illustrated.

53

19.25 cm. long, with thickness ranging from 2.0 to 2.3 cm. (Fig. 25A).

Miscellaneous Metal Objects

In addition to these identifiable tools are several objects, mostly fragmentary. Not all their functions have been determined, but some of them appeared to be broken sections or bits from various articles of the ship's equipment. They are not illustrated.

A latex cast (no. C341-2) was made from the mold in an encrustation that turned out to be a washer, probably of iron, similar to the kind found on the pin of the chain assemblage no. 314-1, 2, 3, described earlier. It measured about 6 cm. across, with a hole of 3 cm. in diameter. The metal had been about 5 mm. thick.

The next, no. 40-5, is a short, curved, rod-shaped segment, made of tin alloy. It is 6.1 cm. long with a diameter of 5 mm.

Two others form a composite object that was found encrusted (nos. 175-3, 175-4). One was a short length of iron wire, 4 mm. in diameter, that was bent at one end into an L-shape; the longer section, 7.3 cm., was found lying beside some wood fragments that were still encrusted. The encrustation itself was designated no. 175-4 and was saved because it retained the mold of the wire. The short leg of the wire piece was wrapped with what appeared to be metal bands 9 mm. wide.

Specimen no. 1444-2 is a solid, cylindrical brass pin or bolt with a round head; a narrow slot perforates the shank near the distal end for the insertion of a wedge. The object is complete, and, except for the small size of the slot, appears much like the pins used for securing the astrolabe sighting devices to their ring centers. It is 3.3 cm. long and tapers in diameter from 1.3 cm. at the head to 7 mm. at the other end; the slot measures 3 x 5 mm. Head diameter is 1.3 cm.

A small, U-shaped iron piece, no. 1464-2, appears to be a shackle that has lost its pin. It has expanded, rounded ends with holes in the center. The shackle is 3.8 cm. high, 2.9 cm. wide, and the perforations are 5 mm. in diameter.

Metal Strap Fragments

There is evidence of at least 75 or 80 pieces of iron straps in the form of badly oxidized fragments or molds left in encrustations. Six of these fragments have been processed and retained (nos. 81-2, 175-2, 323-5, 1458-4 & 5, 1476-5). They must be the remnants of straps used for fastening barrels, casks, chests, or boxes. Most are 2.2 to 2.5 cm. wide and 0.3 to 0.5 cm. thick. The narrowest is 1.8 cm. and the thinnest only 0.1 cm., as compared with the sturdiest fragment, which is 6.5 cm. wide and 1.1 cm. thick. One has the remains of a small rivet or pin driven through it. Latex casts have been made of several strap fragments, and a number of encrustations that preserve good molds have been saved for further casting.

Small Lead Weights

Nine small weights may have been used for fishing, or perhaps for heaving a line (Fig. 16A–H, J). Parry (1969: 72) says that fresh fish were expected to supplement other foods and that fishing lines and hooks were sometimes mentioned as an item of the ship's stores. The shapes vary—cylindrical, conical, rectangular, or oval—but all the weights have some sort of suspension hole. In all but one instance the hole was made in a flattened section near the top, the exception being a sinker that was perforated lengthwise (Fig. 26H). Only one appears to have been cast in a mold (Fig. 26J); the others were crudely made, possibly pounded into their irregular shapes, often lopsided, with rough and uneven surfaces. Their catalogue numbers, measurements, and descriptive details are presented in Table 2.

Other Lead Objects

There are two small special-purpose devices. One is a small solid cone with no suspension hole (no. 57-11, Fig. 26I), that could have been used as a weight if it were tied up in a cloth. The surface is smooth, the base flat, suggesting that it was mold-made. It weighs 43.1 g. The other (no. 1633, Fig. 26K), is a small wedge with a flat circular base and a thin rectangular top. It is 7.2 cm. long and weighs 141.5 g. The top measures 0.2 x 1.0 cm. and the diameter of the base is 1.9 cm. It does not appear to have been cast in a mold.

Other lead objects are what seem to be ingots of various sizes and shapes. Evidently it was necessary to carry considerable quantities of lead along for a variety of purposes. The largest and most impressive of these ingots is a section of a rectangular bar (no. 1497), illustrated in Figure 27. Modern saw marks, evidently made by Platoro, are obvious across one end, suggesting that someone wanted to find out

Fig. 26.—Small lead objects. A–H and J are weights, possibly used for fishing. I is a solid conical piece without perforation that might have been used as a weight. K is a wedge.

whether the lead was camouflaging a central core of gold or silver; smuggling was not at all uncommon. On one side of the bar is a circular mark enclosing a curious design. This may be a shipping mark or it may have something to do with weight. Agricola's *De Re Metallica* (Hoover translation 1950: 499) illustrates some lead pieces that are being weighed as part of the process of using them as alloys. These lead pigs bear marks somewhat similar to the one on the ingot we describe. Its incomplete length is 10.0 cm., and it is 11.5 cm. wide and 9.5 cm. high. It weighs 9.6 kg. (about 21¼ lbs.).

Another lead bar, no. 1625, is longer, slimmer, and triangular in cross-section. The flat ends and smooth surface

0   5   10
centimeters

Fig. 27.—Portion of heavy cast lead ingot (no. 1497) bearing a circular mark with an undeciphered device, possibly a shipper's mark. Line drawing to left shows details of mark. Striations at end of ingot indicate it has been sawn through.

indicate that it was cast in a regular mold. It is 27 cm. long, with maximum width of 3.0 cm., and it weighs 2.38 kg. Neither this, nor the following lead ingots are illustrated.

A third bar-like piece, no. 1626, is roughly rectangular. It measures 8.9 x 5.0 cm., with maximum thickness of about 3.0 cm. and weighs 1035.79 g.

Then there are three ingots of a somewhat irregular disk-like shape. No. 1435 may even be a low grade silver, for a specific gravity test puts it in an indeterminate range of both lead and silver alloys. It is about 10.7 cm. in diameter, with a maximum thickness of 1.5 cm. It weighs 414.35 g. The surfaces are uneven, and there are no signs of a cast and no stamped mark.

No. 1621 is more of a flattened oval, and again there is some evidence of metal other than lead. The surfaces of this piece are also extremely uneven and rough. It measures 20 x 7.8 cm., with maximum thickness of 1.2 cm., and weighs 9014 g.

The third, no. 1489, is smaller—an uneven disk with maximum diameter of 5 cm. and thickness about 0.9 cm. Its weight is only 98.2 g. In this instance, like the others, the specific gravity test was inconclusive, but it is probably lead.

Additional pieces of lead include fragments of thin lead sheeting, nuggets, lumps, chunks, and scraps. There is a strong possibility that the lead sheeting might have been used as sheathing for the ship's bottom or keel. From about 1520 the Spaniards tried by this means to protect their ships from the destructive shipworm *(Teredo navalis)*, which lived in warm waters and had a tremendous appetite for wooden ships (Haring 1964: 277; Marx 1971: 97; Potter 1960: 78; Waters 1958: 92). Haring relates that the first time the hulls of vessels were protected by lead sheathing was on Pedrarias Davila's expedition of 1514, and they used hundreds of pounds of lead for the purpose. According to Waters, the lead sheathing proved to be too expensive for normal use, and the extra weight had a tendency to fall away at the bottom; in addition, the lead set up an electrolytic action with the iron bottom fastenings. Marx writes that the practice of lead sheathing on Spanish ships was discontinued for a time in 1567 because it caused the ships to sail too slowly, but it was again applied to vessels going to Mexico in order that they might be protected during the winter layover in Vera Cruz. By the late eighteenth century copper was being used for this purpose by the French and English, and Potter gives the date 1810 for the year the Spaniards gave up the lead and adopted copper sheathing themselves.

The lead sheets in this collection average in thickness between one-sixteenth to one-eighth inch (3 mm. or less), a figure that is somewhat less than Potter gives for sheathing thickness, one-eighth to one-fourth inch. On a good many of these fragments, patches of thin, black material adhere, possibly tar, but it is more likely to be a naturally occurring asphalt. They are perforated by holes made by large-headed square-shanked tacks. The holes average about 4 to 10 mm. in width; on the larger pieces they are spaced usually 2 to 3 cm. apart, but they can be found at intervals of 1 to 4 cm. Depressions made by the heads often can be seen, sometimes overlapping one another. Impressions of a heavy, coarse fabric are obvious on all of the large sections and on many of the small ones, appearing on the opposite side from which the tacks were struck. The largest of these sheets is illustrated (no. 1457-3) in Figure 28A. It measures about 24 x 19.5 x 30 cm. The piece must be an end section because it has one fairly straight side along which a row of nail holes are evenly spaced about 1 to 1.5 cm. apart. Figure 28B is an enlargement from another sheet (no. 1302-9) to show details of the fabric impression and the seams where the cloth was sewn together. Several other sections are nearly the same size as those illustrated, and as far as appearance goes could all be fragments of the original sheet; in fact, three large segments and a number of scraps were found encrusted with *Verso* No. 1457-1; together they weigh about 1.9 kg. (2¼ lbs.).

A

B

Fig. 28.—(A) Piece of lead sheathing (no. 1457-3B) showing perforations made by square-shanked tacks. Row of tack holes to left probably indicates an end section. Lead sheathing was probably used to protect the lower part of the hull, or the keel, from destructive shipworms. (B) Enlargement of reverse side of a sheathing scrap (no. 1302-9) to show impression of fabric against which the lead sheet was fastened. Seams where pieces of fabric were sewn together are visible at center left and at right edge.

Some of the flat pieces may have been used for patching as well as for sheathing. In 1969 a recovery team brought up the cannons and other materials that Capt. James Cook, the eighteenth century explorer-navigator, had jettisoned off the coast of Australia in 1770 when his ship *Endeavor* went aground. They reported finding a large lead sheet near one of the cannons that was about 2.5 mm. thick, 0.7 m. long, and 0.2 m. at its widest part; it contained 18 circular holes of 6.4 to 10 mm. diameter. But there was no mention of fabric impressions on it. They identified the sheet as a hull patch, or possibly some sort of weatherproofing. Metallurgically it was found to be the same as one from H. M. S. "Looe," which sank in the Florida Keys in 1744 (Pearson 1972a: 106).

The nuggets, lumps, chunks, and other bits and pieces of lead scrap are of irregular shapes and difficult to describe, often contorted and folded, although some seem to be small fragments of lead straps. Others may have been detached from broken ingots or may just represent residue from lead-working operations.

Ballast Stones

Stone, sand, or shingle (a sort of gravel) were all used for ballast in the sixteenth century, but prudent captains were said to prefer stone as it was considered to be much more sanitary than either sand or shingle, even though the latter materials were easier to handle. In spite of the Spanish reputation for filthy ships, the Spaniards usually carried stone ballast, while the English more often used the shingle that was available from their beaches. Since the foul bilges had to be emptied and cleaned out from time to time, the ballast was shoveled out and replaced with fresh sand or stones picked up from whatever beach was nearby. We have to assume, though, that any stone-ballasted ship that had made several voyages would probably be carrying ballast stones from a number of sources—cobbles that other ships had left behind after previous "rummaging" operations.

Not counting the stones that remain in encrustations retained for display or for casting, there are 288 loose ballast stones in this collection. But these were not all the ballast load that the ship carried, by any means, and it is fairly certain that the treasure hunters brought them up only because in the murky waters of the Gulf they were unable to tell what they were recovering. Some of the stones still have patches of shell or other encrusted matter on the surface.

Although most are cobbles (64 to 256 mm.), the usual size for ballast, there are a few of boulder (above 256 mm.) and pebble size (below 64 mm.) as well, along with many fragments of broken larger stones, several of which were definitely derived from the same boulder. The largest stone weighs over 32 kg. (83 lbs.), but there are four others that weigh over 13 kg. The bulk of the stones are smooth from wave action and chemical weathering in the sea.

Even ballast stones may reveal historical information. From analysis of those recovered by the party that found Capt. Cook's cannons, and information from Cook's official log, conservators were able to sort out the stone that was jettisoned (taken on board in the Society Islands and in New Zealand) from that which was native to the Barrier Reef where the cannons were found (Pearson 1972b: 58).

Rod Patten, in 1969 a graduate student in geology at The University of Texas at Austin, undertook to analyze the "smelly old stones." In his words (letter of April 9, 1974):

My intention was to use the composition, sphericity, roundness, and surface features of certain "indicator" stones to determine the geologic province from which they came, and how far they were transported by nature before they were picked up the first time by sailors or ship builders.

Unfortunately, he was unable to complete the project, but he spent many hours examining, measuring, and making a preliminary identification of more than 100 of the stones. Admittedly, the sample is probably too small to be truly representative of the entire ship's ballast, but the information derived from his study is offered here because it may be a start toward a more complete investigation and because it presents some interesting and highly suggestive observations.

Patten found that although several geologic provinces may be represented by the aggregate of ballast stones in the collection, it was remarkable to discover that, at most, only a few sources seem to be responsible for the great majority of them. Most appear to be metamorphic rocks such as schist and gneiss, or igneous rocks such as granite, basalt, or lava, all of which could have come from one geologic province. Neither he nor any of the laboratory crew handling the stones identified any flint among them. Because of their isomorphic structure, the best transport indicators are quartz, granite, and basalt; and based on the shapes of these stones, he believed that they came from a river. He adds:

Judging from the size of some of them, they were picked up not far (a few miles) from their source. This is also indicated by the existence of several fragile, thinly-laminated greenish schists and slate (?). However, they traveled far enough to be sub-round to round (a measure of the angularity of the "corners" rather then an indicator of shape.

The shape, or sphericity, of the indicator stones reveals whether they came from rivers or from beaches; rivers tend to make them rod-shaped, beaches make them disk-shaped. It is possible that these are the kinds that might have washed down the Guadalquivir River in Spain to be picked up on the beach at San Lucar, Spain's port of embarkation for most Spanish voyages to the New World.

Even an estimated weight of the ballast might tell something about the size of the ship. Peterson (1974: 241) calculated from an estimated 50 tons of ballast that a Spanish ship wrecked off the Bahamas in the sixteenth century was probably a vessel of around 200 tons burden, indicating a medium-sized craft that could carry a crew of 35 to 50 men.

If all of the ballast stones were available for study, and the remainder of them proved to be as nearly homogeneous as those at hand, we might infer that they were loaded onto a ship that had been recently built and outfitted near San Lucar. Perhaps there is a document still waiting in the Archives of Seville that could identify the ship whose remains we are now examining.

ARMAMENT AND WEAPONS

Voracious shipworms and savage storms were not the only dangers to ships sailing the Atlantic, for French pirates and privateers were apt to be lurking around the West Indies and across the sea in the vicinity of the Azores and the Canaries where ships customarily put in on their way back to Spain. The prospect of capturing a richly laden treasure ship was a tremendous lure to these marauders, so all ships on voyages between Spain and the Indies had to be armed.

In 1522 an ordinance was issued by the Crown that "prescribed in minute detail the equipment, arming, provisioning, lading, and manning of all vessels sailing to the New World." (Haring 1964: 271). Most of these regulations, Haring relates, were carried over when a new set of ordinances was issued in 1552 for governing shipping practices. According to this order, the ships were at that time grouped into three classes by size: 100-170 tons, 170-220 tons, and 220-320 tons. At that time tonnage was figured on the basis of cargo capacity, not weight—a *tun,* or in Spanish, *tonelada,* was a double-hogshead of wine. A ship of 100 *toneladas,* then, was supposed to carry a crew of eighteen mariners, two gunners, eight apprentices, two cabin boys, and a maximum of thirty passengers (Haring 1964: 274). Such a ship was to be fitted out with two brass guns (but what was then called brass was probably some sort of brass-bronze alloy), which were listed as a *sacre* and a *falconet*—very long, small caliber weapons-along with six *lombards* and twelve *versos,* the latter two types made of iron. Haring notes, though, that from the weights assigned, those called *falconets* were probably larger guns of *falcon* size (1964: 274, ftnt.). In addition to this armament, an assortment of small arms and armor was stipulated: a specified number of *arquebuses* (heavy matchlock or wheellock guns), crossbows, pikes, half-pikes, lances, shields, breastplates, helmets, balls, and the precise amount of gunpowder appropriate for the numbers and kinds of guns to be transported. The larger the ship, of course, the greater the amount of armament prescribed, with the largest vessels carrying a *demiculverin* (a brass half-cannon), two *sacres,* a *falconet* (or as Haring believes, probably a *falcon* instead), and more of all the other equipment, supplies, and personnel.

Ship's Guns

A tremendous variety of guns, both in actual types and in the diversity of fanciful names for them, would have been available for use aboard ships of all nations; they would have included cast iron as well as wrought iron and cast brass pieces, but the eight guns in this collection represent only two types—*bombardetas* and *versos.* All are wrought iron breechloaders that would have been classed as small artillery, anti-personnel weapons, although they could probably inflict some minor damage to another ship that came in close enough for boarding, the usual tactic for capturing and looting a ship. Since these were small guns they were likely to have been among the ones used for firing salutes as well as for defense.

Bombardetas

The three we are calling *bombardetas* (Figs. 29, 30, 31) were originally identified by Platoro, Inc. as lombard cannons, but this apparently was a misnomer, or perhaps a term loosely employed, as in the case of listing *falconets* instead of *falcons* in the 1552 royal regulation. Jorge Vigon, in his

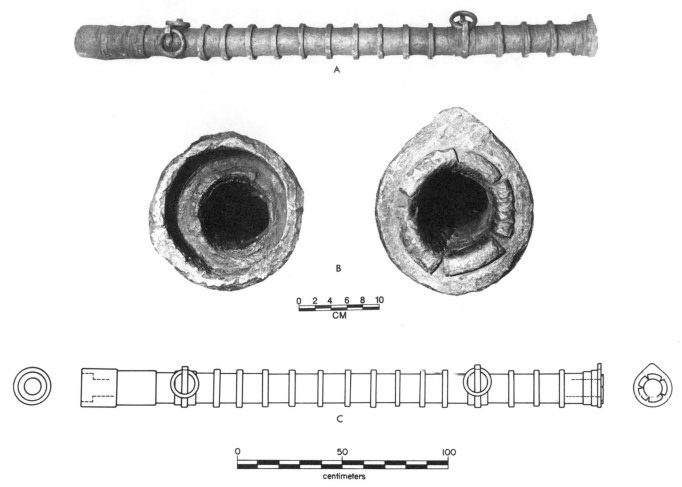

Fig. 29.—Bombardeta *No. 1475-1a, hooped-barrel gun constructed with an interior tube made of five staves. Outer reinforcing rings are placed at the junctures of the bands making up the outer tube. (A) Gun is shown in side view, with breech to left and muzzle to right. Small projection on top of muzzle is probably ornamental. Bore diameter in proportion to barrel length indicates 28 caliber. Fragments of rope were found on underside of barrel just back of the muzzle, probably remnants of lashing to the carriage, and between the second and third reinforcing rings behind the muzzle, at the top of the gun. A few fragments of wood were discovered next to the first set of ring handles back of the muzzle. (B) Close-ups of breech end at left and muzzle end at right. Burred ends of the staves forming the interior tube are evident. (C) Scale drawings of the gun, breech, and muzzle, oriented in the same way as the photograph with muzzle to the right. Bore is indicated by dashed lines.*

Historia de la Artillería Española (1947: 35) based on the collections of the Army Museum in Madrid, the *Museo de Ejército,* explains that the *bombardetas,* although derived from the ancient bombards or lombards dating from the fourteenth century, were of smaller caliber and longer in proportion to the bore diameter than the original guns. Many of the bombards were large enough to be in the "cannon" class of the period, weighing up to several thousand

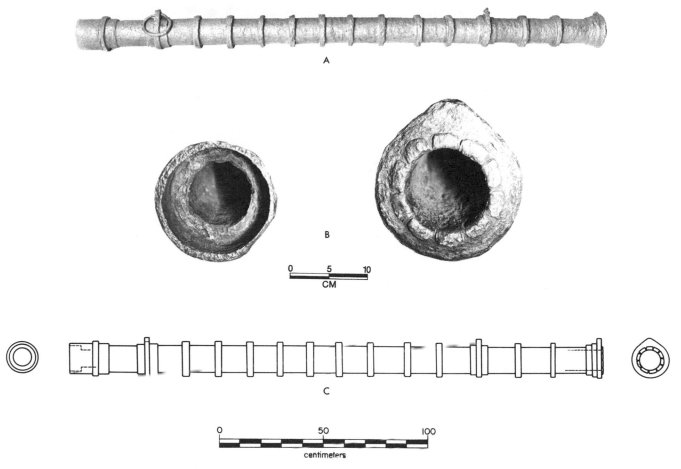

Fig. 30.—Bombardeta No. 1476-1a. (A) Side view of hooped-barrel gun, breech end to the left, muzzle to the right. Slight thickening at top of muzzle is probably ornamental. This gun was built up from an interior tube made of 10 staves, forged around a core, covered by an outer tube of touching bands, onto which reinforcing rings were shrunk at the places where the bands met. Lifting rings were intact at the breech end but broken off at the muzzle. The gun is of 27 caliber. (B) Closeup of breech end at left and muzzle at right. The 10 staves of the inner tube are clearly visible. (C) Scale drawings of gun, breech, and muzzle, oriented as in the photograph. Dotted lines indicate the bore.

pounds and used primarily for battering down walls during a seige. If caliber is figured as the length of the barrel divided by the diameter of the bore, the bombards were fairly short, large-caliber weapons, for Vigon says that none were known whose length was as much as 12 times the bore width. The *bombardetas,* on the other hand, he describes as varying in length between 15 and 30 calibers and thus should not be confused with the small bombards. The *bombardetas* in this collection have calibers of 24, 17, and 28.

Both classes were constructed in about the same manner, however, a subject that will be dealt with later. The terms lombard and bombard (or *lombarda* and *bombarda* in Span-

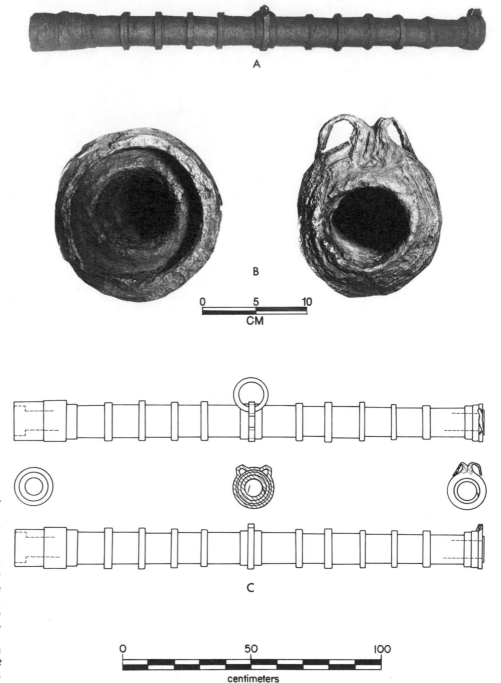

Fig. 31.—Bombardeta *No. 1477-1a.*
(A) Side view of built-up gun, breech end on the left, muzzle on the right. Two-lobed device at top of muzzle is probably ornamental as there is no evidence of a companion sighting piece at the breech. A single set of ring handles had been mounted at the center of the barrel, on the top where rope fragments were found; these were, no doubt, remains of carriage lashings. One handle is still attached to the gun but the other has been broken off. Another handle, however, with its attachment piece, is present and appears to represent the missing half of the pair. Gun caliber is about 24. Unlike the two other bombardetas, the tube of this gun was constructed of a single piece of iron wrapped around a core and lap-welded along its length. Reinforcing hoops were shrunk at evenly spaced intervals along the barrel. The gun was encrusted when received. (B) Closeups of breech end, at left, and muzzle at right. (C) Scale drawings of the gun, oriented as in the photograph. Above, view from the top showing placement of the ring handle. Dashed lines indicate the bore. Center, on left, the breech end; in the middle, cross-section of gun at that point; at right, the muzzle. Below, side view.

ish) seem to have been used interchangeably by many writers, thoroughly confusing both etymologists and historians, for no one appears to know where the name lombard came from. Vigon gives several possible sources for the term but discounts all of them (1947: 47, note 6; McKee 1969: 179 and ftnt). The name *lombarda,* he tells us, is found in early documents along with *bombarda* and quite evidently refers to the same kind of gun. In describing the smaller caliber guns of this type he uses *lombardeta* as well as *bombardeta,* for which there appears to be no English equivalent. A gun of the proportions of the three hooped-barrel pieces in this collection is described as a *bombardeta* in the *Catálogo of the Museo de Ejército* (their specimen no. 5957), which they date at the end of the fifteenth century (1956: 13-14). Since we shall be discussing the guns aboard a Spanish ship, the Spanish terminology will be used and translated when necessary to make the meaning clear.

Both *bombardas* and *bombardetas* are among those known as "hooped-barrel," "made-up," or "built-up," guns because of their complicated construction: rods or staves of iron were laid close together around a core or mandrel and forged into a tube that was open at both ends. *Bombardeta* No. 1475 was made up of five staves; no. 1476 was constructed of ten staves. Over the barrel thus formed (the *caña*) were slipped bands of white hot iron that shrank as they cooled and thus reinforced the tube. The reinforcing hoops were laid so closely together that they made up a complete outer tube in themselves. If gaps were left through imperfect welding, lead is said to have been poured in to close them. Additional reinforcing hoops were shrunk onto the bands, usually at the juncture of the outer tube bands.

A related kind of construction, also strengthened by a set of outer hoops, was revealed by one of the guns from Henry VIII's warship, the *Mary Rose,* which sank off Portsmouth, England, in 1545 while the king was watching from shore (McKee 1974: 260-263). X-rays of the gun that Alexander McKee brought up showed that the barrel had been formed by wrapping a sheet of iron around a mandrel and roughly lap-welding it to make a much stronger tube than the old built-up type. McKee believes that this type of construction was an important innovation for its time and illustrated the English king's interest in improving his artillery. *Bombardeta* No. 1477 was similarly constructed of a single lap-welded sheet, which then had the bands shrunk on to form an outer tube; a series of reinforcement hoops were added along its length. This gun was constructed in the same manner as that described for Type I breechblocks, to be outlined later. Figure 32 shows the X-ray of the forged staves of *Bombardeta* No. 1476 and the single lap-weld of the tube sheet of *Bombardeta* No. 1477.

Extra rings for lifting and handling the heavy iron pieces were added to all the guns of the hooped-barrel type; these

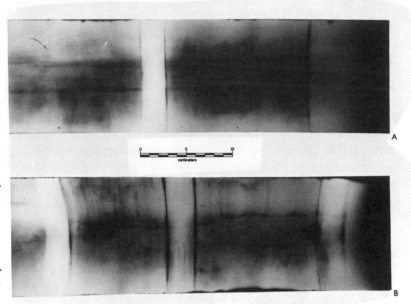

Fig. 32.—X-ray photographs showing two types of bombardeta *construction. (A) Bombardeta No. 1476-1a, made in the standard hooped-barrel manner. The gun is oriented as in Fig. 30 so that the view is downward along the barrel, breech end to the left and muzzle to the right. The horizontal band is one of the 10 staves forming the inner tube. Wide bands of iron were wrapped around the tube to make the outer tube. Where these bands meet, the vertical reinforcing rings, two of which are easily visible, were shrunk on to strengthen the tube. (B) Bombardeta No. 1477-1a, made of a single piece of iron forged around a core and lap-welded along its length. The seam of the weld can be seen as a horizontal line along the barrel. Three reinforcing rings are evident.*

were attached to "eyes" formed in one or more of the reinforcement straps on the barrel. Usually the lifting rings were placed at either end of the tube, as in the case of numbers 1475 and 1476, or in the center, as on 1477.

Such guns, with few exceptions, had to be breechloaders because the gunsmiths of the time could only forge the metal around a straight core, open at each end. In those days nothing was standardized, and consequently no two guns, or

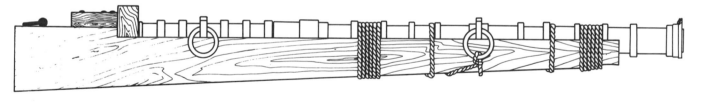

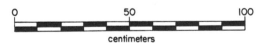

0   50   100

centimeters

Fig. 33.—Artist's rendition of the manner in which a bombardeta *might have been lashed to a wooden stock or carriage. The wooden block back of the breech chamber held the gun tube and breechblock in place against recoil. Some illustrations show wheeled carriages for ships' guns as well as stocks of this type.*

their component parts, were exactly alike. As a highly skilled and valued craftsman, the gunsmith guarded his secrets and made his guns as he saw fit. Charles Ffoulkes, in *The Gun-Founders of England* (1937: 10), says that the hooped-barrel type of construction, especially for ship's guns, was in use until the middle of the sixteenth century.

The gunpowder charge was carried in a separate chamber, the breechblock, which was constructed more or less in the same fashion as the barrel except that it was closed at the back. It was shorter, though, with a smaller bore, designed with a neck to fit into the breech end of the gun tube. Figure 34 shows breechblocks of this type, for which the Spaniards had several names. Vigon (1947: 33) mentions *trompa,* tube or horn; *recámara,* breech or chamber; *servidor,* usually, but not in this context, the person assigned to handle a gun or other device; and *masculo,* translation unknown. Near the back of the *servidor,* which had an inner chamber, was the touchhole (the *fogón*-firebox) that was bored through to the inside, by means of which the charge of gunpowder was ignited. From the middle of the fifteenth century it was generally accepted that the powder should occupy only three-fifths of the volume of the chamber, leaving one-fifth empty—a practice that Vigon says served as a regulator that we would call density of charge (1947: 64-65). The other fifth was reserved for the wooden plug or stopper that was inserted tightly into the mouth of the chamber to contain the powder. This plug was said to be always of a light wood like linden, pine, or willow because it was thought that by using heavier woods one would be running a greater risk that the breech would explode upon firing. Explosion was a real threat as it happened not infrequently and was one reason why each gun was furnished with two or more spare *servidores.* The other reason was that it enabled the gun to be fired more rapidly because spare chambers could be kept loaded, ready to be exchanged quickly in place of one already fired.

The gun barrel was laid in a wooden stock or carriage and held securely in place, apparently with nothing more than rope lashings. The cannon ball, which alone would have fit rather loosely in the bore, was first wrapped with a hemp wadding or wax-impregnated cloth to fill up the extra space and then pushed into the breech end. When the loaded chamber was set in place, the neck was inserted into the bore of the tube at the breech and wedged tightly against it by a wooden block that backed up against the carriage backstop or shoulder and held the two parts of the gun together against recoil.

Not much is known about early gun carriages because, being made mostly if not entirely of wood, not many have survived. Many reconstructions have been made from scanty and scattered evidence, as J. D. Moody, in his paper, "Old Naval Gun Carriages" (1952), points out. He calls the sixteenth century a transitional stage in the development of armament, as demonstrated by considerable variation in the gun mountings. Some had wheels, either two or four, and

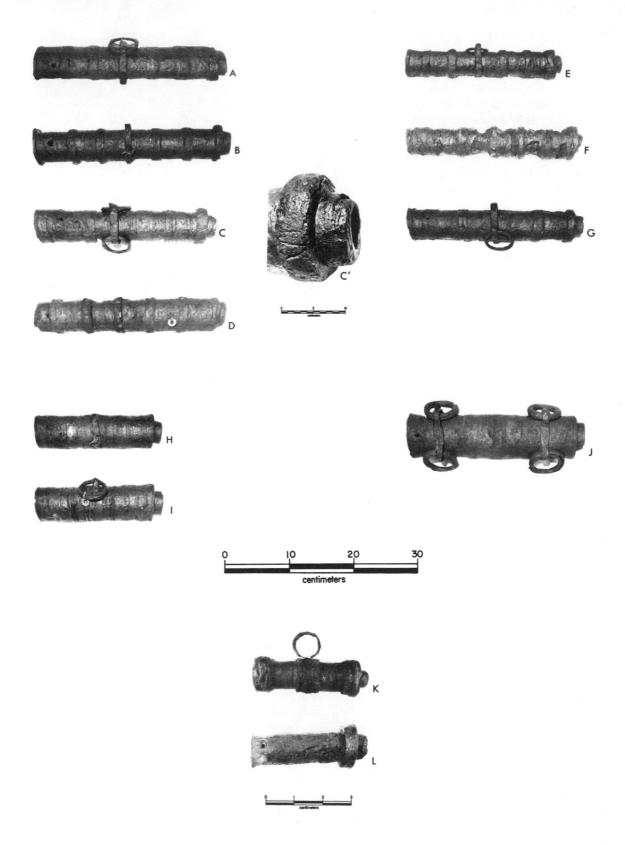

some had none; iron was occasionally used on wheels or trucks, but other carriages were all of wood. He distinguished four main types of carriages, describing them in this way:

The first was the "stock" mounting used for the older wrought-iron breech loaders. The "hall" of the gun was sunk into a solid wooden beam which had a shoulder at the rear end against which the "chamber" was wedged into position. Some, as those recovered from the sea at Anholt prove, had axles and a pair of wooden trucks. Others, like those from the Mary Rose, *had no trucks, but were grooved on the underside, as if to slide along a guide fixed to the deck. I have been able to find no certain evidence for trucks on the three carriages that I have examined, but there may be on some of the others. (Moody 1952: 301-2).*

The Anholt specimens are 10 fifteenth century wrought iron hooped-barrel guns, and one of cast iron, that were recovered from the seas off Denmark between 1937 and 1940. They were still resting in their oaken stocks which, for the most part, were in good condition. The guns and stocks, described and illustrated by Eriksen and Thegel (1966: 11-17), appear as Moody depicted them—solid wooden beams with a shoulder at the rear that served as a backstop. A similar arrangement, shown in Figure 33, was drawn by TARL's artist from these and other illustrations of early stocks. Some of the Anholt guns were held in place with broad iron straps that went entirely around both barrel and stock, while the barrel of another gun had been secured with tarred rope lashing that was found still intact (Eriksen and Thegel 1966: 53-55). Remnants of hemp rope lashing were found on all the Gulf Coast guns; apparently this was all that was used to hold them securely in position in the carriages. There was no indication that the rope had been tarred.

Fig. 34.—Wrought iron breechblocks for bombardetas, *classified into four types, based on variations in construction and size. See text for detailed explanation of the construction.*

Type 1:	(A) No. 316-1a
	(B) No. 321-1a
	(C) No. 322-1a (C') detail of mouth
	(D) No. 325
	(E) No. 1473-1a
	(F) No. 1577-A
	(G) No. 1578-1a
Type 2:	(H) No. 317-1a
	(I) No. 1474-1a
Type 3:	(J) No. 1472-1a
Type 4:	(K) No. 1579-A
	(L) No. 1301-1

Before McKee's recent recovery work on the *Mary Rose,* an English diving crew working in the nineteenth century salvaged several hooped-barrel guns from the ship, one with its wooden stock preserved. The ancient stock has now disappeared and the gun is in poor condition since it received no preservative treatment, as McKee regretfully reports (1969: 47), but he reproduces a water color painting of the gun and stock that was made soon after their recovery 130 years ago. This shows the gun set into the trough of a long, wooden beam, breech chamber backed against the shoulder, with a large, rectangular wooden block holding it in place. Such guns may have been mounted in the waist of the ship, poking out through openings in the hull, for they probably were too heavy to be placed on the castles.

Vigon explains how the charge for the *bombardas* was set off, and presumably this would apply to firing the *bombardetas* as well (1947: 65). The touchhole of the breech chamber was primed with a powder flask or with live powder and lit by a torch, or alternatively by an iron rod with a curved end which was heated red hot and then placed in the touchhole. The latter method of firing must have been in use for a very long period, but probably at some time during the sixteenth century the slow-match appeared and came into general use by the seventeenth century. This was made of a cotton cord or rope, soaked in saltpeter and dipped in melted sulfur, or otherwise treated to burn very slowly, perhaps four or five inches an hour. It was wound around a forked stick long enough to enable the gunner to stand out of danger from the recoil of the piece after firing. By the second half of the fifteenth century the most suitable charge had been proved to be one-ninth of the weight of the ball, and the length of the breech chamber bore should be five times its diameter. After firing, the gun was doused with water to cool it off and to put out the burning hemp left in the bore.

The old-fashioned built-up guns were obsolescent by the middle of the sixteenth century, but according to reports were carried on shipboard occasionally throughout the remainder of the century. Sometimes they were used as part of the ballast. By the end of the century the cast iron and brass guns had about replaced them because of their greater stability and safety.

Breechblocks for Hooped-Barrel Guns

The 12 wrought iron breechblocks of this style represent a minimum of four different types based on their size and manner of construction. Judging from the width and length of the necks, most of them would fit any of the *bombardetas* in the collection, but there are a few exceptions. The breech-blocks are individually described in Table 3 and are illustrated in the photographs in Figure 34. Detailed drawings to scale in Figure 35 illustrate how Types 1, 2, and 3 would have fit into the breeches of the three *bombardetas* and show the elements of construction. Type 4 breechblocks would not fit any of them and must have been used with another gun.

Type 1 consists of seven specimens that are much alike in size and construction. They were made of a single rolled sheet of iron, lap-welded along its length to form an interior tube. This tube was then covered with a sleeve made up of touching bands of iron wrapped around the outside, forming a second, outer tube. Over this was shrunk a series of five to seven reinforcing bands placed at regular intervals along its length. In all cases of this type there was a reinforcing band at the breech, the mouth, and the center; two lifting rings were attached to the center band. The remaining reinforcing hoops were evenly spaced between the others. The Type 1 breechblocks range in length from 55.5 to 84.5 cm., including the neck extension that fit into the breech of the gun. The necks were uniformly 3.5 to 4.0 cm. long and 9.0 to 11.3 cm. wide. They weigh between 52.26 kg. and 77.11 kg. Breechblock No. 1577-A is not a good example of the type, being badly oxidized. These seven specimens would fit most snugly in *Bombardeta* No. 1477, which has a bore width at the breech of 11.3 cm. and a recession of 4.7 cm. to take the neck of the breech chamber. Even in this gun there would be a 1.0 cm. gap between the end of the breechblock neck and the abutment with the breech end of the tube, once the shoulder of the breechblock was secure against the end of the breech. In order to reduce the recoil and prevent escape of the powder gases this space would need to have been securely sealed. Evidently this was closed in some way, probably with oakum in the manner the loaded *verso* chambers were sealed. It is apparent from the fit of these breechblocks that they were ineffectual and dangerous because they frequently backfired.

Both of the Type 2 breechblocks have an inner tube made of a single sheet of iron that forms a solid sleeve similar to Type 1 but lacks the reinforcing bands that project above the outer tube. The bands forming the outer tube are much thicker than the bands that make up the outer tube of Type 1 breechblocks, giving additional support and therefore not

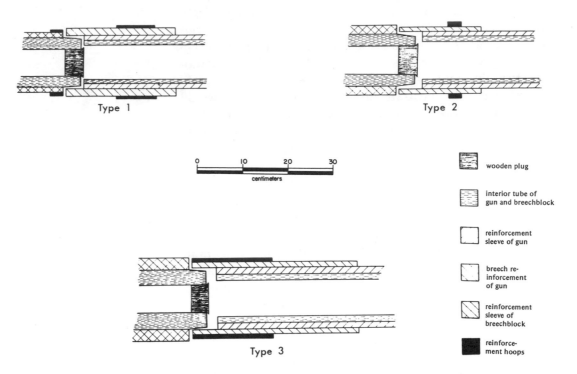

wooden plug

interior tube of
gun and breechblock

reinforcement
sleeve of gun

breech re-
inforcement
of gun

reinforcement
sleeve of
breechblock

reinforce-
ment hoops

Fig. 35.—Details showing how necks of the hooped-barrel breechblocks types
1, 2, and 3 fit into the inset at the breech end of Bombardetas 1477, 1476, and
1475 respectively. Gap between breechblock and gun was probably filled in with
hemp cordage to cut down on the escape of gases after firing.

requiring the extra reinforcing hoops. A single hoop is placed
in the center for the attachment of two lifting rings. The two
Type 2 breechblocks are almost identical in dimensions and
each weighs 55.34 kg. No doubt they were made for the same
gun.

Type 3 consists of a single breechblock, no. 1472, lap-
welded from a sheet of iron and constructed with an outer
sleeve like Type 2, but this has two ring bands, one near
each end, to which a pair of ring handles are attached. This
breechblock would not fit *Bombardeta* No. 1477 but could
be used with any of the others.

Type 4 breechblocks are much smaller than the rest, and
different from each other, but are nearly the same size.
Probably they were intended for the same gun. Breechblock
No. 1301-1 gives every appearance of being a remodeled
version of one made for the long-barreled *versos*—that is, it
has a conical shape, made by welding the iron around a core,
and would originally have had a handle. In this case, however, a thick collar has been added to the simple tube behind
the mouth, thus forming the sort of neck that is characteristic of the ordinary hooped-barrel types. The handle is now

missing, but its stub is present. Perhaps the modification of this piece is evidence of a gunsmith's improvisation in a time of necessity when no breechblock of the usual hooped-barrel type was available. The other breechblock in the class, no. 1579-A, is of the customary lap-welded construction for the tube but lacks the outer sleeve bands. It does, however, have three reinforcing bands placed at the breech, the mouth, and the center; the single lifting ring has broken off from the center band. This might well have been the only ring it had. Neither of these breechblocks would have been suitable for the guns at hand, and their presence indicates a missing weapon of a different size.

Versos

The five swivel guns were of a quite different shape (Figs. 36-40). They represented a light weight, easily portable, rapid-firing type that had a long history of usage by all the European countries on land and sea, beginning at least in the early part of the fifteenth century—possibly even before that—and lasting up to the eighteenth. They were comparable to pieces called bases or slings in England, but the name *verso* is commonly used in artillery literature. Michael Lewis (1936: 338) believes that it is derived from the Latin *vertere*, to turn. The oldest weapons of this type were of wrought iron, like those in this collection, but during the later periods they were usually made of cast iron or brass. On shipboard they would have been mounted on the gunwales so they could be turned at need to repel an enemy attempting to board or be reversed to shoot at invaders already on deck.

There are two sizes of *versos,* the larger ones (nos. 329 and 330) ranging from 264 to 270 cm. in total length and the smaller ones (nos. 1457, 1458, and 1611) ranging from 187 to 195 cm. overall. Each group required a different sized breechblock. The wrought iron barrels were formed by lap-welding a single sheet of iron around a mandrel. At the breech end of the tube a wider, thicker section was added, a sort of sleeve, with the top part left open, or perhaps cut away, to form a trough or cradle to contain the separate breechblock. Two additional strips of iron were forged along the top sides of the trough. Rectangular slots left in these, on each side near the back, were intended for inserting the iron breech wedge that secured the breechblock in position. Figures 38, 39, and 40 illustrate the details of this assemblage. Behind the breech section was a long, narrow tail—the tiller—that provided means for training the gun vertically

A

B

0		50		100

centimeters

*Fig. 36.—*Verso *No. 328. (A) View from the top. (B) View from the side.*

Total length	*270.6 cm.*
Barrel length, tube only	*147.5 cm.*
Diam. of bore	*4.8 cm.*
Caliber	*30.8 (about)*
Weight	*104.32 kg.*
Material	*wrought iron*
Markings	*X's and other marks around top edges of the breech trough and just behind it on the barrel.*

This large verso *was completely encrusted when received, but was found to be in good condition after processing, with the swivel mechanism intact and functional. Construction of the gun apparently was carried out in sections: first, the simple tube was lap-welded around a core, then a sleeve was added about two-thirds of the distance toward the breech, making it thicker from that point on. The trough for the breechblock was a separate section made with two side parts and a cutout base, then additional layers of iron were added to the top rear of the breech. A solid tiller terminating in a knob was welded onto the back of the trough, and still another section forged above the end of the tiller where it entered the trough. An added thickness of metal reinforced the muzzle. Open section at the base of the trough was probably intended for drainage. Two rectangular spaces aligned on either side of the trough were for insertion of the breech wedge. The rope that kept the wedge from flying off after firing passed through a hole in the wedge and went through two small, connecting slits cut under the top surface of the barrel. Caliber was figured for this and the other* versos *by dividing bore diameter into length of tube.*

Construction, size, and markings are almost identical with Verso *No. 330, and probably were made by the same gunsmith. Fig. 37 shows scale drawings and details that apply to both guns.*

---

or horizontally on its swivel. The swivel could be mounted on bearings fitted into holes in the sides of the barrel, or, as in the case of the weapons to be described here, on stubby little cylindrical projections that were like small trunnions. They were placed on either side of the tube, centered just forward of the breech, and served as pivots *(muñones)* that held the barrel in its swivel yoke. This part resembles a mod-

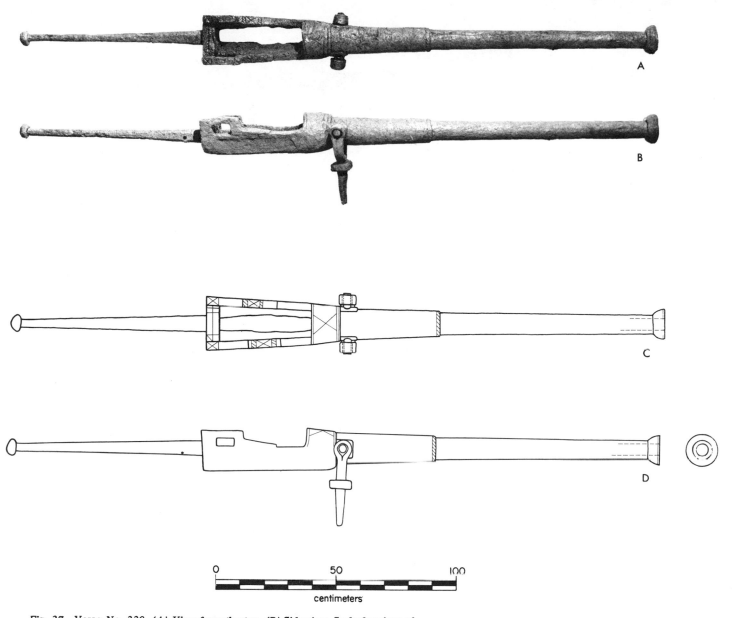

Fig. 37.—Verso No. 330. (A) View from the top. (B) Side view. Scale drawings of top (C) and side (D) view of the gun. Details of the marks are shown in (C), and (D) shows front view of the muzzle. Dashed lines indicate the bore.

Total length	*264.5 cm.*
Barrel length, tube only	*138.6 cm.*
Diam. of bore	*4.5 cm.*
Caliber	*30.8*
Weight	*97.2 kg.*
Material	*wrought iron*
Markings	*X's and vertical marks around top of trough and across its back, diagonals encircling the first added section or sleeve.* 4H *on back of trough.*

The large verso *shown here was also encrusted when it was received, and, like no. 328, was found to be in excellent condition. The two guns are so much alike that the description given for no. 328 will serve for both. The mark* 4H *at the back of the trough appears on both guns and is probably the gunsmith's mark.*

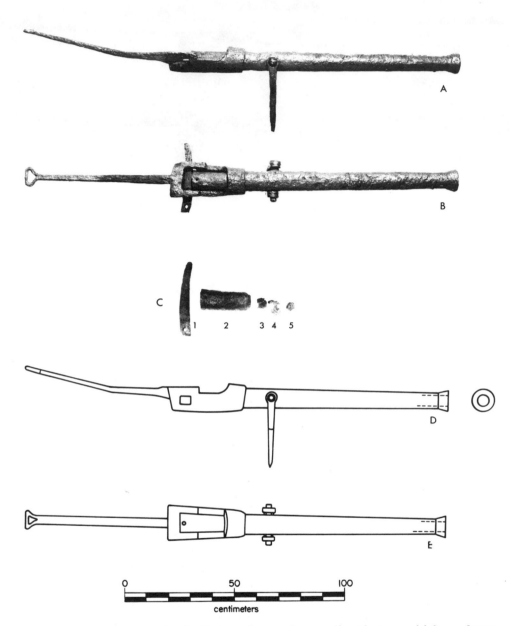

ern oar lock; it terminates in a spike that would have been driven downward into the hull at the gunwale.

Eighteen wrought iron breechblocks, and one of bronze/brass, are of a form that has been aptly described by several writers as "beer stein-shaped," for they were cylindrical and slightly tapering and were furnished with handles. Occasionally they were provided with a small extension, or lip, which underlapped the breech wedge; this locked the breech wedge into place and prevented the breechblock from flying out from the recoil after firing. To the Spaniards these breechblocks resembled oil cans, and they were called by

Fig. 38.—Verso No. 1457-1a and assemblage for firing. (A) Side view of gun. (B) View from top showing firing assemblage in place. Breech wedge at left end of breech trough was inadvertently inserted backward for the photograph; the concave side should face breechblock. (C) Component parts of the firing assemblage, all found in place. From left, 1) breech wedge turned the proper way. It held the breechblock in place in the trough; 2) breechblock with touchhole visible; handle was missing, broken off; 3) wooden breech plug that fit into mouth of the breechblock; 4) hemp wadding that was wrapped around cannon ball, used as a gasket; and 5) cast iron cannon ball found in bore. (D) Scale drawing of gun, side view. At right, muzzle head on; dashed lines indicate bore. Rectangular openings at back end of breech trough are for insertion of the breech wedge. (E) Gun from top. Small hole in bottom of trough probably for drainage.

Total length	*195.9 cm.*
Barrel length	*98.9 cm.*
Diam. of bore	*5.5 cm.*
Caliber	*18 (about)*
Weight	*48.98 kg. with breechblock and wedge*
	42.63 kg. without breechblock and wedge
Material	*wrought iron*
Markings	*none*

The gun was received fully encrusted. It was found to be in good condition with swivel mechanism intact and functional, ready for firing with loaded breechblock, wedge, breech plug, and cannon ball in place. Tube was lap-welded around a core with the trough and other parts added, including reinforcement of the muzzle. The tiller, with a loop handle, was bent slightly upward. This and the other two short-barreled versos have a larger bore diameter than the long-barreled ones.

that name—*alcuzas*. The touchhole was near the back end, and like the breech chambers for the hooped-barrel guns, the mouths were stoppered with truncated, conical wooden plugs. In several instances a short piece of twisted fiber, probably hemp, was found in the touchhole, evidently just to close it. A number of the breechblocks were still loaded, with three still in place in the troughs of the three smaller *versos*. The condition of the breechblocks ranged from excellent to very poor; Breechblock No. 1468 was in such a badly oxidized state that it could not undergo preservative treatment. It was simply consolidated for display purposes and left partially exposed in its enveloping encrustation.

Sizes varied considerably, as will be evident in the examples shown in Figure 41, but all the wrought iron specimens would fit one or another of the five swivel guns in the collection. The brass/bronze example, no. 1416 (Fig. 41E), was much too small to fit any of the *versos* and must have been intended for a very small swivel gun of an unidentified type. In Table 4 the breechblocks for the swivel guns are divided by size into three groups: Type 1 is the largest, 30 cm. or more in length, made for the large *versos;* Type 2 group, between 20 and 30 cm. long, is appropriate for the smaller *versos;* and Type 3 consists of the single, small brass/bronze breechblock. Within each type group the breechblocks are listed by catalogue number and dimensions, with

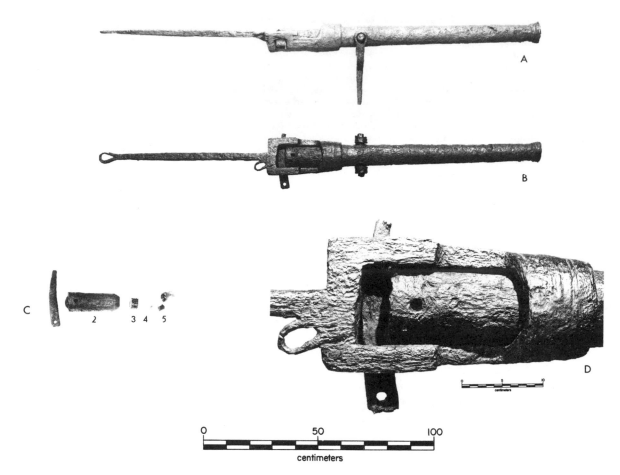

weights and other data given. Most of them will have lost somewhat in weight and size because of surface corrosion, but a good many are still close to their original dimensions.

Breech Wedges for the *Versos*

Nine of these wedges were recovered, three associated with breechblocks mentioned above that were still in place in the gun troughs. Figures 38, 39, and 40 illustrate typical examples. All were of wrought iron, slightly curved, and tapered from a squared-off back to a blunt end. They would have been fastened to the gun by a length of rope passing through a hole in the wider end. As in the case of the breechblocks, their condition and their sizes varied. All are tabulated by catalogue number, with measurements and other details given in Table 5.

Wooden Plugs for Breechblocks

Eleven truncated, cone-shaped wooden plugs were re-

Fig. 39.—Verso No. 1458-1a and assemblage for firing. (A) Side view of gun. (B) View from top showing firing assemblage in place. (C) Component parts of the firing assemblage, all found in place in gun. From left, 1) breech wedge; 2) breechblock, handle missing, broken off; 3) wooden breech plug; 4) small cube of wrought iron from center of cannon ball and fragment of lead that formed part of covering. (D) Firing parts assembled as they were found in gun. Small ring below tiller at back of breech trough was for insertion of the lanyard rope to keep breech wedge from flying out after firing.

Total length	*192.4 cm.*
Barrel length, tube only	*89.9 cm.*
Diam. of bore	*5.1 cm.*
Caliber	*17.6 (about)*
Weight after cleaning	*49.89 kg. with breechblock and wedge*
	43.09 kg. without breechblock and wedge
Material	*wrought iron*
Markings	*none*

Gun was completely encrusted when received. Processing revealed it to be loaded, ready to fire, with breechblock, breech wedge, wooden plug, gunpowder residue in chamber, and a lead-covered iron cannon ball surrounded by wadding was in place in the bore. During processing, lead covering was torn off the inner core of cannon ball, an incident that made it possible to explain for the first time how this type of cannon ball was made. The center of the cannon ball was a wrought iron cube about 2.5 cm. dimension; around it was applied a coating of lead to make round shot. The unevenness of surface suggests the lead was hammered on. The barrel was a simple tube lap-welded around a core, with breech section, tiller, and muzzle reinforcement added, along with pivots or trunnions for the swivel yoke. Rectangular openings in the sides of the breech trough at back were for insertion of the wedge. Like no. 1611, an iron loop was welded between the back of the trough and the tiller for the rope, which passed through the hole in the wedge and secured the wedge to the lanyard ring.

This gun is so much like no. 1611 it probably was made by the same gunsmith. For scale drawings, see Fig. 40, with details that are alike in both guns.

---

covered; some survived in good condition, but others were extremely fragmentary. Four were *in situ* in the hooped-barrel breechblocks and seven were still in the mouths of *verso* breech chambers. In the latter group, three were associated with the completely assembled guns. They are noted in the descriptions of their breechblocks, and those found with the *versos* are illustrated with them.

Breechloading guns had many advantages aboard ship. The most important one, probably, was that the gunner had neither to climb over the gunwale and expose himself to enemy fire in order to load the piece, nor to run it inboard for the purpose; furthermore, the open barrel was easy to inspect and clean, and, if necessary, to remove a possible obstruction. The spare chambers, kept loaded, made rapid firing practical, which was not true of the muzzle-loaders that had to be cleaned and swabbed out every time they were fired. But with all that, these were unstable and dangerous guns, no doubt quite old, and too unreliable for the safety of the gun crew. It was difficult to wedge the breechblock tightly enough behind the barrel to prevent

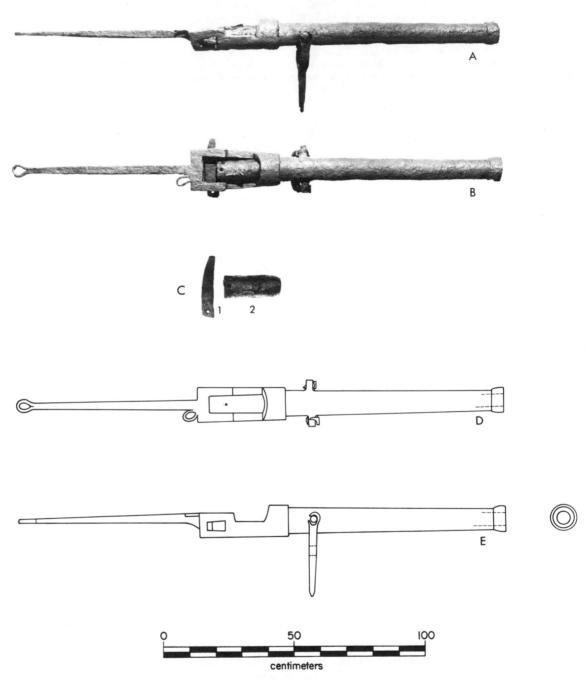

exploding gases from blowing it out of place, and this caused much trouble. Also, too great a charge might cause the barrel itself to recoil fiercely or even blow up. Means for controlling the recoil were primitive, consisting for the most part of the wooden breech wedge block—at least for the *bombardetas*—although ropes and chains may have been utilized to some extent. On the whole, most authorities believe the wrought

Fig. 40.—Verso No. 1611. (A) Side view of gun. (B) View from top. (C) Component parts of the firing assemblage: 1) breech wedge; 2) breechblock. (D) Scale drawing of gun from top; small hole was probably for drainage. (E) Drawing of gun from side; dashed lines indicate bore.

Total length	187.5 cm.
Barrel length, tube only	88.8 cm.
Diam. of bore	5.1 cm.
Caliber	17.5 (about)
Weight	48.08 kg. with breechblock and wedge
	41.73 without breechblock and wedge
Material	wrought iron
Markings	none

The encrustation had been removed from this gun when it was received and it was rusting on the surface; otherwise, it was in good condition. Construction was identical to that of no. 1458-1a.

iron guns were about as hazardous to the gunners as to the enemy.

There is no way as yet of identifying the country where the guns were made—they could have come from Spain, but could as well have been products of England or any of the European gunsmiths. Cast iron or cast brass or bronze pieces often bore the name of the maker or the date of manufacture, and the names of many of the early gunfounders are known, but the only reports we have seen on such information for wrought iron guns comes from the *Museo de Ejército*. Their *Catálogo* (1957: 13) describes a complete *bombarda* with two *recámeras* (their specimen no. 3301); the date 1518 was clearly marked on both breech chambers. A clue to the origin of *Versos* Nos. 329 and 330 is probably found in the figure ⊣

appearing on the back of the breech trough. This may be an ancestor of the merchant's marks and "huismerken" that Sténuit (1974: 243-244) describes as found on brass rings from the Dutch ship *Lastdrager*. This ship that went down off the isle of Yell in Shetland, United Kingdom, in March, 1653 was the oldest wreck of a Dutch East Indiaman discovered in European waters. Such marks, as used in northern and central Europe, had for a long time been a mark of property and identification of houses, tools, various objects, and even on cattle. He says they also became family symbols inherited and recognized by law as an official signature, and also were used by merchants and craftsmen to identify their products. Usually they incorporated the figure ⊣ , which Sténuit explains was just an easy mark to make in metal, although it may have had deeper significance, and along with it might be included initials or

Fig. 41.—Examples of beer stein-shaped breechblocks. All but E are of wrought iron. (A) No. 1512 fits the trough of the large versos, nos. 328 and 330. (B, C) Nos. 1504 and 1519-1 are appropriate size for the smaller versos. (D) was found in place in Verso No. 1458-1a (its specimen number is 1458-1b), but its handle was broken off. The lip extension at bottom of the breechblock on the right served to secure the breech wedge during firing and kept it from flying out. (E) No. 1416; it appears to be made of bronze and is much too small for any gun in the collection but was intended for some sort of swivel gun.

other symbols, or one or more short vertical strokes. The stroke represented an elder son of the family, and the younger sons used additional strokes to indicate their status. The author illustrates such marks in his Figure 23 (Sténuit 1974: 244).

On the guns in question, made more than 100 years earlier, we find the 4 with the extended crosspiece ending in two vertical strokes that might represent a second son or possibly an H. It seems certain that this must be the gunsmith's mark, and from his mark he may have come from anywhere in middle or northern Europe, but most probably from the Netherlands. During the mid-sixteenth century this area was a part of Charles V's Holy Roman Empire and their gunsmiths were famous for good craftsmanship.

AMMUNITION

This category consists of projectiles and the gunpowder for firing them. The projectiles are all round shot, most of them cannon balls. Representative examples are illustrated in Figure 42.

Projectiles—Cannon Balls

Four different techniques of manufacture are evident among the 73 specimens identified in this class: wrought iron, cast iron, lead-covered iron, and stone. Fifty-one of them are of small diameter, ranging from 3.5 cm. to 4.7 cm.

(about 1½–2 in.), averaging about 4.3 cm. That these were intended for use in the *versos* with bores up to 5.8 cm. diameter was proved when round shot in this size range were, in three instances, actually found in place in the gun barrels. This proportion of missile size to gun bore is in accordance with the usual practice of the time to allow plenty of space or "windage" between the ball and the gun bore. Harold Peterson (1969: 24) gives this "windage" as being one-fourth inch or more, explaining that the loose fit would prevent trouble from the irregularities of bore of the gun or of fouling from the gunpowder. The balls usually were wrapped with hemp or cloth to make a better fit. For an example of the actual space that was allowed, the hooped-barrel gun recovered in 1970 from the *Mary Rose* had a bore diameter of 3¾ inches and the cannon ball found within it was 3½ inches (McKee 1974: 260-261).

Some of the 16 medium sized cannon balls, 4.9 to 8.2 cm. (Fig. 42B, F, G, H), would have been appropriate for the two larger-bored *versos* that measured 7.5 cm. and 8.2 cm. at the bore, and any one of the *bombardetas*. The largest of

Fig. 42.—Projectiles, showing the range of sizes and types of round shot. A–J are cannon balls. (A) Shaped limestone. (B, C, D) Wrought iron. (E, F, G) Cast iron. (H, I) Lead-covered iron. (J) All lead. (K) Not quite round lead ball for an unknown weapon. (L and M) Small lead pellets, may be case or canister shot. Barnacles still adhere to the stone shot. Wrought iron has a rough surface texture, but cast iron is smoother and the mold marks are visible. Small cubes of iron covered with lead make the lead-covered iron balls; as the iron oxidizes and expands the lead covering often cracks open. Projectiles of solid lead remain in good condition.

these projectiles were the five made of stone, 9.9—12.7 cm. in diameter, and a lead-covered iron one that measured 10.3 cm. None of the guns recovered was of a caliber large enough to fire any of these.

The seven wrought iron examples (Fig. 42B, C, D) are of unusual interest because no mention of wrought iron shot has been found in the available literature. These examples tend to run a little larger than those of cast iron and have very rough, pitted, uneven, and corroded surfaces. No doubt they have lost more in girth from surface corrosion than any of the other types, but the remaining metal is of good consistency and weight.

The cast iron balls are frequently described in reference works, and 22 of them are present in this collection (Fig. 42E, F, G). Their comparatively smooth surface texture, if not cracked or broken, is very different in appearance from that of wrought iron, and they often show evidence of the casting by their raised mold marks; sometimes the scar from a sprue attachment is also visible. Although a number are very badly oxidized, having undergone extensive graphization, and are consequently light in weight, nonetheless, most of them retain their spherical shape and original surfaces. One cast iron ball that was removed from the bore of a *verso* is still in good condition, doubtless due to the protection provided by the gun barrel being completely closed by concreted matter. One specimen disintegrated during processing and fell apart into fragments, another was broken in two but later glued together, and a third was represented by only one half of a completely oxidized specimen. Wignall (1973: 465-466) points out that the Spanish iron-casting techniques were notoriously deficient during this mid-sixteenth century period, at least in comparison with the English, German, and Flemish work, and the results of their casting processes were poor. Whenever possible the Spaniards obtained their cast iron guns from England or the continent by capture or purchase. The Spanish inability to make good cast iron may partly account for the fragility of so many of these cast iron balls; Wignall contends that the quality of their shot may have contributed to the defeat of the Spanish Armada.

More rare in the literature of round shot ammunition were the 26 specimens made of lead-covered iron (Fig. 42H, I). With one exception, a large ball that measured 10.3 cm. in diameter when received, they all fell into the small-bored *verso* size range. At the center of the small cannon balls was a solid piece of wrought iron. From the cores that remained sufficiently intact to indicate anything about their size, it was discovered that they were usually about 2.5 cm. square and roughly cubical in shape. Where the lead coating could be measured for thickness it was about 0.5 to 0.7 cm., although not of uniform thickness. The uneven, lumpy appearance of the surfaces suggests that the coating had been applied by hammering lead sheeting around the core into as spherical a shape as could be managed. This technique of manufacture, according to Wignall (personal communication 1974) was a relic of the "made-up" wrought iron guns whose barrels were seldom true. The lead coating provided some protection against the scoring that was left by iron shot after firing and provided a cushion against untrue bores. The same situation was probably the case with the wrought iron *verso* barrels too, as their bores were neither true nor smooth.

In all but two instances the corroding iron had expanded and broken, or at least cracked, the lead shell; sometimes only the shell remained and the iron had virtually disappeared or disintegrated into iron oxide powder. The exceptions were a large cannon ball and one of the small ones found in good condition in place of *Verso* No. 1611. A second small one was discovered *in situ* in another *verso* as well, but in this instance the lead covering was torn off the iron core during its removal from the gun and the core was left intact, revealing for the first time the true nature of their construction.

Vigon mentions lead-covered iron balls, using the term *bodoque,* which originally meant a ball of air-hardened clay used for shooting with a catapult (Vigon 1947: 45). They consisted of a given amount of iron covered with lead, the proportion of iron being from one-sixth to one-third the total weight of the projectile. Mendel Peterson also describes cannon balls of this type, with cores of wrought or cast iron, about 2½ inches in diameter (Peterson 1967: 5). These were found in the wreckage of a Spanish vessel tentatively identified as the *San Pedro,* lost near Bermuda in 1594. Dating of the shipwreck depended largely on the nature of its guns, and especially of this type of shot, which he says indicated a period no later than the 1560s or 1570s (Peterson 1974: 236).

The 14 solid lead balls bore no signs of casting either, and they too gave the appearance of having been pounded into shape (Fig. 42K). These were all of the small-bored *verso* size, and, like most of the solid lead objects, were usually in good to excellent condition.

Obviously, the cast iron and the lead-covered iron balls were interchangeable as long as the size was right, and probably this was true of the solid lead ones as well, although none of them were actually found in the guns. The cast iron, lead, and lead-covered balls must still be about their original size, but the wrought iron shot would have been somewhat larger before the badly oxidized surfaces eroded away.

The oldest type, the five stone cannon balls (Fig. 42A), are entirely too large for any of the guns in this collection but were the kind that early, large hooped-barrel pieces would have fired. These were all of limestone, according to Dr. Chris Durden, Curator of Geology at the Texas Memorial Museum, who says that they were probably river cobbles that were pecked and ground into the proper spherical shape. This corroborates Vigon's statement that limestone was most often used for the balls (Vigon 1947: 44). There are records of contracts for quarrying the stone, working it with picks. The balls were classified by size using an iron pattern or calibrator. These five measured from 9.2 to 12.6 cm. in diameter. Stone balls, first used in the early fourteenth century for the great seige weapons, continued as ammunition for the old style guns until the close of the sixteenth century. As they were lighter in weight than iron or lead shot of the same size, they required less gunpowder to propel them; their purpose was achieved when they shattered into fragments on impact. Because the flying fragments could badly damage sails and rigging and severely injure personnel they must have been dreaded as much as the iron or lead projectiles.

Projectiles—Other Round Shot

The three remaining examples of round shot are more difficult to identify with specific weapons. Possibly the two small lead balls (nos. 58-7 and 363-1) represent case or canister shot, or even arquebus shot (Fig. 42L–M). The first is roundish but has a flat base, measures 1.35 cm. in diameter, and weighs 13.8 g. The other is a little smaller, having a diameter of only 1.2 cm. and weighing 8.4 g.; it is completely round. The Encyclopedia Britannica (1969: 801) states that canister shot could be composed or iron or lead balls, metal scrap, or even small pebbles—anything available—that were packed into a metal container of the diameter of the gun bore. Albert Manucy (1949: 64, Fig. 41) illustrates examples of case shot filled with lead balls and a canister containing scrap metal, of the kind used in the American colonies in the eighteenth century. Since this was before standardization, the particular size would have been unimportant as long as the pieces would fit into the containers. The small projectiles, like the shattered stone balls, would scatter in all directions when the container burst shortly after leaving the muzzle, and whatever the composition, they could inflict considerable damage.

The last example of lead shot is even more difficult to identify or ascribe to a particular weapon (no. 58-6, Fig. 42K). It is roundish except for a flattened bottom with a depressed scar in the center. The maximum diameter is 3.0 cm., but it tapers a little toward the top, and weighs 143 grams (just over 5.5 oz.). It is so much smaller than the cannon balls intended for the small-bored *versos* that it does not seem appropriate even for them, but it is larger than the size usually given for the bores of the very early muskets being developed during this period. H. B. C. Pollard (1930: 7) gives about one inch as the largest size for the matchlock weapons then in use. They were so heavy that they had to be propped against a rest for firing, but as time went on they became smaller, more like the modern musket size by the end of the century.

Crossbows

Among the small arms and armor listed in the 1552 regulations issued by the king specifying the armament for overseas voyages were crossbows. Three of these weapons, and a fragmentary portion of a separate crossbow stock, were in the collection (Figs. 43, 44, 45). Specimen no. 1510 was almost complete with most of its wooden stock intact, although the trigger and other outer metal parts were gone; the second, no. 1511, included only the forepart of the stock along with the bow; and the third, no. 1571, was represented by the bow alone as the entire stock was missing.

The first two had been freed of encrustation when the collection was received, but the third, the bow without its stock, was still entirely coated. It was probably the teredo worms that damaged the two surviving stocks as well as the separate encrusted stock section (no. 115-1), and possibly destroyed one stock completely. Crossbow No. 1510 had been attacked on the underside just back of the head, but the devastation there was not great as it extended only partially through the shaft; evidently a few inches also were eaten off the rear end. The second weapon, no. 1511, had the stock severed back of the head in just about the same place as the other was damaged. The separate shaft piece was a short portion of mid-

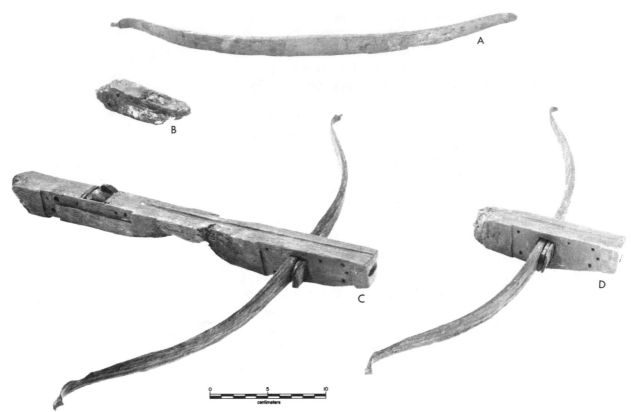

Fig. 43.—Small hunting crossbows and fragment of a stock section. (A) No. 1571, only the bow without a stock attached. (B) No. 155-1, fragment of stock section in the area of trigger mechanism and nut. (C) No. 1510, crossbow with most of stock intact. Teredo worms have eaten away part of the stock behind the head and destroyed an estimated 20 cm. at the back end. Nut for the bowstring is of wood. Holes on the sides were to secure iron cheek plates. (D) No. 1511, bow with head portion of stock remaining, the rest destroyed by teredo worms. Evidently the metal of cheek plates protected wood at this point. The separate stock fragment, B, may have come from this stock, but could have come from Crossbow No. 1571 or another one not recovered.

section in the area of the trigger mechanism and nut. The metal fittings, cheeks, or lockplates that would have been placed on either side of the head and next to the trigger must have protected what wood was left from the worms. Whether the separate section is part of the missing stock, the damaged one for no. 1511, or belongs to an entirely different crossbow, is unknown, but its measurements are about the same as those stocks that were still affixed to the bows when we received them.

These were very simple, small weapons, even rather crude, about the size and type given for Spanish sporting bows that were popular for hunting rabbits, birds, and other small game until about 1725, according to Ralph Payne-Gallwey in *The Crossbow* (1958: 145). He describes such small weapons as weighing eight to nine pounds and measuring 2 ft. 4 in. to 2 ft. 5 in. in length. At the center of the bow the metal was 1-3/8 in. to 1-1/3 in. wide and 3/8 in. to 1/3 in. thick; the Texas Gulf bows, in comparison, measure just under 55.5 cm. (about 21.5 in.) from tip to tip, indicating that they were undersized even for the small hunting type. Their original weight probably was no more than 2.3 kg. or 5 lbs., and their range about 137.2 meters. The small size crossbows could be suspended from a man's belt by a ring at the head and could be cocked and fired from horseback, unlike the larger weapons that required the crossbowman to put his foot through a stirrup at the head and stand on it to "bend" the bow. The arrows were called quarrels or bolts, and were usually steel-tipped, but for birds and very small game they might have the wooden tips blunted so as to avoid damaging their prey.

These bows must have been made of well tempered steel. All three are in excellent condition even now, although there is some damage to the surviving metal at one notched tip of both no. 1510 and no. 1511 where the bow has been slightly corroded, and all have lost at least 0.6 cm. in metal thickness and bow width. The laminated layers wrought by the blacksmith can be clearly distinguished.

Dr. Hamilton, the conservator, carefully studied the Texas Gulf specimens, and X-rays revealed significant details about the construction of the crossbows. For example, the trigger mechanism of no. 1510, although completely oxidized, was revealed so clearly that it was easy to see how it was made (Fig. 45). Since the crossbows are very much alike, the following description of the most complete specimen, no. 1510, will apply to all.

At the fore-end of the stock, a hole was drilled straight into the wood, probably for insertion of an iron hanging ring by which the weapon could be suspended. Only a 3 mm.-wide pin kept the ring in place, a slender attachment that would not, for example, serve to secure a stirrup (cocking aid) under the kind of pressure that it would undergo when it was being cocked. This identification is further confirmed by the splaying out of the wood on either side of the hole where the metal pressed against it.

The stock was mortised on both sides to receive iron side plates at the head and in the area of the trigger mechanism. The front side plate was made of a single continuous piece of metal starting on one side of the stock at the top, covering the bottom, and ending at the top edge on the other side. The back side plate was formed by three pieces of iron, the

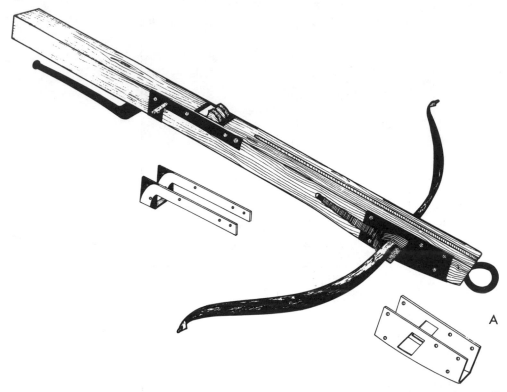

Fig. 44 (A)—. Crossbow No. 1510 as it probably looked when in use. Shaded areas were metal but the remainder was wood except for the sinew that secured the bow to the stock. Metal cheek plate sections are shown separately to illustrate their construction.

long strip extending horizontally along the top edge on both sides of the stock in a strip 1.5 cm. wide, then curving downward and across the bottom forming a U-shape. The second piece was placed to the front of the U-section of the first piece. It has a flat base that goes under the stock like the other, but the vertical pieces that extend up the sides of the stock are triangular, coming to a point at their juncture with the horizontal sections of the longer strip. One small segment of this second strip can be seen in the Figure 44B. Teredo worms destroyed approximately 20 cm. of the length, including the butt end of the stock. When complete, the stock would have terminated in a squared-off end, judging from illustrated examples of similar bows of this period. Along the top of the shaft is a shallow, narrow groove, 0.5 cm. wide, that received the lower part of the bolt; it terminates 3.2 cm. in front of the socket for the nut. Measurements taken between the fingers of the nut indicate that the maximum diameter of the bolt could not have been more than 0.7 cm.

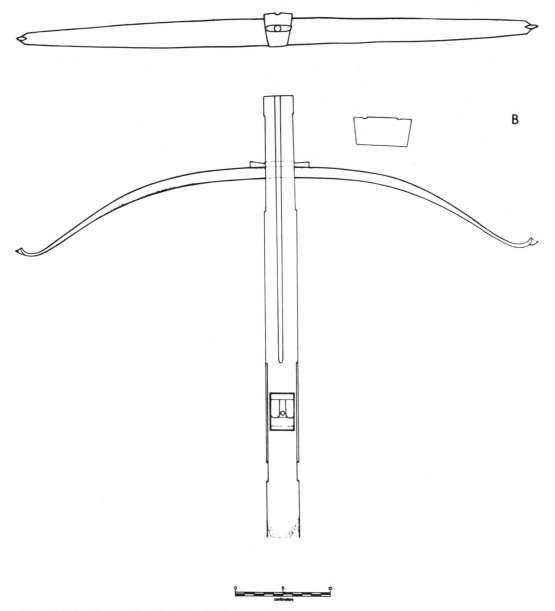

Fig. 44 (B).—View of Crossbow No. 1510 (above) from the front end. Hole for the suspension ring and groove for the bolt shaft are evident. Below, the entire bow and stock, with small metal wedges inserted in front of the bow. Figure to the right is the saddle, a wooden wedge inserted with the bow into the bow aperture; grooves on either side of the saddle were to hold the sinew in place. (Bar scale refers to both A and B in Fig. 44.)

Unlike those described in the literature (for example, Payne-Gallwey 1958: 97), the nut is of wood rather than steel or horn. In fact, steel nuts were not in general use until well into the seventeenth century. But like those made of horn, this wooden one has a steel wedge through its center which engages the trigger. The circular nut was inserted into

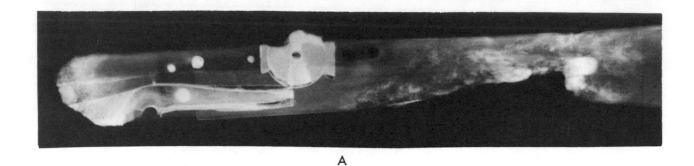

A

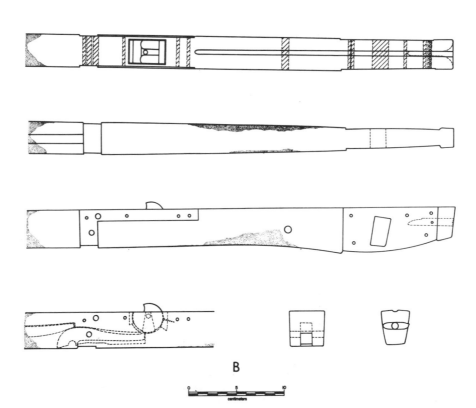

B

Fig. 45.—(A) X-ray photograph shows trigger section on Crossbow No. 1510. (B) Details of trigger mechanism.

a box or socket cut out of the stock to house it and was equipped with concave wedges inserted at the front and at the back, shaped to fit against its sides. The nut was notched at the bottom directly in front of the wedge for contact with the end of the trigger. To assemble this mechanism the front wedge was set in place first and held securely by a small nail; then a nut was inserted into the socket in the middle of the crossbow, and finally, the nut and the back wedge were held together and put into the socket as a unit. Once positioned in its box, between the two wedges, the nut was held loosely in place by them. A blind hole with no outlets was drilled through the center of the nut, not, apparently, as a pivot since there were no corresponding pin openings in the stock; it probably functioned only as a means of attaching the nut to the lathe during its manufacture. There was no need for a pivot or other device to secure the nut in place because of the arrangement with the wedges and the manner in which it was positioned.

The trigger was engaged against the iron wedge in the nut when the weapon was cocked. It will be seen from the drawing (Fig. 45B) that the crossbow was almost in a fully cocked position when it was lost. The trigger was shaped roughly like a Z, similar to others of the period. It was necessary to provide tension against the trigger so that when it was in a cocked position it would be exerting upward pressure. Commonly this was achieved with a steel spring, but in this case a piece of wood was inserted in such a way that downward pressure was exerted against the trigger back of its pivot pin. The wooden piece acted as a leaf-spring which was positioned so space was provided between it and the stock, allowing for some movement. To the back and below the pivot pin of the trigger was a small projection which apparently served as a stop against the end of the slot cut to receive the trigger. This stop limited the upward movement of the trigger end and prevented it from digging into the wood of the nut. A crossbow mechanism of this type, to our knowledge, has never been described previously.

For attachment of the bow, a rectangular hole was cut through the head of the stock at an angle of approximately 75 degrees to receive it; the tips of the crossbow, then, would be about 0.3–0.4 cm. above the top of the stock and the bowstring would not drag across the wood. Back of the hole made to receive the bow, at a distance of 8.2 cm., another hole 1 cm. in diameter was drilled through the center of the stock. A loop of wet sinew was passed through this small hole and both ends were pulled forward around the rectangular opening. The bow and a wooden wedge, called the saddle, placed in front of it were inserted together in the bow aperture through the sinew loops. On either side of the saddle were hollows for holding the sinew in place. Both sides of the sinew loops were next laced tightly to take out the slack, and as they dried they shrank further. This shrinkage pulled the bow securely backward against the stock, allowing the stock to absorb more of the shock of the bow as it was released.

The wood of the crossbow stocks has not been analyzed, but in each case it is quite hard and fine-grained. The bowstring would have been made of several strands of hemp cordage or flax. We were informed that a short length of bowstring was still attached to one tip of no. 1510 when it was recovered, but it was not there when we received the collection.

Small sporting bows such as these would have been effective aginst unprotected Indians and enemies at close range, but would have done little harm to a soldier clad in armor and chain mail. The 1553 wreck story recounts that the survivors recovered two crossbows of finely tempered steel that had washed up on the beach along with a quiver of metal arrows, and these with a few swords were their only weapons against the threatening Indians as they tried to make their way back to Mexico. The crossbows kept their tormentors at a distance for awhile, but when some of the Spaniards were attempting to cross the mouth of the Rio Grande on a makeshift raft the weapons, wrapped in rags, were thrown overboard by mistake. This disaster ultimately sealed their fate (Newcomb 1969: 3).

Since even small hunting bows would have been difficult to cock by hand, cocking devices known as goat's foot levers were provided for the crossbows. They consisted of a system of claws and levers that could be attached to the top of the stock in order to stretch the drawstring back to the wooden nut that held it in place until released by the trigger. Laboratory personnel at TARL first became aware of the presence of a goat's foot lever when a shapeless piece of encrustation was cut open and iron oxide was cleaned out, revealing crisp markings on the interior. When the spaces were filled with casting material and the resulting parts were assembled, there was no doubt that we had a replica of the long-lost original object. The reconstructed device, no. C-84, is illustrated in Figure 46, showing how it would have been placed on a crossbow and illustrating details of construction. Its measurements correspond closely to those described by Payne-Gallwey for the kind to be used with the small sporting bow of the sixteenth century (Payne-Gallwey 1958: 86). One of these levers was actually fixed in its proper position on Crossbow No. 1510 when the ship went down because three chunks of Platoro's cleaning debris containing disintegrated metal indicated from the X-ray that there were parts of the hinge section outlined in them. The pieces of

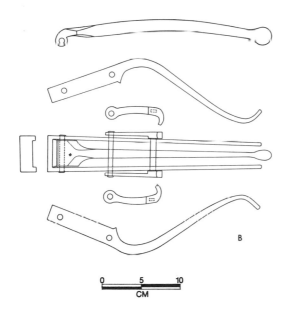

0   5   10
CM

Fig. 46.—(A) Crossbow No. 1510 with replica of the cocking device, a goat's foot lever, in place. (B) Component parts of the goat's foot lever as revealed by latex casts made from hollow molds left in the encrustation by the oxidized iron of the original object.

encrustation fit together precisely over the exact place on the shaft, with the lug holes in the shaft perfectly aligned with the transverse pins of the cocking mechanism. The design was slightly different from the one of which the replica was made, however; unfortunately, not enough remained to enable a second reconstruction. Evidently in cleaning the weapon Platoro had knocked the encrusted device off the crossbow shaft thinking it was just another chunk of concretion. X-ray photographs of the trigger mechanism of no. 1510 and detailed drawings are shown in Figure 45.

The name for the cocking instrument comes from a fancied resemblance to a goat's hind foot, but it was also called *pied-de-chienne* (female dog's foot), *pied-de-biche* (doe's foot), and *pied-de-chevre* (nanny goat's foot), says Claude Blair (1962: 37), so it must have looked like the foot of several different animals to various imaginative people. In England it was known as a gaffle or bender. In Spanish it was called *arbaleste.* By whatever name it was called, the goat's foot lever was a popular device with huntsmen well into the seventeenth century, and for target shooting until almost the end of the eighteenth century.

PERSONAL WEAPONS

Knife or Sword Blade Fragment

A thin, slender fragment of metal protruding from an encrustation (no. 1593) proved to be the remnant of a sword or knife blade, badly oxidized. When the encrustation was removed, stamped letters could barely be made out along the center of the blade, but the metal was so corroded they could not be identified. Fortunately, however, the encrustation was saved and the impression of the letters remaining on the interior, although in reverse, was much clearer than on the metal itself. Five letters were visible: N I M U, in that order, from the left; a fifth letter at the right end is composed of two uprights, | | , that could represent an eroded N, an H, or possibly an O with straight sides, similar to the style of the U. They were block capitals, about 5 mm. high and spaced about 1 cm. apart in a straight line down the blood groove of the blade. The first N was so close to the left end of the piece that it hinted other letters might have preceded it, but the last letter at the right end was well over a centimeter from the broken edge, suggesting that the lettering terminated there—at least on this part of the stamped legend, if that is what it was. If the piece is turned upside down, other letters suggest themselves, especially the M, which becomes a W. The I remains the same either way, as does the N, but on the actual object the diagonal of the N would have been going in the wrong direction no matter which way one looks at it because the impression in the encrustation is in reverse. Since there is no letter W in Spanish, the M is probably correct as oriented in the photograph. The Spanish, moreover, were acclaimed for their skill in making fine steel, and although it is not certain this was made in Spain, the stamp might represent the maker, the owner, or possibly a well-known phrase or motto of the period. The letters as they appear in the encrustation are illustrated in Figure 47

A

B

along with the actual blade fragment. What remained of it after cleaning was only 11.9 cm. long, 2.8 cm. at its widest, and 0.3 cm. thick, but the impression left in the matrix indicated that the blade had originally been about 2.5 cm. wide.

Cast of Sword or Knife Blade Fragment

This is a replica made from a mold in an encrustation that contained potsherds and natural molds of nails or spikes along with the oxidized sword blade fragment. The iron oxide rust was cleaned out and filled with casting material, and the resulting cast (no. C-217A) indicates that the blade remnant was 6.2 cm. long, 2.3 cm. wide, and had a maximum thickness of 1.24 cm. at the center (not illustrated). In cross-section the shape was like an elongated diamond. On the surface of the cast an impression that resembles fabric can be seen; this may be from the fabric lining of a scabbard.

Chain Mail

It is certain that at least one man aboard ship, perhaps a military officer or a returning adventurer, had personal armor

Fig. 47.—(A) Corroded fragment of a sword or knife blade, no. 1593, on which several letters had been stamped. (B) A good illustration of how much clearer the impression can be seen in the encrustation that had enveloped the blade remnant. It is evident that the letters had been stamped down the blood groove of the weapon. Seen from this orientation they appear to be N I M U and a fifth that is of uncertain identification. Turned upside down, the M becomes a W and the fifth letter is still a puzzle.

with him. Twenty-nine small rings of brass chain mail were discovered in one of the concretions (no. 1579-1). Chain mail probably would have been proof against arrows even if it were not used as part of plate armor, and Ffoulkes (1967: 48) documents the fact that shirts of mail were in use until the first decades of the seventeenth century. Most chain mail, however, was made of iron and was very susceptible to rust, so special precautions had to be taken to keep it in good condition. The iron rivets that once fastened this brass mail together are gone and the fabric has separated into seven small groups of one to nine rings, but it is obvious that the construction was of the usual type as described by the noted authority on arms and armor (Ffoulkes 1967: 44-45). Some of the chain pieces and line drawings of its construction are shown in Figure 48. Each ring originally passed through four others. No contemporary works describe the details of construction, but from examination of surviving chain mail, Ffoulkes believes that wire was twisted spirally around a rod of the diameter of the ring that was required, then cut off into rings with overlapping ends. "The two ends were flattened and punched or bored with holes through the flat portion. A small rivet, and in some cases two, was then inserted, and this was burred over with a hammer or with punches." (Ffoulkes 1967: 44-45). The rings were interlaced with one another before the ends were joined. In this case the rings were slightly more ovoid than circular, measuring about 5 to 7 mm. across their widest dimension. The wire was less than 1 mm. thick.

Since these remnants are of brass instead of iron they might indicate special decorative usage, or perhaps they belonged to someone of high or wealthy status. Not enough exists to suggest how or where it was used—whether as a complete shirt, or in gauntlets, as a neckpiece, or elsewhere.

CARGO

Gold, silver, and other treasure must have made up the major part of the cargo, although there probably were some household goods and other personal belongings being carried back to Spain by passengers and crew. In these early days of colonization the New World had little but treasure to export, but the ships arriving from Spain were heavily laden with necessities for the colonists—manufactured goods such as tools, household items, clothing, and weapons, along with wine, oil, and other luxuries. Much of the treasure no doubt was being shipped in payment to Spanish merchants for these

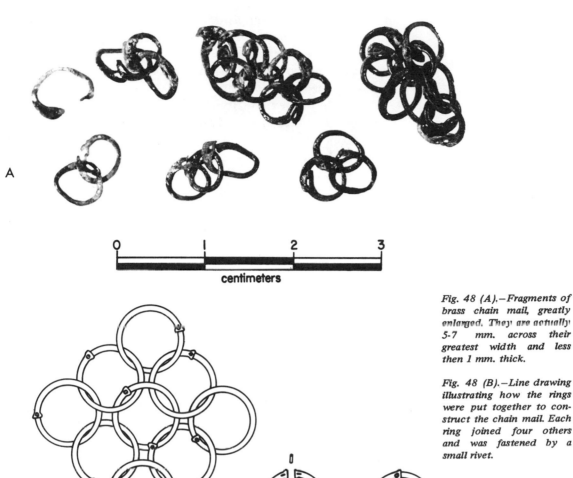

A

B

Fig. 48 (A).—Fragments of brass chain mail, greatly enlarged. They are actually 5-7 mm. across their greatest width and less then 1 mm. thick.

Fig. 48 (B).—Line drawing illustrating how the rings were put together to construct the chain mail. Each ring joined four others and was fastened by a small rivet.

imported materials and the remainder for taxes and royalties that were due the king.

Much of the valuable cargo consisted of silver coins and gold and silver ingots. Figure 49 shows a sampling of the treasure. There were a few copper coins, but it is unlikely that they were a part of the treasure shipment because they had little monetary value and were never listed in the records of valuables carried on the ships; probably they were on board only incidentally as minor personal property. Nevertheless, for convenience, these coins will be described along with the silver ones.

No gold coins were in this collection, and if any were minted in Mexico during the period, they have disappeared, as none has ever been found. Not until 1679 were gold coins officially minted in Mexico, but Dr. Albert F. Pradeau

(1938: 46) found implied evidence that some gold coins may have been minted in Mexico City during 1536. His evidence is based on a royal decree of May 11, 1535, stating that no gold was to be coined in New Spain; a subsequent decree issued on February 28, 1538, prohibited the minting of gold in Mexico City. Dr. Pradeau reasons that if none was being minted it would not have been necessary to issue the second decree.

Gold bullion was represented by a single cigar-shaped ingot (Figs. 49K, 62). Silver ingots were in the shape of crude disks, large and small, some whole and others broken, and a few lumps and nuggets. Some of the disks, including two that have been left encrusted, also are shown in Fig. 49.

Coins

Judging from the unworn appearance of most of the silver coins, and the identification of the assayer's marks, the major portion of the hoard probably had been recently struck at the Mexico City mint before being packed away for shipment to Spain. The silver coins and fragments totaled 884, but in addition there were some 231 in which the metal had decomposed and converted to sulfide to the extent that little or no actual silver remained. About 90% of the silver coins were whole, or nearly so, making it possible to identify 862 of them as representing denominations of 2-, 3-, or 4-reales. The remaining fragments ranged in size from a tiny scrap to more than half of a coin, but usually enough was left of a recognizable design element in even the smallest ones that they could be at least partially identified. Only eight that were processed by the laboratory were so fragmentary that no identification of any kind was possible. More than 82% (711) of the silver coins were of the 4-reales denomination, nearly 18% were 2-reales, and a single, very rare, 3-reales piece accounted for the tiny fraction remaining. Most of the disintegrated coins were X-rayed, and because they contained either such a small bit of silver that it would have been useless to try to recover it, or there was no good silver at all, they have been left encrusted just as they came up from the sea. They are interesting artifacts in themselves because they show how the action of the sea converts the circular silver pieces into objects that now look more like cookies than anything else. A cluster of these encrusted coins is shown in Figure 49N. The reverse mold of one side of a coin was evident in 170 encrustations that were retained; in some instances this imprint was from coins that had been removed at the laboratory or from coins that had completely disintegrated.

All the identifiable coins, both silver and copper, are known by numismatists as Carlos and Johanna pieces, and with one exception the entire hoard was issued by the Mexico City mint. This first mint of the New World was founded under the direction of Charles I of Spain (Charles V of the Holy Roman Empire) in the spring of 1536. His mother, Johanna (called "la Loca"), daughter of Ferdinand and Isabella, was still living during part of Charles's reign, and nominally the queen, but she was mentally disturbed and her son shared the Spanish throne with her as co-ruler until her death. Carlos and Johanna coins, in denominations of one-fourth, one-half, one, two, and three-reales pieces, were the first silver monies to be struck at this new mint. The larger 4-reales denomination probably was not made until 1538 when the 3-reales coins were discontinued because they were easily confused with the 2-reales pieces.

Even after Johanna's death the coins continued to bear the legend CAROLVS ET JOHANA REGES around the edges of the obverse side. In the center of the well-formed circular piece the quartered royal shield features the lions of Leon and the castles of Castile in the four sections, with a pomegranate representing Granada in a small triangle at the base. Atop the shield is a crown. On one side or the other of the shield, and occasionally on both sides, appears:

$$M, \overset{\circ}{M}, \text{ or } \underset{\circ}{\overset{\circ}{M}},$$

indicating the Mexico City mint. On the reverse of the coin appears the legend HISPANIARVM ET INDIARVM (Spain and the Indies) surrounding the rim, the Pillars of Hercules, and across or behind them the motto of the throne: PLVS VLTRA, thought to be an adaptation of Alexander the Great's motto, NE PLVS ULTRA, proudly asserted when he had conquered the known world. The Spaniards were able to say, in effect, "There is more beyond" when they laid claim to the New World. Depending on the particular design, which varied only in detail through time, the assayer's mark can be found either on the obverse opposite the mint mark or on the reverse below the pillars. This is represented by the initial of his first or last name. The denomination was always placed on the reverse between the pillars, either above or below the motto. Figure 50 shows enlargements of both sides of a typical 4-reales coin in which these details can be identified easily.

CM

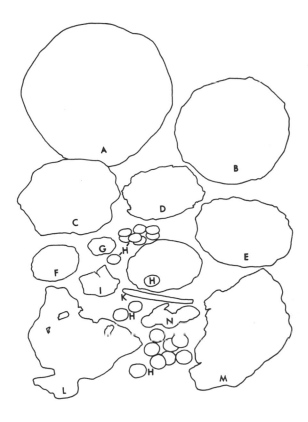

Fig. 49.—(Facing page) Sampling of the treasure cargo: silver coins, a gold ingot, and silver bullion in various shapes. Diagram, right, identifies the treasure pieces: (A) Large silver disk, no. 1417. (B) Large silver disk, no. 1424. (C) Medium silver disk, no. 1418. (D) Medium silver disk, no. 1423. (E) Medium silver disk, still encrusted; note shells on surface; no. 1639. (F) Small silver disk, no. 1412. (G) Small silver disk, no. 1410. (H) Scattering of Carlos and Johanna 2- and 4-reales silver coins. (I) Small silver disk, no. 1414. (J) Small silver disk, 4-reales coin encrusted on surface, no. 1426. (K) Gold ingot, no. 1437. (L) Irregularly shaped silver ingot, no. 1421. (M) Fragmentary large silver disk, no. 1425. (N) Cluster of encrusted silver coins, turned to sulfide, no. 1640.

A similar coin design was also in use for the island of Santo Domingo (Española), where a mint may have been authorized about the same time as in Mexico City, but not actually established until 1542 (Burzio 1958: 362). It is appropriate to discuss the Santo Domingo mint here because one of the most interesting and rare coins in the collection is a Santo Domingo 4-reales piece. After much confusion it was finally identified by the "S" and the "D" appearing on either side of the pillars. The "S" is reversed and looks somewhat like a tilted 8, and the "D" is so indistinct it could be taken for a "P" with a short leg (Fig. 51). The coin will be described in detail later.

The existence of a mint in Santo Domingo during this period has been a matter of considerable doubt among the coin experts (Vives 1899: 671-676; Medina 1919: 142; Nesmith 1944: 94-96). It is known that silver and copper coins (the latter were actually *vellon*, an alloy of silver and copper) were exported to Santo Domingo, probably coined in Spain. These were in use soon after the island was settled and circulated after 1505 for several decades. Documents are on record giving directions for the establishment of a mint there along with details concerning the design (Vives 1899: 691-676; Adams 1929: 485-486), but none has been discovered that provides information on the actual operations of the mint. What is widely recognized, though, is that the silver coins of Santo Domingo are unusually crude as compared with the Spanish and Mexican coinage of the time. They are well rounded, like the Carlos and Johanna coins of Mexico City, but the designs are executed in a most eccentric fashion. Robert I. Nesmith, in 1955, was able to record only 17 of these coins, of which seven were 4-reales pieces (1944: 95). He says of these Santo Domingo coins:

Almost, if not every example is different in spelling, style of lettering and in the designs of the stops between words. The coins look to the writer as if punches were assembled and dies made by workmen handicapped by not having the proper punches, and if they were passed by an official examiner to circulate as coins of the crown, he must have had some explaining to do to the authorities for their imperfections.

Nesmith noted lions and castles transposed to the wrong quarters, "V's" that were sometimes inverted and used for "A's", reversed "S's", and a Gothic "D" that might be placed upside down to take the place of an "E" or laid flat for an "M". Inasmuch as the Spanish mints had been turning out excellent coins for a long time, and the Mexico City mint, although newly established, was issuing fine coins too, it seems more reasonable to suppose that the peculiar coins of Santo Domingo were being produced there under primitive conditions than that the other establishments were turning out poorly made coins for the island. Burzio (1958: 363) believes that a mint really was established in Santo Domingo in March, 1542 for coining silver and *vellón,* and because of defective coining techniques, lack of instruments, and inadequate equipment, the silver coins were crude and clumsy. They probably circulated during the decade of the 1540s but no more were made after 1552. Copper coins of a debased nature continued to be struck for some time thereafter, though, and were notorious for their lack of value.

Even the well made and handsome Carlos and Johanna coins from Mexico City varied considerably, one from another, although the general pattern remained fairly uniform throughout the sequence of three sets of punch designs used during this coinage. We are indebted to Nesmith for most of what is now known about these coins, for he spent 15 years in research on them and published his comprehensive and definitive work, *The Coinage of the First Mint of the Americas at Mexico City, 1536-1572,* in 1955. The coins were not dated, but based on known assayers and a distinct change in the design details, Nesmith (1955: 16-25) divided them into an Early and a Late Series. He dated the Early Series as beginning in 1526, when the mint was established, to about 1542, and the Late Series from that time to 1572. In the Early Series, the mark of the assayer might be found on either the obverse or the reverse side, depending on the issue, but in the Late Series it is always on the obverse, on one side or the other of the shield. The motto is placed on a panel or ribbon behind or in front of the pillars in the Early Series; it disappears entirely in the Late Series, and the letters of the motto are found on either side of and between the pillars. Waves of the sea, representing the Atlantic, are present

A

0 1 2 3

centimeters

Fig. 50.—Enlargement of typical Late Series (1545-1572?) Carlos and Johanna silver coin, 4-reales denomination, to show details of obverse and reverse sides. Two-reales coins are similar, although somewhat smaller, and denomination is indicated by two small dots between the pillars above the motto instead of the 4 below it. Motto on the 2-reales is abbreviated to PLV SVL TR. (A) Obverse side, beginning with the central shield and moving outward on the coin:

Shield of Charles V of the Holy Roman Empire (Charles I of Spain). Devices within shield represent different kingdoms of Spain.

Lions of Leon in upper right and lower left quadrants.

Castles of Castile in upper left, lower right quadrants.

Pomegranate of Granada above point of shield at base.

M for the Mexico City mint, left of shield. This can be found on either side of the shield and is often rendered:

$$\overset{\circ}{M} \; or \; \underset{\circ}{M}$$

L, initial of the assayer, right of shield but also can be on other side.

Legend around edge of coin, with spacing devices between words:

    CAROLVS ∘ ET ∘ JOHANNA ∘ REGES

Crown on upper edge above shield.

(B) Reverse side, beginning with the pillars at center and moving outward:

Crowned Pillars of Hercules

Across coin, on either side of and between the pillars, PLV SVL TRA (Plus Ultra), motto of the Emperor-king.

Between pillars, near base, the denomination mark 4, representing 4-reales coin.

Waves of the sea, below pillars, stand for the Atlantic Ocean.

Legend surrounding edge, with spacing devices between words:

    ✠ *HISPANIARVM ⁚ ET ⁚ INDIARVM*

B

A

A'

B

B'

Fig. 51.—Santo Domingo 4-reales Carlos and Johanna coin, no. 8-1. A and B (left) show actual size. A´ and B´ (right), enlarged to show details. The reverse S and the D on either side of the shield on reverse identify the Santo Domingo mint. Four vertical strokes between right side of shield and legend indicate the denomination. Assayer is unknown. Coin was probably made between 1542-52.

centimeters

centimeters

at the base of the pillars in the Late Series. Other changes in detail, too numerous to mention here, also can be found, most noticeably in the style of the pillars. In both series there is a great variation in the spelling, amount of abbreviation, style of crowns, castles, lions, and pomegranates, and the use of an assortment of spacing devices. In the Late Series alone, Nesmith noted 46 different ways of rendering both the obverse and reverse legends.

To appreciate and understand why each of these coins is in its own way unique, it will be helpful to know something of how they were made, and we can follow this best as Nesmith describes the process (1955: 30-35). Silver bullion to be made into coins was first cast into thin bars, then hammered or rolled into strips. From these, blanks (called planchets or flans) were cut and rounded. After the weighmaster determined that they averaged correctly in their required amount of silver, they were sent to the coining department for heat treating and annealing.

The dies for stamping the design would already have been prepared for the next operation. The pattern was punched, not engraved, into the steel. It took 15 letters and 11 other devices to make the design on the dies, and for each of these there was an individual punch. Element by element, these had to be hammered into the die, and because it was impossible to place each punch exactly, no two dies were just alike. Carelessness in spacing the legends could leave gaps at the end which could be filled in by various devices—rondules, annulets, lozenges, etc.—or if too much space was used up, the words could be abbreviated in a number of ways. Dies were not collared, and with heavy usage they broke frequently so that new ones had to be made. Individual punches wore out too, or broke, and they also had to be replaced. The lower die, which was the obverse and more elaborate design, was sunk into an anvil and held in place by a tongue at its base; this die was called the *pila,* or "pile." The upper die for the reverse was cut into the end of a rod called the *troquel* or "trussel." None of the original Mexico City dies has survived, but Figure 52 from an illustration used by Nesmith (1955: 34) from dies of a similar kind at the Vienna Mint Museum, shows what they were like. Because the strongest force of the blow fell on the upper die, it was in greatest danger of breaking. Nesmith notes that according to English records two upper dies were issued to the provincial mints for every lower die, where hand hammering of coins took place (Nesmith 1955: 34, ftnt. 11). Figure 53 shows the hand hammering coin operations as performed in an Austrian mint during the reign of the Emperor Maximilian I (1493-1519). At this mint, though, it can be seen that the silver is being hammered into thin sheets of a generally uniform thickness, then trimmed with shears into circular shapes before being stamped in the dies. With the Carlos and Johanna coins it did not seem to matter how the obverse was oriented with the reverse, so that when the coins are turned over, the pillars, in relation to the shield on the other side, might be right side up, upside down, or at any angle. It took a good hard blow to get a perfect result, and there must have been many weak blows because overstriking was common. The coins were blanched to clean and whiten them after the discoloration that developed from making them,

Fig. 52.—Reproduced from Nesmith's The Coinage of the First Mint of the Americas at Mexico City 1536-1572 *(1955: 34), used by permission.*

Hand Hammering Dies at Vienna Mint Museum

The upper dies (A and C) were held over the lower dies (B and D) which were set in a hole in an anvil. The designs for the coins were punched into the lower ends of A and C and into the tops of B and D. E illustrates how a reverse die of a one real of the LATE SERIES would appear.

and finally they were weighed to make certain they averaged the standard 67 reales to the mark, a weight that was equal to a half pound of silver. The assayer guaranteed by his initial in the die that the silver was of the authorized fineness and purity. Indians and Negro slaves furnished the hard labor in minting under the direction of Spanish supervisors.

Since the coins were not dated, the problem of setting up a chronology for them was extremely difficult, but Nesmith has developed an approximate sequence for them by examining changes in the design. He believes that the first viceroy to Mexico, Pedro de Mendoza, probably brought the first dies, or more likely the first punches, with him when he arrived in 1535, establishment of the mint having been authorized by queen's decree on May 11, 1535 (Nesmith 1955: 8). If not, they were sent over soon afterward. The punches, he says, for the earliest *R* coins (those with the assayer's initial *R*) were certainly of Spanish manufacture, with letters, lions, and castles of typical Spanish design at that time. The square Gothic letters were characteristic. As time went on, and native labor was taught to cut punches for the die elements, letters were simplified, castles became more Aztec than Spanish, and lions resembled no known animal.

The chronology of the assayers was constructed through correlating the design elements with documents recording assayers' terms of office (Nesmith 1955: 17-22). The sequence begins with Francisco del Rincón (whose mark is *R*), documented with certainty as assayer from the opening of the mint in the spring of 1536 until some time after March 22, 1538. Following Rincón came Juan Gutiérrez *(G)*, but the date on which he took office is unknown. Third was Esteban Franco *(F)*, who appears to have served only temporarily, probably around 1538-1540. The author says that the rare coins with the mark *P* are probably those of Pedro de Espina, the fourth assayer; his signature appears on a voucher dated October 22, 1541, and he too seems to have been on the job only a short time. With the *P* coins, the Early Series ends. Figures 54, 55, and 56 illustrate examples and details of coins from the Early Series assayers *R*, *G*, and *P*; there are no *F* coins in the collection.

The Late Series begins with Gutiérrez on the job again, serving a second term which lasted from March, 1543 to January 7, 1545. There seems to have been some overlapping and confusion concerning the office during this period, because Rincón was to have begun his second term in August, 1543 and served until at least March 18, 1545. But Nesmith believes that the assayer whose initial was *A*, whom he was unable to identify, held the office some time between Rincón and Gutiérrez. In connection with *A*, Burzio (1958: 1) mentions information furnished to Dr. A. F. Pradeau that *A* was the licentiate Aleman who was assistant to Rincón. Probably following Rincón's second term came another unidentified assayer whose initial was *S*. The seventh assayer was Luis Rodríguez *(L)*, around whom a problem of dating revolves. The assayer whose mark is *O*, still unknown, was evidently the last of the Carlos and Johanna assayers and the first of the new coinage which had a different design entirely and bore the name of Philip II. Assayer *O* may have alternated with *L* at the last, because pieces are known with both *L* punched over the original *O* on the die, and *O* punched over the *L*. Documents show that Luis Rodríguez's death was announced in May, 1570. Examples of Late Series coins, with

Fig. 53.—A mint during the reign of Emperor Maximilian I (1493-1519) of Austria, from the Weisskunig. *Reproduced by permission.*

111

A   B

C   D

Fig. 54.—Examples of Early Series Carlos and Johanna silver coins (1536-1545). Assayer R. Upper, 4-reales; (A) Obverse legend reads: KAROLVS ET IOHAN, Gothic K, double rondules between words, M—M. (B) Reverse legend: HISPANIE ET INDIARV R, double rondules and other devices between words. Motto: PLVSV in oval panel; R between pillars. Specimen no. 8-5, diam. 3.0 cm., 11.1 g. Lower, 3-reales; (C) Obverse legend reads: KAROLVS ET IOHANA, Gothic K and H, N reversed; M—M. (D) Reverse legend: HI SPANIE ET [INDIAR]VM, Gothic H, double rondules and other devices used to divide words. Note Roman numeral III. Motto: PLVSV [L?]. Specimen no. 8-3, diam. 2.9 cm., 7 g.

details, bearing initials of assayers *G, A, R, S,* and *L,* are illustrated in Figures 57, 58, 59, and 60.

Because *L*'s term as assayer is directly involved in our attempts to date the shipwreck, his time in office is of special significance. More than 90% of the coins in this collection bear his initial, and it appears that more known Carlos and Johanna coins have been attributed to him than to any other single assayer. Nesmith examined more than 2,400 coins in preparation for his book on the coinage of Mexico City during this period and noted the following percentages assayed by the various officials whose initials were found on the Late Series coins (Nesmith 1955: 95):

G:	12%
A, R, and *S,* together:	3%
L:	43%
O:	41%

In comparison, these are the approximate percentages for the Late Series coins in this collection:

G:	6% (46 coins)
A, R, and *S,* together:	3% (22 coins)
L:	91% (698 coins)

[No *O* coins are in the collection]

There are additionally nine probable *L* coins and two possible *G*'s. Nesmith believed that the *L* and *O* coins fell at least partly, and possibly completely, into the first period of the reign of Philip II, 1556-1570. But the question of when Philip ordered a change in the design to show his own name and crest has been, and continues to be, another point of uncertainty and disagreement among the coin experts, because, again, no definite document has ever been found. Nesmith concedes that his evidence for Rodríguez's beginning his term of office about 1556 is more negative than positive, but is based on the fact that Philip did not order a new design put into use in American mints until March 8, 1570 (Nesmith 1955: 39), citing Herrera in *El Duro* (1914, I: 13). Even in the Spanish mints, Philip did not order a change in the coinage design until 1566, some ten years after he became king. Nesmith therefore concludes that the large proportion of *L* coins can be reasonably accounted for because of Rodríguez's possibly extended period in the office of assayer—much longer than that of any of the others. A. J. S. McNickel (1962: 9) confirms this opinion, bringing up the point that "coins bearing the name of a defunct ruler are known to have been struck as long as two years after the new monarch ascended the throne." He adds, "The longest period in which the Mexico mint struck coins of the regular issues not in the name of thc reigning monarch was during the reign of Philip-the-Second (1556-1598) when from 1556 to 1571, inclusive, all coins issued bore the name of Carlos and Johanna."

Dr. Pradeau, however, is of a different opinion. In a letter of June 4, 1972 (personal communication), he writes:

Philip II was 29 years old when he ascended the throne in 1556 and granting a year or at most two for the change of dies, I would consider 1557 or 1558 the end of the Chas. & Johanna coinage, therefore your identification of the 1553 wreck would be in line. . . I speculate that the hoard was the property of a private individual and I venture the thought that said coins were minted in 1550 at the latest except the three reales which were discontinued about 1538. The subject of coinage in New Spain for the first and second centuries has been the subject of deductions and conclusions mainly because of lack of records; the edict of March 8, 1570 authorizing thc change of design does not specify that the Chas. & Johanna series were struck up to that time. Whether acceptable or not, these are my opinions.

If this wreckage can some day be dated with certainty, it may help to determine at least the year when Luis Rodríguez's term as assayer might have begun.

Only 20 Early Series coins have been recognized in this collection, but among them are represented three of the four Early Series assayers. The first to hold the office, Rincón, was responsible for one 2-reales, one 3-reales, and four 4-reales pieces. For Juan Gutiérrez there are four 2-reales coins and one 4-reales. Pedro de Espina's *señal* (mark) is on more coins than either of the other assayers: five 2-reales and four 4-reales.

The single 3-reales coin (Fig. 54) is of particular interest because this denomination was minted for such a short time, 1535 to 1537, and thus is extremely rare. According to the records the viceroy ordered their discontinuance in late 1537. Because they were so nearly the size of the 2-reales pieces the coins were easily confused. Three vertical strokes, signifying the Roman numeral III, indicate the denomination. This detail would make it the last design of the 3-reales coins, according to Nesmith (1955: 68) because the earlier ones had three dots between the pillars to show the denomination, corresponding to the two dots that denote the 2-reales coins. As previously mentioned, the coin was assayed by Rincón, the first assayer of the mint, whose initial, apparently

A   B

C   D

Fig. 55.—Examples of Early Series Carlos and Johanna silver coins (1536-1545). Assayer G. Upper, 4-reales; (A) Obverse legend reads: KAROLVS ET IOHAN, Gothic K, lozenges between words, M—M. (B) Reverse legend: HISPANIARVM ET INDIARVM RE. G between pillars, lozenges between words. Motto: PLVS in oval panel. Specimen no. 8-4, diam. 3.2 cm., 10.3 g. Lower, 2-reales. (C) Obverse legend: KAROLVS ET IOH[ANA], Gothic K, lozenges between words, M—M. (D) Reverse legend: HISPANIARVM ET INDIARV, rondules between words. Motto: PLVS in rhomboid panel pointing right. Two dots indicate denomination, G between pillars. Specimen no. 10-14, diam. 2.6 cm., 4.1 g.

A   B

C   D

0   1   2   3
centimeters

Fig. 56.—Examples of Early Series Carlos and Johanna silver coins (1536-1545). Assayer P. Upper, 4-reales; (A) Obverse legend reads: KAROLVS ET IOHANA RE, Gothic K, lozenges between words, M–P. (B) Reverse legend: HISPANIARVM ET INDIARVM RE, lozenges between words. Motto: PLVS in rhomboid panel pointing right. Specimen no. 8-7, diam. 3.1 cm., 10.19 g. Lower, 2-reales; (C) Obverse legend: KAROLVS ET IOHANA RE, Gothic K, double annulets between words, M–P. (D) Reverse legend: HISPANIARVM ET INDIA [RVM], mascles between words. Motto: PLVS in rhomboid panel pointing right. Two dots indicate the denomination. Specimen no. 8-13, diam. 2.6 cm., 5.3 g.

double stamped, appears below the pillars on the reverse. The N of IHOANA in the obverse legend is reversed. The motto PLVSV appears on a panel mostly between the pillars, although the P is actually on the left hand pillar itself.

Not until November 18, 1537 did the king order the Mexico mint to coin 4- and 8-reales pieces. But if allowance is made for the time it took for the order to reach Mexico and the new dies to be made, it was probably the spring of 1538 before the fours *(reales a quatro)* actually appeared. There is evidence that an attempt was made to manufacture 8-reales pieces, but fashioning the large blanks and striking coins of this size by hand hammering was "too slow, difficult, and costly for the mint to support" (Nesmith 1955: 37). The famous "pieces-of-eight," it seems, were not struck at the Mexico City mint until 1580, although trial pieces may have been made. No authenticated ones from the earlier period have yet been recognized.

The 4-reales coin from the Santo Domingo mint is considerably larger than the corresponding ones from Mexico, as can be seen in Figure 51. This can probably be accounted for by the differing evaluations in terms of the assigned values as directed from Spain. Thirty-four *maravedíes* (a Spanish unit of value) per real were assigned to the Mexico City coins, but the Santo Domingo money circulated at 44 maravedíes to the real. This was seemingly a holdover from the time when the additional value was assigned because of the risks and expense of importing it (Burzio 1958: 363-364). The reversed *S* and *D* with a long upright, flank the pillars on the reverse. The lions and castles can be seen on the obverse shield. To the right of the shield appears the Roman numeral IIII, indicating the denomination, but whatever letter represents the assayer to the left of the shield is indecipherable now. It may well have been an *F,* since that seems to have been the only assayer's initial recorded for this mint. Occasionally an *E* is shown on the coins of this origin, but it is generally agreed by the numismatists that it was just another of the frequent errors made by the die sinkers and should be translated as *F.* There is documentation confirming that one Francisco Rodríguez was appointed assayer of this mint in March, 1542 (Dasí 1950: 89); no others are named in the records. Dasí points out, however, that Vicente Blasco Íbañez, in a passage from *El Caballero de la Virgen,* mentions a man named Fermin Cado who was assayer and purifier of metals. His initial also could have been *F.* This coin bears out the Santo Domingo mint's reputation for eccentricities. The shield is crudely delineated with wavering and uneven lines, the *S* is made in reverse each time it appears, and the legends are unusual indeed. The obverse reads CAROLVS ET IHOANA RE, the remainder of the last word appearing in the reverse legend, making it read GI SPANIA ET INDIAR, but the *A* of SPANIA is just an inverted *V*. The *L* in CAROLVS is in the Gothic style as is the *H* of IHOANA. The letters PLV of the motto on the reverse are placed on a rhomboid panel with the *P* on the left pillar; there may have been an *S* to complete the word on the right pillar, but it cannot be distinguished now.

The four copper coins should not be considered part of the treasure shipment but may have come from someone's purse or pocket. They were made for short periods only so that the Indians would have coins of small denomination available for minor market transactions (Nesmith 1955: 40-45), but the Indians disliked them as they considered copper of little or no value. In spite of severe punishment, they refused to use copper coins for trade, and instead threw them into the gutters or into Lake Texcoco. Only luck has preserved a few of them in this collection.

All the copper coins appear to be of the 4-maravedíes denomination. Coins of 2-maravedíes value are known to have been made, but none seems to have survived. Although they had been authorized in Mexico from the time the mint was founded, evidently the officials did not get around to making them right away, and no copper coins were actually struck in Mexico until after June 28, 1542, the date of the viceroy's edict of authorization. It is believed, however, that copper coins from Spain, some designated for Santo Domingo, were circulated for a time. In 1542, 4-maravedíes coins were struck at the Mexico City mint from dies made with a series of punch designs that were sent over for the Early Series *G*, *F*, and *P* silver coins. At this time they were valued at 34 maravedíes to 1 real, reduced from the earlier 44 to 1. Since the copper coins had no silver content it was not necessary to assay them and they bore no assayer's mark.

The early square Gothic *K* can be seen on one of these copper coins, no. 1447-2; it is in unusually good condition. Other design details conform exactly with the Early Series 4-maravedíes coin illustrated by Nesmith (1955: 129 and Fig. 6). When the third series of punches arrived from Spain the details of the dies were changed accordingly, and the copper coins then resembled the Late Series *G* silver coinage of small denominations. They were made in values of 2- and 4-maravedíes, and possibly even of 1-maravedí, but as no examples of the 1-maravedí have ever been seen, they may

Fig. 57.—Examples of Late Series Carlos and Johanna silver coins (1545-1570?). Assayer G. Upper, 4-reales; (A) Obverse legend reads: CAROLVS ET IOHANA REGES. (B) Reverse legend: HISPANIARVM ET INDIARVM. Single or double annulets between words in both legends. Motto: PLV SVL TRA. Specimen no. 11-4, diam. 3.2 cm., 9.6 g. Lower, 2-reales. (C) Obverse legend: CAROLVS ET IOHANA REGES. (D) Reverse legend:

HI[SP]AN[I]RVM ET INDIARVM

Single or double annulets between words in both legends. Motto: PLV SVL TR. Specimen no. 10-20, diam. 2.7 cm., 4.5 g.

115

Fig. 58.—*Examples of Late Series Carlos and Johanna silver coins (1545-1570?). Assayer A. Upper, 4-reales. (A) Obverse legend reads: CAROLVS ET IOHANA [RE]GES, single rondules between words. (B) Reverse legend: HISPANIARV ET IN[DIAR]VM, single or double rondules between words. Motto reads: PLV SVL TRA. Specimen no. 11-6, diam. 3.4 cm., 10.1 g. Lower, 2-reales. (C) Obverse legend: CAROLVS ET IOHANA REGES. (D) Reverse legend:*
   HIS[PA]NIARVM ET INDIARV[M]
Single rondules and annulets between words in both legends. Motto: PLV SVL TR. Specimen no. 8-12, diam. 2.8 cm., 4.6 g.

Fig. 59.—*Examples of Late Series Carlos and Johanna silver coins (1545-1570?). Assayer R. Upper, 4-reales. (A) Obverse legend reads: CAROLVS ET IOHANA REGES, single rondules between words. (B) Reverse legend: HISPANIARVM ET INDIARVM, single annulets between words. Motto: PLV SVL TRA. Specimen no. 11-33, diam. 3.3 cm., 9.69 g. Lower, 4-reales. (C) Obverse legend reads: CAROLVS ET IOHANA REGS, double annulets between words. (D) Reverse legend reads: HISPANIARVM [ET] INDIARVM, single annulets between words. Motto: PLV SVL TRA. Specimen no. 42-12, diam. 3.3 cm., 13.29 g.*

never have been struck at all. Insofar as the other three copper coins in this collection can be identified they are of this later period, but two of them are fragmentary and the other is in very poor condition because of surface erosion, so few details are discernible.

The continued resistance of the Indians to the copper coins forced their discontinuance around 1551 or 1552. Officially outlawed in 1565, copper coins were not minted again in New Spain until 1814. Only unusual circumstances of preservation enabled even this single coin to survive in

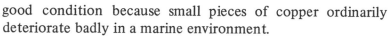

A   B

C   D

Fig. 60.—Examples of Late Series Carlos and Johanna silver coins (1545-1570?). Assayer L. Upper, 4-reales. (A) Obverse legend reads: CAROLVS ET IOHANA REGS, single rondules between words. (B) Reverse legend: HISPANIARVM ET I[N]DIARVM, single rondules between words. Motto: PLV SVL TRA. Specimen no. 17-6, diam. 3.1 cm., 9.4 g. Lower, 2-reales. (C) Obverse legend reads: CAROLVS ET IOHANA RE[G]S, single annulets between words. (D) Reverse legend reads: HISPANIARVM ET [I]NDIARVM, single rondules between words. Motto: PLV SVL TR. Specimen no. 13-11, diam. 2.8 cm., 6.1 g.

Fig. 61.—Early Series 4-maravedíes copper Carlos and Johanna coin (no. 1477-2) from the Mexico City mint. The square Gothic K on the obverse side identifies it as an Early Series coin, struck only in 1542. Copper coins bear no assayer's mark. (A) Obverse side. Legend (letters in brackets are missing):

    KAROLVS [ET] IOHANA [RE]GES
Mint mark:
           °
        M

                       is at the bottom, just left of center. (B) Reverse side. Legend:

    HISPANIARVM ET INDIARVM,
with quatrefoils between the words. Denomination mark 4 is at base of the large I, with sets of four small rondules on each side.

good condition because small pieces of copper ordinarily deteriorate badly in a marine environment.

The following list sums up the coins in the Texas Gulf collection by denomination and condition:

1.   TWO-REAL CJ COINS, MEXICO CITY MINT, LATE SERIES

1)	Whole, good condition	111
2)	Whole, poor condition	2
3)	Fragmentary, good condition	14
4)	Fragmentary, poor condition	9

2.   PROBABLE TWO-REAL CJ COINS, MEXICO CITY MINT, LATE SERIES

1)	Fragmentary, poor condition	2

3.   TWO-REAL CJ COINS, MEXICO CITY MINT, EARLY SERIES

1)   Whole, good condition   6
2)   Whole, poor condition   1
3)   Fragmentray, good condition   1
4)   Fragmentary, poor condition   2

4.   TWO-REAL CJ COIN, SERIES UNKNOWN

1)   Partially encrusted, left as is for display   1

5.   THREE-REAL CJ COIN, MEXICO CITY MINT, EARLY SERIES

1)   Whole, good condition   1

6.   FOUR-REAL COINS, MEXICO CITY MINT, LATE SERIES

1)   Whole, good condition   516
2)   Whole, poor condition   69
3)   Fragmentary, good condition   12
4)   Fragmentary, poor condition   95
5)   Whole, good condition, left partially
     encrusted for display   1

7.   PROBABLE FOUR-REAL CJ COIN, MEXICO CITY MINT, LATE SERIES

1)   Fragmentary, poor   12

8.   FOUR-REAL CJ COINS, MEXICO CITY MINT, EARLY SERIES

1)   Whole, good condition   8
2)   Fragmentary, good condition   1

9.   FOUR-REAL CJ COIN, SERIES UNKNOWN

1)   Fragmentary, poor condition   8

10. PROBABLE FOUR-REAL CJ COIN, SERIES UNKNOWN

1)   Fragmentary, poor condition   1

11. FOUR-REAL CJ COIN, SANTO DOMINGO MINT

1)   Whole, good condition   1

12. UNIDENTIFIED CJ COIN, LATE SERIES

1)   Fragmentary, poor condition   1

13. PROBABLE CJ COINS, DENOMINATION & SERIES UNKNOWN

1)	Fragmentary, poor condition	9

14. FOUR-MARAVEDÍES COPPER CJ COINS

1)	Whole, good condition	1
2)	Whole, poor condition	3
3)	Fragmentary, poor condition	1

TOTAL COINS AND FRAGMENTS   889

15. DISINTEGRATED SILVER COINS CONVERTED TO SULFIDE   231

Most were left encrusted as X-ray showed little or no silver remaining. Includes one cluster of nine coins.

16. MOLDS OF COINS FORMED BY ENCRUSTATION   172

These show the reverse imprint of one face of a coin on one side, the other side being the protective encrustation. Often the mold is more clear and crisp than the design on the coin itself.

Gold and Silver Ingots

Gold

The gold cigar-shaped ingot (no. 1437) is a slender bar, flat on the bottom and rounded across the top, evidently the end section of a longer piece originally cast in a mold, then divided into segments (Figs. 49 and 62). One end is evenly rounded, but the other end was cut with a chisel halfway through, then hit against something to snap it off. The piece is 14.9 cm. long and tapers in width from 1.5 cm. at the rounded end to 1.2 cm. at the cut end where it bends slightly upward. Thickest at the rounded extremity, 0.9 cm., it thins out to 0.6 cm. at the other. It weighs 181.6 grams. Near each end on the upper surface appears a stamped mark:

A V
S

Another mark,

XV :

signifying an assayed value of 15¾ carats, is stamped twice, in corresponding positions, a little closer to the center, but the lower dot of one mark is almost obliterated. Between this imperfect stamp and the center of the bar appears the Roman numeral VIII. Aside from a little pitting on the surface, the ingot is in excellent condition, almost unaffected by its long period under the sea.

119

Fig. 62.—Gold ingot, no. 1437, upper and lower sides shown actual size. Marks on upper side: Roman numeral VIII, probably a tally mark; XV with three small dots toward each end indicating 15¾ carats; AVS, appearing next to the value stamps may represent the assayer or the owner, or may be an abbreviation for AVREUS (AUREUS), Latin for gold. The ingot weighs 131.6 grams and was probably the end piece of a series of eight.

The VIII was no doubt a tally mark of some sort. A. J. S. McNickle examined and described the various marks appearing on a 72-pound silver bar dated 1652, that had been recovered from the sea, and noted: "Each bar bore its own number under which it was entered in the books of the Treasury together with such particulars as its fineness, weight, date, origin and name of owner" (McNickle 1953, unpaged). He explained that Roman numerals were used for the sake of clarity and because large punches with Arabic numerals would have worn out quickly. The metal used for punches possessed some of the qualities of steel, but "was to all intents and purposes wrought iron." The tally number, he says, was never changed and no other number which could be confused with it could ever be used on the surface. We do not know just when this system went into effect, and this figure VIII probably just indicates the identifying segment of a series. What the letters indicate is open to speculation, but Clyde Hubbard, noted numismatist, believes they stand for AVREVS or AUREUS, the Latin word for gold (personal communication 1971). It might also be the assayer's mark that was required on all pieces of gold and silver bullion, or might indicate the owner.

Silver Bullion

The silver bullion is of tremendous interest because few such crude ingots have survived in their original form. Ordinarily it was melted down for fabrication into coins, plates, or other objects of the silversmith's art in Mexico or sent on to Spain where it soon suffered the same fate. Rarely has an opportunity arisen to examine the actual objects as they appeared in the treasure shipments. The complete pieces were almost all in the form of rough disks that had not been cast into regular molded shapes but appear instead to have been poured out into sand, or perhaps into depressions in rock, and allowed to cool, taking on thin, more or less circular shapes. Figure 63 illustrates the upper and lower sides of two disks, one large (no. 1424) and one small (no. 1410). The upper surfaces often show striations, swirls, lumps, and bumps that were probably formed as the metal cooled after melting. Evidently in later years the bullion was cast into uniform bar- or wedge-shaped ingots. The large silver bar that McNickle described, dated 1652, had a rough appearance on the underside, which he said was caused by the soft stone molds in which all such ingots were cast. That specimen represented a boat-shaped form, called the "Guanajuato" type of ingot because it was at the mining center of that name in Mexico that this shape was first tried out. It was found to be so convenient and easy to handle that this shape eventually became the standard form throughout the Spanish Americas, according to this authority, and no other molds of any other shape were permitted by law. The early, irregular, and non-uniform disk shape that we find was probably as convenient as any for stacking and transporting the silver to Vera Cruz and stowing away on the ship.

No two of the disks are exactly the same shape or size; and the color and weight of the silver differs from one piece to another, possibly indicating differences in the mineral composition. There is a wide range in size, from maximum diameter of 40.5 to 5.2 cm., and in weight from 13.131 kg. to 15.3 g. The thickest is 2.0 cm. and the thinnest, 0.2. The whole ones can be sorted by size into large, medium, and small, using maximum diameter as the measure: [1] four large disks (30.4 to 40.5 cm.) [2] three medium disks (22.5

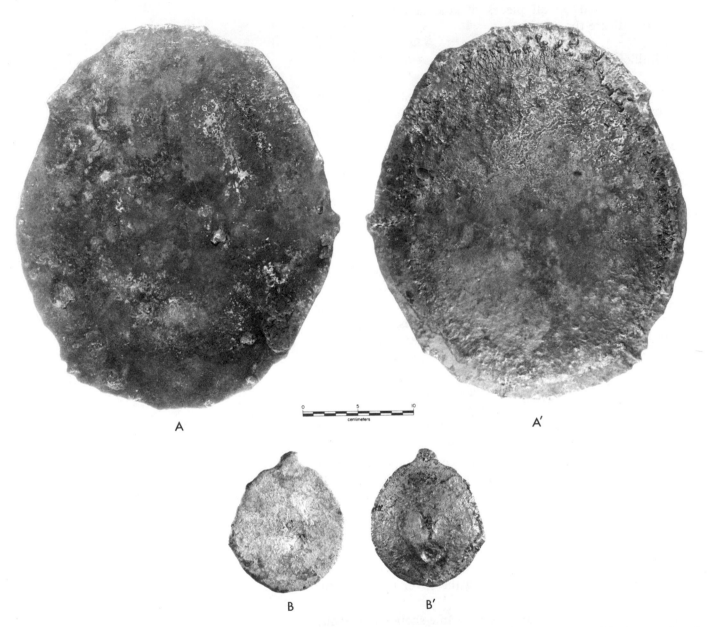

A   A'

B   B'

Fig. 63.—Silver disks. A, upper side of large disk no. 1424. A stamped mark can just be made out near the upper right. A' is the reverse side of the disk showing impressions made by sand as the disk cooled after smelting. It weighs over 4.8 kg. (nearly 11 pounds). B and B' are upper and reverse sides of small disk no. 1410. Stamped marks can be seen on top of the surface and the reverse illustrates the same type of sand impressions found on all the disks. This one weighs 0.449 kg. (about 15.9 ounces).

to 25.0 cm.) [3] twelve small disks (5.2 to 17.0 cm.).

In addition to the complete disks, there are fragments of broken ones, large and small, and a number of irregular little lumps or scraps of silver—altogether adding up to some 32 diverse non-disk pieces. A complete tabulation of the silver bullion is given in Table 7, with measurements, weights, and other pertinent data.

Most of the disks and disk fragments, and even many of the small lumps and odd pieces, have one or more stamped marks on the surface. These are usually found on the upper side, but occasionally occur on the underside too. The chances are that originally most of the complete specimens were stamped at least once, but erosion has obliterated the marks. Faint, indistinct markings are still visible in some instances, but it is almost impossible to make much out of them. Among those stamps that are clear enough to show some details, ten different designs have been distinguished. These are illustrated with identifying numbers in the drawings and photographs in Figures 64 and 65, and noted in the description of the individual pieces in Table 7. Some pieces were stamped as many as four or five times, often one mark struck over another, and sometimes the same mark appears more than once on a single ingot. The various stamps obviously were intended to convey specific information about the bullion, and could probably reveal much about their history if their significance were known. All silver and gold was supposed to have been marked at least once by the Royal Assayer, but from the variety of stamps to be seen there must have been reasons for using other marks as well.

On the 72-pound silver bar that McNickle studied, there appeared a number of stamps: the year in which the ingot was cast; the tally number; the value of the bar (expressed in reales); a name in the form of a *sigla* (an abbreviation in initials); the weight of the bar in marks (a mark was equal to one-half pound); the stamp of the Royal Foundry; the Royal Seal; the mark of an assayer; the "bite" of two different assayers; chisel marks obliterating the results of the first assay; and at least two unidentified marks. The mark of the Royal Foundry at this time was a cross with small bars at the ends. McNickle was able to trace the history of the ingot by means of the stamps; and by the name of the second assayer, which was quite clear, he identified the silver as coming from South America. It probably was cast at Santa Fé de Bogatá in the New Kingdom of Granada (McNickle 1953: unpaged).

There is little to go on in our quest for knowledge about

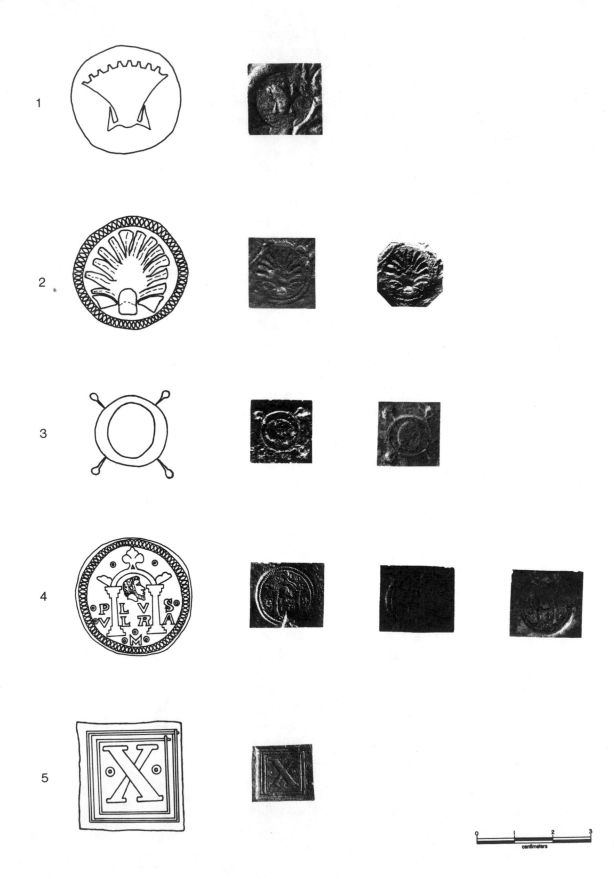

the silver pieces in this collection—where they came from, how they were made, and something about sixteenth century technology. P. J. Bakewell, during extensive research for *Silver Mining & Society in Colonial Mexico: Zacatecas 1546-1700* (1971) searched the archives of Spain, Mexico, and the United States and found not a single contemporary work from the first 200 years of Spanish occupation. Apparently the old mining records are lost or destroyed. E. J. Foscue (1947: 20), writing of *Taxco, Mexico's Silver City*, quotes Chism (1899: 197-199) as saying that revolutionaries burned the archives in Taxco in the early nineteenth century.

It is certain, though, that by 1553 at least 20 silver mines were active in Mexico (Ingerson 1971: personal communication), and by 1555 a good many more were in operation (Bargalló 1955: 64). The silver bullion pieces could have come from any of these, or from Peru, whose mines were flourishing by that time. The most productive and important mines in New Spain at this period were those in the Zacatecas district, but other prominent mining centers were operating in the Guanajuato, Pacheco y Real del Monte, and Taxco districts as well (Bakewell 1971: 222); and besides

---

Fig. 64.—Drawings of stamped marks found on upper surfaces of silver disks and other silver pieces, with accompanying photographs of the actual marks. Because some were not clear or were fragmentary, two or more were required to complete the design. On occasion the full pattern was put together using stamps from disks in the State of Texas collection (41 KN 10) along with incomplete marks from the collection at hand.

1. *This may represent the Shell of St. James, symbol of the patron saint of Spain. In this stamp the shell rim has 10 scallops. If correctly identified, it is probably an official mark, and appears seven times among the pieces.*

2. *A more elaborate version of the Shell of St. James, this stamp has a border of touching lozenges and 12 scallops on the shell. It was found six times and it too is probably an official mark.*

3. *The unevenly shaped circle or wheel with four short spokes features four short spikes, each ending in a knob, evenly spaced around it. It has not been identified, but might be an assayer's mark. It was located four times.*

4. *The most complicated stamp discovered is undoubtedly an official stamp because it bears elements from the coins and what looks like a bearded profile of Charles V between the pillars. The Pillars of Hercules, the royal motto— PLVS VLTRA— and the M, with rondules above and to each side, indicating Mexico City, establish its importance. This design appears 20 times, more frequently than any of the others, and is sometimes stamped over another mark. It may be the stamp that indicates the 20% tax, the* Quinto, *had been paid to the king's treasury.*

5. *An X, with a rondule on either side all set within a nested square, may possibly represent the* diezmo *stamp, indicating the silver was taxed at one tenth instead of the usual one twentieth. If not, it remains unidentified. It was found five times.*

1

2

3

4

5

these, a number of small mines were also producing. Among the disks in the collection are one each from the Taxco and the Guachinango mines or mining districts. So far as is known, no studies have been made on which mines produced silver of specific mineral composition. It is possible that metallurgical analysis of these pieces could match them with silver from currently producing mining centers.

Another tantalizing but highly unlikely possibility would be determining whether this silver was refined by smelting, the long-established technique, or by amalgamation with mercury, a process which was not introduced into New Spain until 1556. This would confirm a date for the collection. Recovery of silver ore from the rock matrix and the subsequent breaking up, grinding and pulverizing of the stone for smelting or amalgamation, was hard, dangerous, and tedious work performed at first by Indians and later by Negro slaves. Smelting required mixing and melting the crushed material with lead ores or litharge (a lead monoxide) in small furnaces in order to extract the silver. But as Bakewell points out (1971: 146), there was no need for elaborate equipment or much capital outlay. It could be carried out in either large or small scale operations. The amalgamation process (called

Fig. 65—Drawings of stamped marks found on upper surfaces of silver disks and other silver pieces, with accompanying photographs of the actual marks (see also Fig. 64).

1. *This obviously represents either the Tasco mine or mining district where a mine was established in 1543. The rectangle bearing the name is outlined by beading, and a Maltese cross is placed to the right of the name. It was discovered only once in this collection, but its counterpart was found in the State of Texas collection.*

2. *The crowned LVIS may refer to one Luis Rodríguez, who was the royal assayer for silver before he became assayer for the coins. It must be associated with a royal official because of the crown. This mark, and all the remaining ones, were recognized a single time apiece.*

3. *GUACHINANGO, separated in two lines, must be the mark of a mine that was, like the Tasco mine, recorded as being established in 1543. It appears once.*

4. *This mark, with an A in the eroded extension above the main rectangle, has been overstamped by the Pillars of Hercules which almost obliterate it. The letters CA can be seen on the left side of the stamp adjacent to the circle of the second stamp. What remains of some sort of figure to the right of the upper A has not been identified. A remote clue is that a Peruvian mine named CARABAYA was operating in 1545; but not enough is left of the word to tell what it actually was. Found once.*

5. *This heraldic shield or banner is the most elaborate stamp discovered except for the Pillars of Hercules. Double joined Xs are suspended from the top of the shield and an unusual figure that might include an A is below it, extending to the point. If the mark is turned to the side, the A becomes a P with a long, curving crosspiece. This too remains unidentified but may be an owner's mark. Found once.*

the "patio process"), on the other hand, required the addition of mercury, which was then scarce and expensive, and the performance of a complicated series of procedures (Bakewell 1971: 140-144). Amalgamation was a far more efficient system of refining silver, revolutionizing the production of metal in New Spain and Peru so that before long, vast quantities of treasure were shipped off to Spain. Mercury amalgamation was called the patio process because the slush of ore, water, salt, and mercury was spread out into semi-liquid cakes *(tortas)* contained in temporary circular curbs of wood or stone set in a courtyard (Bakewell 1971: 140). The *tortas* were mixed or stirred several times a day for up to two or three months to incorporate the mercury thoroughly into the mixture. The mercury was eventually distilled out and the fine silver melted down into bars of standard size. The mercury, fortunately, could be saved and used again. If casting the silver into standard bars was the usual practice in all the refining plants employing the patio process, it is reasonable to assume that the crude disks with which we are concerned were simply smelted and poured out into some sort of basins to cool, each taking on a different form as it hardened.

The various stamps on the silver pieces offer an even more interesting challenge of interpretation. A few clues have turned up, as we have seen, and there are many possibilities for speculation. To begin with, as Bakewell explains, the precious metals, both silver and gold, were divided for taxing purposes into two categories: *plata* (silver) or *oro* (gold) *del diezmo,* which was taxed at 10%, and *del quinto,* taxed at the basic rate of 20%. Both tax schedules, however, fluctuated somewhat at various places and at different times, depending on circumstances—scarcity, difficulty of production, and so on. Silver taxed at the 10% rate (which in Zacatecas was established in 1548 and continued for some time) was produced by a recognized, licensed miner in his own smelting or refining plant with ores from his own mines. After the silver had been taken to the nearest *Caja Real* (Royal Treasury), it was melted (or perhaps only a small sample was melted to test for quality), assayed by a royal official, and imprinted with a stamp called *el diezmo;* the tax was collected and it was then known as *plata dezmada.* But since it had been taxed, and bore a stamp to prove it, the piece was also recognized as *plata quintada,* although it was taxed at the lower rate. The term evidently signified the tax had been paid, at whatever rate was approved. The silver could then be sold, traded, taken to the mint for coining, or to the silversmiths to be fabricated. This mark was identified as the Royal Arms and featured the Pillars of Hercules.

There was also a variation of the *diezmo* marking system, which Bakewell describes as a special stamp called *la marca del diezmo*. It was another way to register the bullion without paying the tax, and meant that the silver was legitimately produced by a regular miner but the tax was not yet paid. The stamp consisted of the name of the town where a special receiver *(receptor)* appointed by the Crown had his office and the necessary authority to register the bullion. Sometimes instructions also required that the name of the miner be stamped on the silver, but as usual with the numerous Spanish regulations, this was not always observed. This silver, untaxed but carrying the *marca del diezmo,* could then circulate freely but at a reduced value. The tax had to be paid eventually by anyone wanting to have the metal coined or worked by a silversmith.

Then there is the famous *quinto,* the standard tax (usually 20%) applied to all other silver, and of course to gold and jewels. In the case of silver it was mainly metal bought from the Indians or acquired from non-regular small operators who smelted in back yard furnaces. This tax stamp is uniformly described as bearing the royal arms (Beals 1966: 50; Oman 1968: 39, 48; Pradeau 1972), "a small punch bearing a design of a crown and the Columns of Hercules," according to Beals. From this it appears that whether the 10% or 20% tax was assessed, the royal arms indicated the tax was paid and the silver was *quintada.* The royal seal found on the silver bar described by McNickle consisted of the coat of arms that appears in the shield: lions, castles, and pomegranate. But McNickle notes that it is not to be confused with another royal seal featuring a small crown, with or without the Columns of Hercules, "used originally on all metal but later only on manufactured articles of gold and silver and on ingots, which, although registered and assayed, had not yet passed through the royal foundry and upon which the royal dues were still owing" (McNickle 1953).

Lawrence Anderson's book, *The Art of the Silversmith in Mexico 1519-1936,* Vol. I (1941), focuses on hallmarks discovered on silver objects, but much of the information is applicable to bullion as well. He reports (1941: 282-285) that the earliest information on hallmarks came from Proceedings of the Municipal Council of Mexico City, dated January 24, 1533. At that time one Pedro Despina was to be appointed *veedor* (inspector) and *alcalde* (chief) for the silver trade and assay-master of the city. The mark and die (that is, the punch) of the city was delivered to him. Then, it seems, either the die was changed or for some reason was taken from him, because on July 17, 1537 Antonio de Carbajal, an assemblyman, brought the "die of this city which the silversmiths are to stamp on the pieces they make" to the municipal council. On April 6, 1537 Luis Rodríguez, a silversmith (who may have been the Luis Rodríguez who was later assayer), was named *alcalde* for the silversmith's trade and marker for the city "of the silver fabricated here." The next one was Francisco Hernandez, who replaced Rodríguez in February or May, 1538. Gabriel de Vallasana (also spelled Grabriel de Billasana) seems to have held the offices from 1554 to 1557—at least no one else is listed for this period.

But in addition to the *alcalde*, there was at least one Chief Assayer, and probably several assistants. "It was the duty of the Chief Assayer," says Anderson (1941: 305), "to examine (to make certain that the Royal tax had been paid) all the precious metals which were brought for assay, whether to be made into ingots or plate or coined." At times he could also stamp the hallmarks, seals, and royal marks—which would indicate there must have been different kinds—and act as *Juez Veedor* (Judge Inspector) of the Noble Silversmiths' Art. For the period with which we are concerned, Anderson cites documents listing Francisco de los Cobos as holding this office in 1522, and Diego de los Cobos in 1552. But there probably were other assayers on hand as well. From 1524 to 1637 it appears that only one official mark was required on any kind of silver—the one that certified that the tax was paid and the metal used was of the required standard (Anderson 1941: 303). Since silver brought in for further processing was melted down for assaying, thus destroying the original tax paid mark, can we assume that after being cast into ingots for coining or other use the assayer stamped it again, using his individual mark, properly registered? The dies were kept in a locked chest, and the keys were distributed to three specified officials who were required to be present when the chest was unlocked.

The first mark stamped on gold and silver was described by Bernal Diaz (quoted by Anderson 1941: 286-287), as "bearing the royal arms like a *real* and of the size of a fifty cent piece or four [reales]" (brackets by Anderson). This was for use on bars of precious metals, and was stamped originally on Moctezuma's gold which was melted down.

As Anderson illustrates the mark from information furnished him by the Royal Library in Madrid, it bore the device of two columns, a band across two serpents' heads, and the lettering *PLUS OULTRE*, with water beneath, all inside a border with the letters *ESPANA NUEVA*. Silver plate, on the other hand, was hallmarked first with an *M*, later surmounted by a crown, signifying Mexico City. This mark appears, in the publications available, as a square with the design in the center. Anderson shows it on page 288 of the cited publication, and Oman (1968: 39, 48) illustrates a variation of the same mark as it appeared on a chalice (no. 104) and a monstrance (no. 137). In the latter two instances the Columns of Hercules are supporting a crown above a head, and at the base is the *M*. The chalice was dated in the last quarter of the sixteenth century, and the monstrance about 1602.

With this background in mind, it may be possible to interpret some of the marks found on the silver and illustrated in Figures 64 and 65. It is known that some sort of official mark was required on all bullion, but it is not clear whether there was just one acceptable design. It seems more likely that the Chief Assayer and his assistants had their own recognized symbols. Individual owners, says Anderson, were allowed to have dies cut for themselves, but usually they were more elaborate than the official assayers' marks, which were always simple. He illustrates various marks, but attributes them to a period later than we are considering. In addition, the various mines and provinces could have their own identifying stamps.

The design shown in number 4 (Fig. 64) must be an official mark, and may well be the standard tax-paid stamp, for it features variations of the royal arms—the Pillars of Hercules are most easily distinguished even when the mark is incomplete. The design is a small circle, not quite as large as a dime, which surrounds the pillars; between them, near the top, is a crowned profile head, and at the base:

$$\circ \, M \, \circ \quad \text{or} \quad \overset{\circ}{M}$$

This is the complete stamp with all of its elements. Sometimes the entire circle is discernible, but the details are flattened and blurred; frequently only parts are visible, but enough are sharp and easily recognized so the entire design can be pieced together from the parts. One variation has the letters PLVS across the pillars, as in some of the coins. This may be one of the emblems used by the *Casa de Contrata-*

ción in Seville, for a mark almost exactly like it appears, along with three other, different, stamps on the title page of a compendium on the art of navigation, published by the *Casa* in Spain, in 1588. The only difference between the mark illustrated in the compendium and the one we find is that, in the former, the pillars are crowned and there is no evidence of a profile head. Destombes reproduces the page (1969: 61) because this mark was stamped on the 1563 astrolabe that he identified as belonging to the *Casa*. The Pillars of Hercules stamp appears on the silver pieces more frequently than any of the others—20 times altogether.

The next most frequently seen stamp is shown in Figure 64, No. 1. It occurs seven times and might be identified as a scallop shell, which would suggest St. James, the patron saint of Spain, whose emblem was a scallop shell. This was one of the stamps that Destombes found on the Spanish astrolabe illustrated in his publication (1969: 64).

Another version of what may be the scallop shell is represented by No. 2 (Fig. 64), although it is a little more elaborate. It was found marked on the ingots six times and may be another St. James symbol.

The "X" in a square with a small circle on either side (Fig. 64, No. 5) occurs four times. This might be the mark that signifies the silver was produced at a registered mine by a registered miner, and therefore could be taxed at the 10% rate, *la marca del diezmo*. Admittedly, this is highly speculative, but it might be a fairly reasonable deduction as to its identification.

As for the circle or wheel (Fig. 64, No. 3), with small knobs on the ends of four straight strokes, faintly resembling an anachronistic pilot's wheel, there are no clues at all. It appears four times.

Small rectangles of various sizes with faint, indecipherable letters are found three times, and also a few faint circles, but we have not assigned a number to them since they give us no information at all.

The remaining devices appear only one time apiece. Taking them in numerical order (Fig. 64):

Number 6 is definitely TASCO, although in this instance the T has been almost obliterated. The first three letters of the identical mark were discovered on a silver disk in the collection recovered from another ship of the same fleet by the Texas Antiquities Committee, and the two marks together confirm the identification of the stamp. TAXCO is an alternative spelling, and the stamp represents the town, the mine, or the mining district of that name.

Number 7 is strongly suggestive of one of the royal assayers since it bears a crown over the letters LVIS [LUIS]. It is fairly certain that a crown could not be used unless the stamp pertained to official business, and the records show that a Luis Rodríguez held the office of *alcalde* and silver marker for the city (of Mexico) from 1537 to 1538, as has been related previously. It seems reasonable to infer that this might be his stamp.

Number 8, GUACHINANGO, spelled out in two lines, represents the mine of that name, established in 1543 (Bargallo' 1955: 64). Like the name TASCO, this one also has an alternative spelling, sometimes found as HUACHINANGO on the maps. According to the dictionaries, it was a nickname that the Cubans and Puerto Ricans called the Mexicans, and the Mexicans of Vera Cruz called the people in the interior. It means a crafty person, or one who is brusque or crude. On the disk where it appears, the mark has been overstamped by the familiar Pillars of Hercules.

Number 9 presents another instance of overstamping by the pillars. This is a long rectangle with two squarish protrusions in the upper center, but the original mark has been almost covered by the pillars stamp. An *A* appears in the upper left section and the remnant of another, unidentified letter in the right one. The letters *CA* can be made out just to the left of the overstamped circle. We could find no mine listed for New Spain whose name began with *CA*, and without the remainder of the letters it is impossible to tell what the word was. A Peruvian mine called CARABAYA was operating in 1545 (Haring 1964: 438), but there is no way to connect it with this piece of silver.

Number 10 is the most elaborate design discovered except for the pillars. It resembles a heraldic shield or banner, with attached XXs across the top and an intertwined, complicated device in the point at the base. If the design is turned sideways one might interpret one of the figures as the Greek Chi Rho, part of the symbol for Christ. This is another mystery, but because of its intricacy seems most likely to be an individual owner's stamp.

Many times in removing the encrustation around the silver pieces it was discovered that the impressions left in the matrix, although in reverse, were clearer and better detailed than those remaining on the object itself. Although it is quite possible that because of various circumstances not all the disks were encrusted when first recovered, one can only suspect that had all the protective coating debris been saved, as it was removed by Platoro, a great deal more information might have been salvaged during the processing. In several instances a more complete design and sharper letters would have added details that would help in identification.

Some suppositions can be made from the information available. Considering only the complete, unbroken pieces, for there is no way to tell what stamps might be missing on the others, we find that the Pillars of Hercules device appears as the only stamp on five disks, although it may be on there several times. It is found in combination with one or more other marks on four other pieces. The possible shell of St. James (Fig. 64, No. 1) is the single stamp on one large disk and on two small lumps of silver that have no particular shape but are apparently intact. The other possible scallop shell (Fig. 64, No. 2) is found alone on one large disk and in combination with unidentified figures on two other disks. The eight other stamps are always discovered in combination with one or another of these three: Nos. 1, 2, or 4 (Fig. 64). It seems certain that the Pillars of Hercules was an official stamp and probably signified that the king's 20% tax had been paid, or in other words, the silver was *quintada*. Since the other two marks stand alone on several pieces, it may be assumed that these were official marks too, and reinforces our attempts to identify them with the similar St. James stamp illustrated by Destombes. It is strongly suggested that these marks were used by the royal assayers. Undoubtedly all the devices we find were properly registered in several places, but aside from those already identified, guessed at, or described from other publications, the rest must remain enigmas for the present. It is hoped that their presentation here will be a start toward recognition as additional clues from other early shipwreck materials are recorded.

As a sort of historical detective game, and in no way approaching the scholarly work of McNickle (1953) in researching the 1652 silver bar and its history, we might be able to offer a hypothetical outline for the career of no. 1417 (Fig. 66), the large disk that bears four stamps. This is the one with the TASCO mark, so we can assume it came from that district where a mine was established in 1534 and bonanzas were discovered in 1542 and 1544 (Bargalló 1955: 64). Foscue (1947: 10) says it was "commonly considered that the first silver shipped from Mexico to Spain came from the Taxco district," so it had a long history. Having been struck with the TASCO stamp, the disk might have circulated for awhile as *plata dezmada*, registered by a licensed miner, but still untaxed. Then our licensed, registered miner, if our speculation about the X-in-the-square mark is right, paid his 10%

centimeters

Fig. 66.—Stamped marks on Silver Disk No. 1417.

tax, *el diezmo*, and the piece was duly stamped to prove it. Or perhaps it was delivered at the mine to one of the capitalists who, as Hamilton (1929a: 443) says, financed small mining operations through advances of subsistence and equipment for mining. Only the wealthier miners carried their own metals to the assay offices for it was an expensive procedure to transport and protect it. Eventually it turned up at the mint headquarters in Mexico City where LVIS, the Royal Assayer, determined its silver content and applied his mark with the crown above his name. It may at last have been ready for the Pillars of Hercules stamp, certifying it had been officially registered and taxed.

The gold ingot, the silver coins and disks, and the miscellaneous pieces must represent only a small portion of the treasure cargo that was on its way to Spain. All versions of the 1553 or 1554 wreck story relate that most of the treasure was salvaged by the Spaniards within a year after the disaster. If, indeed, we are dealing with a ship from this fleet, as seems likely, the greater part of the cargo is not present in the collection, although the liklihood is that it is a fair sampling. Hamilton (1929a: 468) gives the proportions of silver and gold shipped to Spain between 1551 to 1560 as

87.672% silver, by weight, and 12.328% gold. According to these figures, then, there should have been more gold in the collection, but perhaps it was easier for the Spanish salvage crew to recover the gold than the silver. In spite of strict rules on unregistered treasure, Hamilton (1929a: 448) found that soldiers and sailors were always permitted to bring in small amounts without penalty, as were passengers who could carry enough for traveling expenses for themselves and their families. This amount was fixed later by an ordinance of May, 1646. Soldiers and sailors could carry a sum not in excess of their salaries; travelers could carry no more than the sums they registered. Some of the unmarked silver pieces may be from these "traveling accounts." The chances are that a good many items of personal jewelry also were either returned to New Spain or still lie on the bottom of the Gulf.

SHIPBOARD LIVING

Food

It would be surprising to find much evidence of foodstuffs preserved after all this time, although the ship would have been carrying all sorts of perishable rations for the long voyage—beans and peas, oil, vinegar, rice, flour, biscuits, olives, cheese, onions, garlic, wine, salted meat, and fish, among other provisions. No doubt officers and affluent passengers could make arrangements for special delicacies that would not be available to the crew. It is possible that this ship was carrying fresh meat on the hoof, because a bone fragment from a juvenile pig, no. 1596 *(Sus scrofa,* right calcaneum) and another fragment identified as probably cow, no. 1492-11 (left proximal end of an ulna or radius) were discovered in the collection. On the other hand, the meat may also have been butchered and salted. Five additional pieces of bone were found, but several of them were heavily mineralized and none could be identified as to species.

It is known that olives were among the stores, from the impression of an olive pit in an encrustation (no. 609). Scientific proof for this identification was demonstrated by the conservator, who compared a contemporary olive pit with the 400 year-old impression. Olives were a staple of the Spanish diet and could be kept safely in oil or brine for a long time.

The only other evidence of food has not been identified but it looked like a wrinkled seed, something like a dried watermelon seed (no. 501-3).

Containers

Shipping containers were represented by 790 earthenware potsherds from an unknown number of vessels. There were no whole pots and the fragments were small and badly eroded, some not much larger than crumbs. The largest single piece measured only 10.5 by 7.3 cm. A few rim sherds that could be fitted together indicate the shape and size of several jar mouths and suggest the contours, in two instances, of the neck and shoulders. Not enough remained of any vessel to give a hint as to the capacity.

The great majority of the sherds appeared to be fragments of what are usually called Spanish Olive Jars, a term first used by Goggin, who published the most thorough study of these useful vessels (Goggin 1964). He traced their ancestry to the ancient Mediterranean "amphora" type of container. There was some evidence that the glazed types may have been used for wine, while the unglazed ones could have been serviceable for heavier liquids such as olive oil and olives in brine. There was also some indication that condiments and dried or prepared vegetables, such as beans and chick peas, may have been carried in them as well. Sherds of these jars are characteristic of Spanish colonial sites in the Americas dating from about A.D. 1500 until after 1800, and they frequently appear in Indian and English sites of the period too. In fact, because they seem to have been universally useful for so many purposes, modern commentators have called them the five-gallon can of colonial times.

Using style as the basis, Goggin separated the vessels chronologically into Early, Middle, and Late Style Olive Jars. From archeological evidence he placed his Early Style in the first three quarters of the sixteenth century and described it as a "medium-sized globular vessel with a small, flaring, or collared mouth, having a loop handle on each side" (Gog-

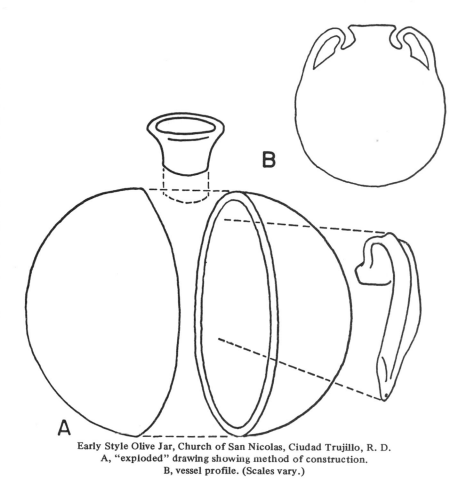

Early Style Olive Jar, Church of San Nicolas, Ciudad Trujillo, R. D.
A, "exploded" drawing showing method of construction.
B, vessel profile. (Scales vary.)

Fig. 67.—Reproduced by permission from Goggin's "The Spanish Olive Jar" (1964: 259).

137

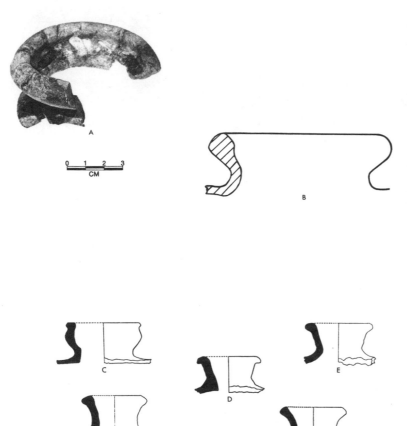

Mouth Details, Early Style Olive Jars. A, La Vego Vieja, R.D. B, C, Nueva Cadiz (Tr. 6, 10-12 m., 0-15 cm.), Ven. D, Panama Vieja, Panama E, Nueva Cadiz (Tr. 6, 2-4 m., 0-15 cm.), Ven (1/3 size.)

Fig. 68.—Upper, Early Style Spanish Olive Jar Rim fragment: (A) Partial reconstruction from three sherds. (B) Outline of rim shape. Lower, mouth details as illustrated by Goggin (1964: 261), used by permission.

gin 1964: 258). Each half of the vessel was thrown on the potter's wheel and the two pieces were joined by slip after drying. The collared mouth was applied to a cut made in the mid-line where the halves fit together. The bottom appeared to be rounded. A white slip was usually applied to the exterior, and when glaze was used it was typically applied to the exterior and sometimes splashed around the mouth. This glaze ranged in color from an emerald to an olive green, and on to a light brown. The exact place of manufacture was not located, but Goggin thought it was probably Spain. The only vessel of this Early type that he was able to measure stood about 25.5 cm. high and had a capacity of 5.4 liters (Goggin 1964: 259). Figure 67 is reprinted from Goggin and illustrates how the jar was constructed.

From what we can make out of the fragments at hand, the sherds for the most part meet Goggin's criteria for the Early Style vessels as to surface and interior color, composition of the paste, thickness of the body fragments, and shape of the mouth. The color varies on the surface from yellowish tan to pink, but the interior paste is usually a light to dark gray. Throwing rings are evident. The sandy paste is fairly compact, and the surfaces, when not too badly eroded, are smooth. Traces of white slip and eroded lead glaze appear on a number of sherds; where any color remains the glaze is brown. But no handle fragments have been found and no basal sherds are recognized. Thickness of what appear to be body sherds ranges from 3 mm. to 14 mm., with most of those that we measured falling between 6 and 9 mm., a range that agrees with Goggin's overall range of 4 to 11 mm. (from 12 vessels), with the majority falling between 5 mm. and 9 mm. (Goggin 1964: 260).

The largest reconstructed mouth fragment from the collection (nos. 320-9c, 320-4a & b, and 365) is illustrated in Figure 68. It stands 23 mm. high and falls within the range of those that Goggin examined, although he found that most of them appeared to fall between 34 and 38 mm. in height. While it is not exactly like any that he illustrated, it is very similar and does not at all resemble those of the later periods.

Goggin says also (1964) that other types of vessels were made on olive jar paste, and one of them may be represented by rim sherd no. 610-3. It has an everted, flaring lip, but it was not thickened as were the others. The surfaces are pinkish orange with a gray-brown sandy paste interior containing a few tiny air holes. Hardness, like that of most of the sherds, is about 2.0 on the Moh's scale (Fig. 69).

Several rim sherds from a distinctly different kind of vessel were recognized and assembled (nos. 610-1 and 229-1) to form a portion of a vessel mouth (Fig. 70). In this instance the paste is dark, terra-cotta red, unlike the others, of compact texture with some small inclusions of coarse sand. Traces of a brown lead glaze remain on both interior and exterior surfaces. The rim makes a straight collar 3.8 cm. high, with a thickness of 8 to 16 mm. and the lip edge is flat. Its curvature suggests that this was a wide-mouthed vessel, perhaps about 15.3 cm. in diameter. Another sherd (not shown) may possibly be a lug from this container, for the thickened area on the left of the photograph suggests the base of some kind of lug whose shape has not been determined.

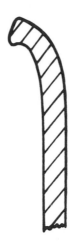

Fig. 69.—Sketch of rim sherd with everted, flaring mouth. This fragment may represent a different kind of vessel than the olive jar although it is made of the same paste.

Utensils for Cooking and Eating

Cooking arrangements on board ship were primitive in the 1500s, consisting of a firebox set into several inches of sand or earth. Morison (1971: 130) explains that on the smaller ships a hooded box was placed athwartship at the forward end of the spar deck where it would be protected to some extent by the forecastle. It was attended by the steward, or the cook if the ship carried one, probably assisted by the ship's boys. The steward was responsible for looking after the provisions as well as the lamps, sand-glasses, and other such necessities. Food for the crew was probably served in wooden bowls, and if they had plates at all they were of wood too. But the ship's officers and at least some of the passengers would have been served with a certain degree of elegance. They were called to meals by a ship's boy who had memorized a regulation formula.

Only a few objects in this collection fit into the category for cooking and eating: two pewter plates, small fragments of what appear to be a third plate, and an encrusted serving spoon bowl. Pewter plates like these seem to have been used

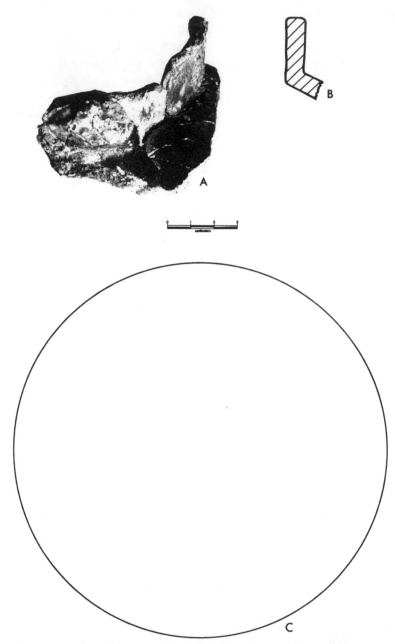

Fig. 70.—(A) Partially reconstructed rim fragment with part of shoulder from vessel made of hard paste, dark red earthenware. It had a straight, collared mouth, and probably a lug handle as suggested by the thickened area on the left. (B) Outline of rim shape, with exterior to the right as in the photograph. (C) Curvature of rim fragment indicates a jar with a very wide mouth, 15.3 cm. in diameter. Reconstruction was made from fragments no. 229-1 and no. 610-1.

on shipboard for several hundred years, for they are illustrated frequently in published accounts of salvaged shipwreck materials covering a very long period of time. Perhaps they were used by the ship's officers or some of the passengers. They are almost the same size and closely resemble modern soup plates with their shallow bowls and wide, flat rims. Figure 71 shows the top of no. 1619 and the bottom of no. 1618 with an enlarged drawing of the pewterer's touchmark found on the back rim of both. The plates are 22.7 cm. wide across the top, with a rim width of 3.0 cm. and a depth of 2.2 cm. The surfaces are badly pitted and eroded from long immersion, and in some places the bottom of the bowls has been warped upward. The most significant information to be gained from the plates is the pewterer's mark, a crowned Tudor Rose, a mark of the English pewterers' guild. The initial *R* appears on the left side of the rose and a *V* on the right. The rose was traditionally rendered as a flat, five-petaled flower beneath a high-standing crown, and the let-

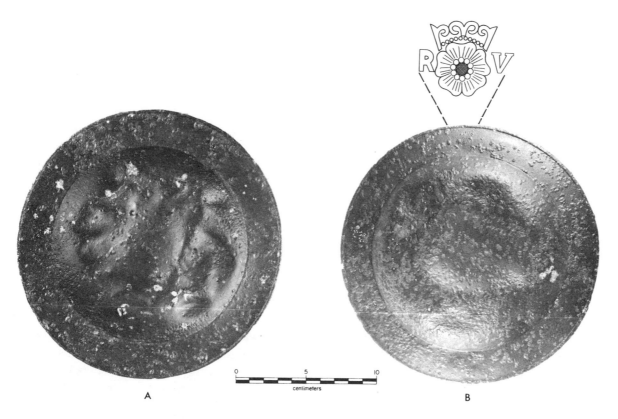

Fig. 71.—*Two pewter plates. (A) The upper side of no. 1619. (B) Bottom of no. 1618, with drawing depicting the pewterer's touchmark that appears on the back of the rim on both plates. It represents the crowned Tudor Rose, and the initials RV are those of the pewterer. Placement of the initials on either side of the rose indicates English manufacture.*

ters were within small, wing-like triangular spaces.

Old Pewter: Its Makers and Marks (Cotterell 1963) describes and traces the history of English pewterers' marks. From this source came the information that each pewterer had his own distinctive mark or "touch," which was duly stamped on a large pewter plate or plaque upon his acceptance into the Worshipful Company of Pewterers. This was kept in the guildhall and carefully preserved. In addition to this touchmark, the mark of the Tudor Rose was applied to their objects, perhaps as a mark of quality, because the pewterers of the time were meticulous in supervising the work of guild members and in assuring the quality of the metal. In early times, though, it appears that the Tudor Rose with initials could be used by itself by a pewterer. According to Cotterell (1963: 47), the Tudor Rose denoted various things before 1564; the "Mark" for goods exported, the "Mark of the Hall," and a maker's "Proper Touch." Evidently the addition of the maker's initials could mean that this was his "Proper Touch," and this is what the initials probably represent on these two plates. In 1564 it was forbidden to use the mark in this way except by special permission, which was rarely granted. Whoever was represented by the initials *RV* could have been identified at one time, but the great fire of London in 1666 destroyed the Pewterers' Hall and along with it, no doubt, all records, for neither the master plate with all the marks stamped on it nor the book in which every man's mark was registered has ever been found. As soon as possible after the fire all the living pewterers restamped their marks on a new plate, but the old one with the earliest stamps probably was melted and gone forever. The earliest master plate now surviving shows marks from 1635 to 1680—long after the period in which we are interested. Among the marks to be seen, however, Cotterell (1963: 326-327) lists a Richard Vallet (or Vallatt), his number 4862, who came from Cork and was first mentioned in 1637, and a Walter Vaughan of London (Mark No. 4871), who in 1591 was fined by the guild for absence without leave; and there also was a Richard Vernon of London, 1650, (Mark No. 4870). By wishful conjecture we might speculate that the *RV* of the pewter plates in this collection could have been an ancestor or distant relative of the pewterers with surnames beginning with *V* who were later recorded.

As for the plates being carried on a Spanish ship, it would have been quite in order, since English pewter was recognized for its quality and was widely exported in those times.

The remaining utensil is a large spoon bowl (no. 494), the

right size for a serving piece or tablespoon. It is shown in Figure 72 as it appears now, fully encrusted, and in an X-ray photograph. The metal, probably pewter or silver, is completely corroded but the shape of the bowl can be seen easily in the X-ray.

A

Fig. 72.—(A) Encrusted serving spoon bowl, possibly of silver or pewter. (B) X-ray of photo of spoon bowl showing outline of the piece although the metal has disintegrated.

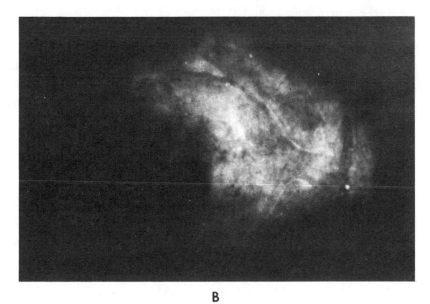

B

0   1   2   3
centimeters

Fig. 73.—*Two small, hollow cylinders (left, no. 1500, right, no. 1444-1), made of brass, identified as candle prickets. These were sharp devices that penetrated the bottoms of large, thick candles to keep them in place in their candlesticks.*

Candle Spikes

Religious services were as much a part of shipboard life as was eating. The captain or master led morning and evening prayers if no clergymen were on hand, and, as Morison relates (1974: 165), the youngest boys aboard, "the *pajes de escobar* (pages of the broom)," performed special observances every time the half-hour glass was turned.

Two small brass objects have been identified as altar candle spikes or "prickets" (nos. 1444-1 and 1500), shown in Figure 73. They probably could have been used in other places than the altar but they would have been an appropriate size for securing very large, heavy candles in their holders. For that reason they could be classed here, somewhat arbitrarily, as religious paraphernalia. Both are cylindrical and hollow, tapering from the head to what would have been a pointed tip, although in both cases the shanks are broken off above the end. They were not encrusted when we received them and were in fairly good condition in spite of some corrosion.

Pricket No. 1444-1 is 8.6 cm. long, 1.4 cm. wide at the top opening, and 0.4 cm. wide at the broken end. About 0.4 cm. below the top a thin, narrow, flat collar, 3 mm. to 5 mm. wide, surrounds the cylinder. A second collar, only about 1 mm. wide, is placed about 1.0 cm. below the first, then the rest of the shank is smooth.

The other pricket is 7.8 cm. long, about 0.9 cm. wide at the top opening, and 0.55 cm. at the broken end. The collar just below the top is uneven and damaged, but at its greatest width it measures 1.7 cm. Below the collar the cylinder bulges outward a little for a short space, the bulging area being set off above and below by small, very narrow ridges. Except for a patch of corrosion that has damaged the shank from about the middle to the broken end, the remainder of the piece is smooth.

Personal Possessions

Pitifully few personal effects of passengers or crew from the ill-fated ship were recovered, but among them is one of the most beautiful and fascinating objects in the entire collection—a tiny gold crucifix (no. 1436), shown in Figure 74. That it was not created by the Indians of Mexico but rather by a skilled European artisan is evident.

The cross itself is only 2.7 cm. long and 1.74 cm. wide at the arms. On it is the small figure of Christ, 1.6 cm. in length; the head droops to the right, and nails pierce the

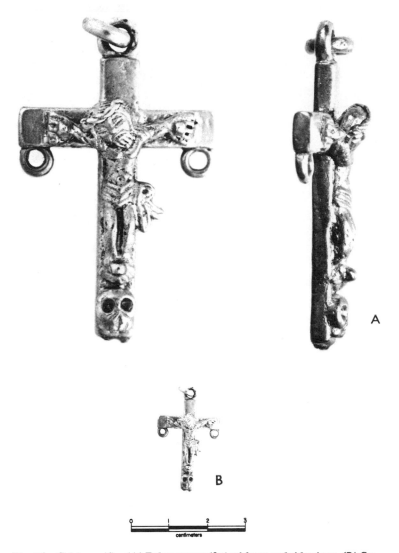

Fig. 74.—Gold crucifix. (A) Enlargement (2x) of front and side views. (B) Crucifix shown actual size. The piece was probably made in Spain, the separately applied figure cast by the lost wax process. Crown of gold wire, nails in hands and feet were added after casting. Death's head at the foot was probably attached separately too. The stub of a third ring remains at the base of the cross. Pearls or other jewels, or perhaps small crosses, would have hung from the rings.

hands and feet. At the foot of the figure is a skull that probably signifies Christ's triumph over death. Atop the cross is a hanging ring, with a smaller ring suspended below each arm; remnants of a third ring can be seen at the base. Undoubtedly jewels, or perhaps miniature crosses, once hung from them. Other than the broken ring, the crucifix is in excellent condition, almost undamaged by its long sojourn under the sea. What may be the *burilada*—the small mark made by the assayer's bite in taking his sample—shows up as a scraggly line on the back of the cross, but can be seen only under a microscope.

Austin goldsmith Phil Shaw, who has made a study of jewelry of the period, both Mexican-Indian and European, examined the exquisite piece and kindly gave us the benefit of his expertise (Shaw 1970; personal communication). He says that the style is baroque and that the basic cross and the figure were cast in separate molds by the lost wax process. The figure and the rings then were soldered onto the basic cross. This complicated technique was made obvious by the undercutting that is particularly evident in the corner under the right armpit and below the droop of the sash. The crown is a spiral twist of drawn gold wire, also separately applied, and probably the skull was separately added too. The entire piece manifests a high technical skill of a style that indicates non-Indian manufacture. There may have been other figures cast from the same mold, for it probably was not a one-time casting. Shaw guesses that the gold is about 16 carats, alloyed with copper, and he notes that the gold of the upper ring appears to be different from the rest. The crucifix weighs only 5.2 grams.

Also among personal possessions is a badly deteriorated silver thimble, of a dainty size suitable for a woman's finger. Figure 75A illustrates the piece (no. 74-1) and a drawing of the pattern found on it. The thin, fragile walls were almost crushed together in the encrustation that formed around it and were in such poor condition that no attempt was made to restore the thimble to its original shape. Instead, the interior was filled with microcrystalline wax, and the walls were strengthened to preserve the decorative designs that could be made out in the outer layer of silver sulfide. It is about 2.1 cm. long, with a basal diameter of about 4.0 cm. Filling a circle at the top is a flat flower with six round petals and just below that is an area punctated for pushing the needle head. Next, two concentric lines encircle the piece; between the lines are evenly spaced horizontal dashes. Below in a wider band, diagonal sections with punctations alternate with sets of three parallel diagonal lines. Around the base is a chevron design formed by short lines and bordered above and below by horizontal concentric circles. Altogether, it was a rather intricately decorated example of a very useful device for hand sewing.

A third item (no. 195a) looks like part of a clothing fastener or clasp, possibly a piece of the "eye" section of a hook-and-eye assemblage, but the actual eye is broken

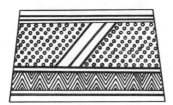

A

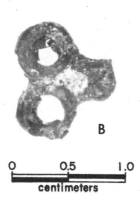

B

Fig. 75.—Small silver thimble for a woman's finger (no. 74-1), somewhat flattened and in fragile condition. Left, the thimble as it actually appears. Center, line drawing showing details of the pattern as though the thimble were laid out flat. Right, decoration at the top. (B) Probably part of a hook-and-eye clasp, fragment of the "eye" section. Shown here greatly enlarged as it is only 9 mm. long and 11 mm. wide. Material is not identified but may be lead or pewter.

off and only the part to be fastened down to the cloth remains. Metal composition is uncertain; it is definitely not iron or steel since it does not react to a magnet. It may be lead or pewter. If so, it would not be sturdy enough to withstand much weight or pull, but might be part of an ornamental trim. The incomplete length is 9 mm., and its maximum width is 11 mm. It is illustrated in Figure 75B.

The fourth and last in this short list may be a button fragment (no. 501-3). It is very small, extremely thin and fragile, but traces of a design can be detected on the surface. The pattern appears to be something like a shamrock or four-leaf clover—or would be if the circle were complete, but only about three-fourths of it remains. Two small holes pierce it near the center, although they may be the result of corrosion rather than intentionally made for sewing it to cloth. If it is not a button it may be a small ornamental device. The metal is probably copper or brass, but it is so dark and discolored that this cannot be identified with any certainty. It is not illustrated. A design that appears to be somewhat similar is illustrated by Di Peso (1953: 206) on a small button of lead that he dates to the Spanish occupation of

147

the Upper San Pedro River Valley in Southeastern Arizona during the seventeenth and eighteenth centuries (Di Peso 1953: 201). In this instance the flat, four-leaved figure is in the center of the button with a different pattern around it.

Other Materials

This is a catchall category including all items not fitting one of the previously described categories. It includes cloth, rope and other fibrous materials, small concretions, wood fragments, and samples of other organic matter.

It seems almost miraculous that even five tiny, fragile scraps of cloth survived, but they were all found in protective encrustations. All were loosely woven in a simple over-and-under technique. Under the microscope the individual strands appear to be made up of S-twisted fibers. The fabric seems rather thin and light for canvas or sailcloth and may be remnants of clothing. Four of the fragments came from a small conglomerate (no. 578) containing oxidized nails and metal straps, five potsherds, and several small bits of shredded, matted hemp fibers that may have been oakum. The largest piece of woven material measured 2.2 x 1.2 cm. (Fig. 76A), and the smallest only 0.9 x 0.5 cm. The fifth cloth scrap is of the same construction as those described, but was found embedded in another small piece of debris, no. 608. What is visible, about 1 cm. square, has been left partially encrusted.

An example of the rope used as lashing for the guns is shown in Figure 76B. These pieces (no. 345-2) were removed during the cleaning of *Bombardeta* No. 1477-1 but were given à different catalogue number. Aside from other rope fragments found with the guns, and the fibrous materials already mentioned that were associated with breechblocks, cannon balls, and beneath heads of spikes and pins, a few fibrous fragments were encrusted by themselves in cleaning debris. Among these were the thickest examples of rope and the smallest samples of cordage. The heaviest (no. 476) were five fragments of what had been a single rope section, made in standard rope construction—that is, three S-twisted strands of Z-twist yarns laid together to make a three-ply Z-twisted piece about 2.8 cm. thick. The alternate Z-S-Z twists serve to strengthen the rope. Each of the three component strands was about 1.2 cm. in diameter. Thin cordage, S-twisted, lay in three parallel sections within an encrustation, and what is left of the fiber is in very good condition (no. 578). The fragments were given preservative treatment and left partial-

Fig. 76.—Miscellaneous materials:

(A) *Enlargement of tiny cloth fragment measuring about 2.2 x 1.2 cm., from small conglomerate no. 578.*

(B) *Set of rope fragments, no. 345-2, that had probably been used to lash Bombardeta No. 1477-1 to its wooden carriage. These and a few other rope pieces were discovered as the encrustation was removed from the gun during cleaning.*

(C) *Impression of X-mark left in the encrustation that came off one of the large versos, either no. 328 or no. 329. Catalog number of the specimen is 527.*

(D) *Piece of wooden planking perforated by the hole made by a large pin or spike, no. 1583.*

ly encrusted. The longest segment is about 2.7 cm., and the pieces are uniformly 2 mm. wide. A slightly larger scrap of cordage (no. 511) is 3.5 cm. long and 1.5 cm. wide.

The remainder of the fibrous materials appear to be just scraps of shredded hemp, probably oakum. Some of the fragments have been freed from the encrusted matrix but others have been left, after treatment, as they were found.

The largest group of miscellaneous objects is composed of 45 concretions, left "as is," that have been saved either for display or for making reproductions. Many of them contain molds that could be cleaned out and the hollows used in casting. Over 200 such conglomerates were discarded after X-rays showed they contained nothing of interest. With the exception of a natural concretion, all the rest contain singly or in various combinations: oxidized metal or molds of ring fragments, cannon balls, spikes, straps, or unidentified objects, potsherds, lead scrap, wood fragments, and ballast stones. The most interesting among them are: 1) the impression of an olive pit briefly noted under "Food;" 2) the impression of a wooden mid-section of a crossbow stock from the area of the trigger mechanism and nut; 3) the inside edge of what looks like a box, including two pieces of wood and a nail penetrating a piece of lead sheeting; 4) two marks left in pieces of concretion. One is an X that matches the X-marks to be seen in the upper section of the breech troughs of the large *versos* (nos. 328 and 329, shown in Fig. 76C), and the other is simply a diagonal line that probably represents half an X and must have been removed from one of the same guns.

There are also the following: 39 wood fragments that include three twigs possibly used for stuffing between the hull planks; a section of planking with a hole through it that was left by the head of a large pin (no. 1583, Fig. 76D); one fragment that may be part of a deck plank, about 21.5 cm. long, 5.5 cm. wide, and 3.5 cm. thick; three smooth, probably worked, fragments, and numerous small scraps. Many pieces have been riddled with worm holes and are very fragile.

Twelve marine shells and shell fragments have been retained. Those identified are mussel, scallop, clam, and possibly oyster. A fragment from the edge of a turtle shell and a few pieces of coral complete the list of miscellaneous materials.

SUMMARY

Grave misfortune overtook the Spanish voyagers long ago, but the disaster that befell them has left a priceless legacy of the objects that made up their seagoing environment. Travelers, vessel, and cargo constituted an active, functioning community until the ship had to be abandoned just offshore. Passengers and crew made their way to what they hoped would be the safety of the island, and as the ship broke up, pieces of its hull, spars, equipment, armament, and cargo were strewn over the ocean floor. Since then, well over four centuries have passed; winds, currents, and tides have shifted the wreckage, burying most of it—especially the heavier pieces—on the sand and clay bottom, scattering the smaller articles near and far, even depositing some on the Padre Island beach. And through the long years teredo worms feasted on the wood and electrochemical corrosion of metal objects in the sea water created its own selective damage.

Still, many of the overall associations of cultural material were preserved on the sea bed. Through careful archeological excavations various aspects of the shattered community can be put together to suggest what the ship must have been like when it was intact; often, however, too much time had gone by and too much damage had been done to provide the complete picture. Added to the initial breakage and displacement that took place at the time the vessel sank, and the deterioration in a harsh environment through the succeeding centuries, were the unfortunately destructive techniques of excavation carried out by Platoro, Inc., whose emphasis was directed toward the salvage of treasure rather than the recovery of archeological and historical knowledge. They probably did not document the location and associations of objects as they were found *in situ,* or with one another as they were processed later, for this information has not been available to our laboratory. Large, amorphous, concreted masses of encrustation may contain a number of different kinds of things, often unseen or unrecognized from the surface; necessarily, a large part of the actual excavation and identification of the findings must take place in the laboratory as the artifacts are extracted. Platoro's inadequate or careless conservation methods may have destroyed a number of relationships between objects that could have been significant for their interpretation. An example is the encrusted portion of the goat's foot lever, discovered among Platoro's cleaning debris, that had been fastened onto the shaft of a crossbow when the weapon went into the water.

Charged by the court with the responsibility of recording, preserving, and studying the collection, the Texas Archeological Research Laboratory of the University of Texas at Austin has established a conservation facility that is now recognized as among the best in the world. Research developed in carrying out the court's mandate has brought TARL widespread renown for modern and effective techniques of treating the materials found in the collection, especially for its work with iron. The actual cost of processing the collection was borne by the Texas Antiquities Committee, which at this time has jurisdiction over the artifacts. Six years of research by members of the TARL staff have gone into the identification and interpretation of the objects and in putting together associations that might enhance the significance of the individual items. Yet there is no way of knowing how much irretrievable information was lost or discarded through ignorance or unthinking handling before the collection reached us.

Undoubtedly, there are many articles of interest and importance still lying at the bottom of the sea on the site of the shipwreck or in its general area. Among them would probably be very large items difficult to bring up—anchors, and quite likely additional guns, perhaps even some of cannon size. There must be weapons for the breechblocks at hand that do not fit any of the three *bombardetas* or five *versos* herein described, and for the large cannon balls. There may be other large concretions containing additional navigational devices, tools, ceramics, and artifacts of many different types. Many smaller artifacts may have been dispersed toward the beach by the violent excavation techniques employed by Platoro. Nevertheless, the large and assorted collection we have been privileged to study has presented a fascinating challenge and we believe it is entitled to a special place in the interest and imagination of scientists and romanticists alike.

A mid-sixteenth century dating of these antiquities is certain, bracketed securely between the year 1550 and close to 1570. This is proven by the 1550 date on two of the astrolabes and the year 1570 when Luis Rodríguez, the prolific coin assayer whose initial was *L,* is known to have died. The remainder of the artifact categories all can be placed comfortably within that time span, although some had a history beginning much earlier and some were in use well into the eighteenth century and even later. The lead sounding weights are examples of devices still used that have been around since the days of the seafaring Phoenicians and Greeks.

Little is known about ship construction in the sixteenth century because shipwrights kept their knowledge and skills in their heads, passing them on only from father to son, or to workers in the same company. So, the survival of only a few key examples of gear and rigging parts may provide valuable clues for naval architects and historians. Although contemporary paintings and woodcuts are illustrative of the general appearance of the ships they are not necessarily factual about the details, for artistic license tends to distort the image, making a truly accurate rendition unlikely. Representations showing details of the stern are especially hard to find, and for that reason the preservation of a complete rudder gudgeon from the ship is unusually important. From the conformation it can be assumed that the gudgeon was fastened to a flat section of the stern, probably near the top, and may even indicate a flat stern. The fragmentary rudder pintle, unfortunately, was too incomplete to give much information aside from its identification. Various sizes and styles of chains used for the standing and running rigging, the copper sleeve bearing, and the assorted planking nails and spikes were probably standard equipment for their time; their counterparts doubtless could be found on almost every wooden ship for hundreds of years. The long iron through-pins that penetrated the hull indicate that the sides, including bracing members, were about two feet thick. It appears certain that the bottom of the hull or the keel was covered with lead sheathing, fastened through fabric (possibly old sailcloth) by large-headed square shanked iron tacks that have disintegrated through electrolytic action between the lead and the iron.

Tools and other equipment for wooden ships are not good dating indicators since they did not change much over the centuries. For example, the lead sounding weights and small fishing weights are as common today as they were in 1550 and could go right to work again tomorrow if they were needed. But some tools in the collection are enigmatic, such as the wrought iron L-shaped implements with sharp curved heads; they might have been used for digging out old caulking. It is our hope that someone may some day recognize and identify them.

The three navigational astrolabes in the collection must take the place of honor for scientific and historical value. They hold the distinction of being the three oldest dated sea-astrolabes in the world at this writing. Two special points of interest might be brought out. One is the difference in size and weight between the large, thick instrument dated 1545 and the other two dated 1550. The second difference is between the styles of peepholes on the two alidades that survived. The 1545 alidade has large holes, both the same size, while that for the later astrolabe has extremely small holes, one even smaller than its partner. Was the difference in overall size and weight between the larger, older instrument and the two others just an evolution toward a more easily managed device on shipboard? Did the very large sight-holes on the former reflect a dual function whereby it could be the more easily used for both stellar and solar observations? Whatever these differences may mean, the three ancient instruments are extremely significant representatives in the development of navigational instruments and will be recognized as such and acclaimed by scholars all over the world.

Armament carried on the ship, although not exceptional in the same degree as the astrolabes, is notable in its own right because the excellent condition of the guns makes apparent that they were put on board for defense and not as old rusty pieces brought along as part of the ballast. The three short-barreled *versos,* fully loaded and ready to fire, prove the case without a doubt, at least as far as they were concerned, and loaded breech chambers the right size for the two large *versos* were present, although not actually in place in the guns. At least four of the hooped-barrel style breechblocks also were loaded. The two long-barreled *versos* are so nearly identical in construction, size, and decorative markings that they must have been made by the same gunsmith. Two of the others also are nearly twins; again, both probably made by the same person, but since they lack any decorative markings there is no reason to think they were constructed by the gunsmith who made the larger pieces. Remnants of the rope lashing around two of the *bombardetas* reveal how at least those pieces were secured in their wooden beds or carriages, long since gone. X-rays illustrated in detail two types of construction for the *bombardetas.* The first type was made in the usual way with forged strakes arranged lengthwise to make the inside tube; next, wide bands of iron were welded around it, one next to the other, to form an outer tube; then additional, thick rings were shrunk over the seams where the inner bands joined one another, serving to reinforce the entire piece. The other type of construction seems to have been unusual for its day, for the entire inner tube was made of a single sheet lap-welded in a seam along its length; the outer bands were then forged on, as in the other style, for the outer tube, and then the thick outside rings reinforced the seams where they joined.

Many large and beautifully ornamented military and hunting crossbows can be seen in museums and illustrated in armament catalogues, but seldom have small, plain, utilitarian crossbows designed for the ordinary hunter been identified. Three, possibly four, such everyday weapons, or parts of them, in this collection have given us an opportunity to understand how they were made. X-rays show the manner in which the rather complicated trigger mechanism was put together on two of the stocks. Both stock fragments had a wooden nut, contrary to the commonly found description that calls for a nut of horn or ivory at this period. The reconstruction of a complete goat's foot lever, by making a cast from its mold, was a happy bonus. These artifacts give us incontrovertible evidence that the ship's defenders were armed with small, light, crossbows ordinarily used for hunting birds, rabbits, and the like.

The treasure cargo that never reached its destination brought to light a fascinating sample of the coins and the forms in which the bullion was shipped. The bulk of it was silver, with some gold, as was common in the cargoes sent back to Spain from Vera Cruz at this period. In this collection, the percentage of gold to silver was skewed, as only one gold ingot was present among the large quantity of silver. The stories of both 1553 and 1554 wreck versions say that most of the treasure was recovered by the Spanish salvage crew from New Spain within a year, so we can assume this is only a small part of the original shipment and speculate that they retrieved most of the gold.

Among the 900-odd silver Carlos and Johanna coins, dating from 1536 to not later than 1570 are a number of rare and unusual examples that would put sparkles in the eyes of numismatists. These include coins from Nesmith's Early Period (1536-1545), some bearing the assayer's initial *R* (for Rincón), the first to hold this office at the Mexico City mint. One of these is a three-reales piece, only a few of which are known to exist. Other Early Series coins were assayed by *G* and *P*. Then there were a number of infrequently seen Late Series (1545-1572) *G, A, R,* and *S* specimens along with the well known and common *L* coins. Unusually interesting and of great rarity too is a four-reales Santo Domingo Carlos and Johanna coin that was struck during the brief 10-year period during which that strange mint turned out its peculiar silver coinage. Very little monetary but great historical value attaches to the few copper four-maravedíes coins from Mexico City. They probably were not considered "treasure" by the Spaniards (and certainly not by the Indians), but they are very rare now. One is in especially good condition, a most fortuitous occurrence because copper is dangerously vulnerable to undersea corrosion. The preponderance of silver coins assayed by *L* (Luis Rodríguez), most of which show little or no sign of wear, indicate rather strongly that they were part of a consignment shipped out not long after they were minted. Luis's death was announced in May, 1570 and assayer *O* followed him in office. Whoever *O* was, he became the first assayer for the new Philip II coin design, presumably initially struck in 1572. For at least one period, and possibly others, *O* and *L* overlapped in holding the assayer's office before *L*'s death. Since there were no *O* coins in the collection, their absence supports our inference that the large hoard of *L* coins was probably struck well before 1570, before *O* was in the picture at all. If time and funds permitted it might be possible to segregate *L* coins struck from specific die lots. This would be of great interest and value to coin enthusiasts and historians, but it would be a tremendous undertaking with so many coins to study in the necessary detail. Once the shipwreck is documented with a precise date we can provide a definite early year when Luis must have been at work, and very likely the recent research conducted in the Spanish Archives will establish it. Then we shall have something more to say about *L*'s term as assayer other than to substantiate the great quantity of coins for which he was responsible.

Photographs of treasure recovered from the famous Silver Fleets of the eighteenth century show the silver bullion cast into regulation-size bars and wedge shapes, but the ingots in this collection give evidence of earlier silver mining processes. With the exception of a few small lumps or chunks they are all in the shape of irregular disks, small-to-large in size, that were poured out into shallow sand molds, rather like pouring pancakes, and allowed to cool into crude discoid forms. This was probably a simple enough way to prepare them for stacking, storage, and transportation prior to shipment. The stamped marks on the surfaces are the most challenging and tantalizing features they present, for very little has been published about them. The most easily recognized, most frequently found mark has to be an official stamp because it bears elements found on the coins: the Pillars of Hercules, PLVS VLTRA (or some abbreviation of it), the Mexico City *M,* and in addition, a bearded profile head bearing a strong resemblance to portraits of Charles V. Two other stamps represent the Tasco and Guachinango mines or mining districts. Scallop shells in two different styles may represent St. James, patron saint of Spain, whose symbol this was. If so, the stamps probably would indicate another official mark, especially in the situations where it has been discovered. The other possible official stamp may be the crowned LVIS, as Luis Rodríguez at one time was official assayer of silver bullion. The remainder of the marks are open to even more question and speculation. The chances are they stand for either assayers or individual owners. The single gold ingot tells little except that it is of 15¾ carats in value, was stamped with Roman numeral VIII—probably a tally mark—and bears near each end, the stamp:

A
VS

This quite possibly is the abbreviation for the Latin AUREUS meaning gold, and may also represent the assayer's mark. It could be inferred that this is number 8 of a series of similar ingots, originally poured into the same shallow, open mold, and eventually cut into regular lengths, all numbered in sequence. Since this is an end piece, there must have been seven others.

The exquisite gold crucifix and the little silver thimble stir our imaginations, for these are intimate objects that help to bridge the gap between those who treasured them so many years ago and those of us who handle them now. We wonder whose meal was served on the pewter plates from England, and what happened to the rest of the spoons and other tableware they must have used.

We can conjure up only part of their story now, but as we look at these relics we can almost hear the wind in the sails and the creaking of the rigging, the shouts of the crew and the chants of the ship's boys. Fragmented as it is, the collection is unique in America. Had scientific archeological techniques been employed during the excavation, its significance would have been increased immeasurably. We can only hope that in time the remainder of the sunken Spanish legacy will be properly recovered, for it seems certain to reveal absorbing details of everyday life beyond our capacity to visualize or even imagine today.

Appendix

Tabular Data:

1
Wrought Iron Spikes, Nails, Pins
Page 161

2
Small Lead Weights
Page 165

3
Chambered Wrought Iron Breechblocks for
Hooped-Barrel Guns
Page 166

4
Chambered Breechblocks (Beer Stein Style)
for *Versos* or Other Swivel Guns
Page 169

5
Wrought Iron Breech Wedges
Page 172

6
Ammunition
Page 173

7
Silver Bullion
Page 177

TABLE 1

WROUGHT IRON SPIKES, NAILS, PINS

Measurements maximum after processing, in centimeters
*Illustrated in Fig. 24, identified by italicized letter under Cat. No.
†Previously described as part of chain assemblage; Fig. No., if any, given under Remarks

Cat. No.	Length	Shank Diam. or Width	Shank X-Section	Head Diam. or Width	Remarks
83-1	35.5, incomplete	2.6	Round	------	Spike or pin with head missing, one end flat.
83-2	30.0	2.5	Round	------	Spike or pin with head missing, both ends flat.
95	9.0, incomplete	1.4	Square	2.1	Fragmentary spike.
107-1* *G*	33.5, incomplete	4.2	Round	9.3	Large pin or spike with very large head, shank broken.
174	6.1, incomplete	2.0	Round	3.2, incomplete	Fragmentary spike or pin, only a piece of head and small shank section remaining.
201	11.1, incomplete	1.8	Round	------	Fragmentary spike or pin, head missing.
C217a	5.2, incomplete	1.4	Round	3.0	Cast of fragmentary pin or spike, made from mold in encrustation.
234-4a	50.0	2.6	Round	6.0	Through-pin with 1 cm. square hole at distal end for key; fibrous gasket material found under head.
314-1a†	62.0	3.5	Round	6.8	Eye-pin with 3.4 x 4 cm. oval space in head, attached to chain; broken rectangular slot at distal end for insertion of key. Pin is almost complete.
315-1†	32.0	2.5	Round	6.0	Eye-pin with 4 washers and key in slot at distal end. Part of chain assemblage Fig. 22A.
318-2	32.5, incomplete	2.5	Round	6.0	Pin or spike.
320-6	22.0, incomplete	2.0	Not determined	------	Frag. section of pin or spike shank, badly corroded.
323-2	14.0, incomplete	1.2	Not determined	------	Frag. section of pin or spike shank, badly corroded.
333	17.0, incomplete	2.4	Not determined	------	Frag. section of pin or spike shank, badly corroded.
479	3.6, incomplete	1.2	Square	------	Spike or nail fragment, head broken, found lying across and still adhering to a piece of lead sheeting perforated by a small square nail hole.

Continued on next page.

Cat. No.	Length	Shank Diam. or Width	Shank X-Section	Head Diam. or Width	Remarks
530* K	16.5	1.0	Square	3.0	Planking spike, badly corroded.
531* L	13.0	2.4	Square	2.7	Planking spike, badly corroded.
575	16.0	1.0	Square	------	Planking spike, badly corroded, head broken.
588	15.0, incomplete	1.2	Square	2.6	Planking spike, curved a little, head twisted and bent over.
602* M	9.5	1.0	Square	2.3	Planking spike, badly corroded.
603	10.0, incomplete	2.0	Round	------	Spike or pin, shank fragment, head missing.
1305* D	60.0	2.5	Round	7.0	Eye-pin, heart-shaped "eye" slot at distal end for wedge or key. Piece almost complete.
1472-4* N	8.5	1.5	Prob. square	2.6	Badly corroded spike.
1476-4	29.0	2.5	Round	5.6	Spike or pin, fibrous material found beneath head.
1477	Not measured	1.8	Round	4.9	Fragment of spike or pin, with only the head & a small section of shank remaining. Badly oxidized but treated to retain shape.
1507	31.0	2.4	Round	5.5	Through-pin with small pin inserted in hole at broken distal end. The small pin may not be of iron.
1520* F	43.2	3.0	Round	5.7	Through-pin with slot at distal end for key.
1521* P	59.0	3.1	Round	5.4	Large spike or pin; "wraparound" construction of head is obvious.
1522a* B	57.0	4.2	Round	8.7	Large through-pin; frag. of oakum gasket material found under head.
1523* E	53.5	3.2	Round	6.0	Large through-pin.
1524	44.0, incomplete	3.0	Prob. round	4.9	Spike or pin, badly corroded.
1525* J	20.5	1.5	Square	3.1, incomplete	Spike, head broken.
1526	33.5, incomplete	3.2	Round	------	Spike or pin, head missing.
1527	47.5	3.0	Round	5.1	Spike or pin.

Continued on next page.

Cat. No.	Length	Shank Diam. or Width	Shank X-Section	Head Diam. or Width	Remarks
1528-1	36.0	3.0	Round	7.75	Spike or pin with badly corroded shank; "wraparound" construction quite evident; wood and rope frags. found under head.
1529-1* H	36.0	3.4	Round	6.5	Through-pin, slot at distal end partly broken.
1530	37.0	3.5	Round	5.4	Spike or pin.
1531* C	30.0	3.0	Round	8.2	Spike or pin, badly corroded, trace of fiber beneath head; "wraparound" construction of head is evident.
1532	38.5	3.2	Round	5.4	Spike or pin.
1533* A	68.0	3.5	Round	8.5	Large through-pin, somewhat curved slot for key partly broken.
1534	28.0	2.5	Round	4.7	Through-pin, corroded; slot for key.
1535	34.0	2.5	Round	*ca.* 4.0, incomplete	Spike or pin, badly corroded, head broken.
1536* I	19.5	1.9	Round	4.0	Spike or pin, badly corroded; "wraparound" construction of head is evident.
1537	12.7, incomplete	1.7	Not determined	Not measured	Spike or pin badly corroded, head broken.
1538	18.2	1.3	Square	2.4	Spike, corroded.
1539	15.8	1.8	Square	2.9	Spike, corroded.
1540	8.6	0.8	Square	2.2	Planking nail or spike, corroded.
1541	10.2	1.1	Square	------	Planking nail or spike, corroded, head broken off.
1542	7.4, incomplete	1.3	Square	3.0	Planking nail or spike, corroded; head irregular in shape.
1543	6.2	1.0	Rectangular	1.3	Planking nail or spike, corroded; head irregular in shape.
1544	11.4, incomplete	1.0	Square	------	Spike, corroded, head broken off.
1545* O	7.6, incomplete	1.0	Rectangular	1.8	Planking nail or spike, corroded; head broken.
1580+	46.0	2.5	Round	3.7	Eye-pin, part of chain assemblage Fig. 23.
1585	4.6, incomplete	1.0	Square	2.5	Spike fragment, badly corroded.
1589	15.0, incomplete	2.6	Round	5.4	Spike or pin, shank broken; "wraparound" construction of head evident.

Continued on next page.

Cat. No.	Length	Shank Diam. or Width	Shank X- Section	Head Diam. or Width	Remarks
1590	18.6, incomplete	2.5	Round	------	Spike or pin shank fragment, head missing.
1603	17.7, incomplete	2.0	Round	------	Spike or pin shank frag., badly corroded; head missing.
1604	15.2, incomplete	2.7	Round	------	Spike or pin shank frag., head missing.
1605	20.6	3.0	Round	------	Spike or pin shank frag., badly corroded; head missing.
1606	15.3, incomplete	1.8	Round	------	Spike or pin shank frag., badly corroded; head missing.
1609	Not determined	1.3	Not determined	------	Shank frag. of spike or planking nail penetrating what appear to be remains of 2 wooden planks. Left encrusted for display.
1628-1	5.1, incomplete	2.0	Round	2.4	Spike or pin frag., head broken but may have been square.

TABLE 2

SMALL LEAD WEIGHTS

Measurements maximum in centimeters, weight in grams.
Illustrated in Fig. 26, identified by italicized letter under Cat. No.

Cat. No.	Length	Base Size or Diam.	Cross-Section of Body	Diam. of Suspension hole	Weight	Remarks
1472-3 *A*	7.5	1.7	Rectangular	0.9	649.2	Narrow rectangular top spreads out to bulbous base with small depression in bottom.
1479 *G*	4.3	1.3	Cylindrical	0.4	39.0	Rounded bottom.
1480 *E*	5.9	1.9x 2.1	Rectangular	0.5	109.4	Shallow groove across bottom.
1481 *F*	5.3	1.6	Cylindrical	0.9	57.5	Flat bottom.
1486 *C*	8.2	2.3x 2.7	Rectangular	0.6	254.7	Flat bottom.
1577-8 *J*	5.5	1.6	Cylindrical	0.4	62.8	Cylindrical body below a rectangular top; bottom flat. Vertical striations surround surface below suspension hole. Appears from its regularity to have been mold-made.
1623-2 *H*	2.7	----	Cylindrical	0.6	26.7	Oval, with hole running from one end to other, diam. 1.7 cm. May be net sinker.
1632 *D*	5.25	2.5	Cylindrical	0.45	141.5	Flat bottom.
1634 *B*	8.0	3.6	Cylindrical	0.85	240.55	Vertical mark incised down one side in form of arrow pointing downward with shaft terminating at top with single stroke on right like half an arrow pointing upward. Flat bottom.

TABLE 3

CHAMBERED WROUGHT IRON BREECHBLOCKS FOR HOOPED-BARREL GUNS

(Measurements in centimeters, weight in kilograms)
(All illustrated and identified in Fig. 34)

Cat. No.	Max. Length includ. Neck	Outside Diam. of Tube	Reinforcing Bands	Diam. of Bore	Ring Handles	Weight	Remarks

Type 1. Inner tube of single rolled sheet, lap welded. Outer tube made of touching bands. Additional reinforcing bands spaced down the length of the breechblock.

Cat. No.	Max. Length includ. Neck	Outside Diam. of Tube	Reinforcing Bands	Diam. of Bore	Ring Handles	Weight	Remarks
316-1a	80.5	13.2 behind front reinforcement band ———— 14.6 across front band	7 bands	6.0	2 rings near center, but 1 is incomplete	71.67 (158 lbs.)	Neck extension 4.0 long. Neck diam. 10.5. Extra reinforcing bands at breech & muzzle ends. —1b: fragment from broken left ring handle.
321-1a	55.5	12.4 behind front reinforcement band ———— 15.4 across front band	7 bands	6.0	Originally 2 rings, but both broken off	77.11 (170 lbs.)	Neck extension 4.0 long. Neck diam. 10.5. —1b: left ring fragment. —1c: right ring fragment.
322-1a	77.5	12.95 behind front reinforcement band ———— 15.2 across front band	6 bands	5.9	2 rings at center	70.76 (156 lbs.)	Neck extension 4.0 long. Neck diam. 10.4. Extra reinforcing bands at breech and muzzle ends. Roman numeral VI on front reinforcement band. Charged with gunpowder. —1b: wooden plug found in mouth. —1c: residue of powder from chamber. —1d: fibrous material in touchhole.
325	84.5	13.9 behind front reinforcement band ———— 15.0 across front band	7 bands	6.0	Originally 2 rings at center but both broken off	67.13 (148 lbs.)	Neck extension 3.7 long. Neck diam. 11.3. Good condition.

Continued on next page.

Cat. No.	Max. Length includ. Neck	Outside Diam. of Tube	Reinforcing Bands	Diam. of Bore	Ring Handles	Weight	Remarks
1473-1a	74.1	13.0 behind front reinforcement band _____ 15.1 across front band	7 bands	5.9	Originally 2 rings at center but right ring broken off, now in 2 pieces.	63.50 (140 lbs.)	Neck extension 3.5 long. Neck diam. 9.8. Charged with gunpowder. −1b: fragments of broken ring. −1c: wooden plug found in mouth. −1c: residue of powder from chamber. −1e: remnant of fibrous material in touchhole.
1577-A	76.6	13.2 behind front reinforcement band _____ 14.0 across front band	7 bands	5.65	Originally 2 rings at center but both gone.	52.62 (116 lbs.)	Neck extension 3.5 long. Neck diam. 9.0. Very badly oxidized.
1578-1a	75.4	12.6 behind front reinforcement band	6 bands	5.85	Originally 2 rings at center but left ring broken off.	61.69 (136 lbs.)	Neck extension 3.5 long. Neck diam. 10.0. Charged with gunpowder. −1b: remaining handle ca. 2/3 complete. −1c: wooden plug found −1d: gunpowder residue from chamber.

Type 2. **Inner tube of single rolled sheet, lap welded. Outside this tube, touching reinforcement bands make up an outer sleeve. No additional reinforcing bands. Illustrated in Fig.**

Cat. No.	Max. Length includ. Neck	Outside Diam. of Tube	Reinforcing Bands	Diam. of Bore	Ring Handles	Weight	Remarks
317-1a	55.5	14.1, diam. of sleeve back of shoulder _____ 15.5, diam. back of neck	Sleeve construction, estimated 13 bands	5.2	Originally 2 rings at center but both broken off.	55.34 (122 lbs.)	Neck extension 4.0 long. Neck diam. 10.3. Fibrous material in touchhole was removed but not saved. −1b: right ring handle fragment.

Continued on next page.

Cat. No.	Max. Length includ. Neck	Outside Diam. of Tube	Reinforcing Bands	Diam. of Bore	Ring Handles	Weight	Remarks
1474-1a	54.5	14.2, diam. of sleeve back of shoulder 15.6, diam. back of neck	Sleeve construction, estimated 13 bands	5.27	Originally 2 rings at center but right ring now broken off.	55.34 (122 lbs.)	Neck extension 4.0 long. Neck diam. 10.3.

Type 3. Sleeve construction over lap welded single sheet as above, but has four ring handles. Illustrated in Fig.

Cat. No.	Max. Length includ. Neck	Outside Diam. of Tube	Reinforcing Bands	Diam. of Bore	Ring Handles	Weight	Remarks
1472-1a	73.8	17.9, diam. of sleeve back of neck	Sleeve construction, estimated 18 bands	6.1	4 rings, attached in pairs.	124.74 kg. (275 lbs.)	Neck extension 3.75 long. Neck diam. 12.3. Charged with gunpowder —1b: wooden plug found in mouth. —1c: residue of gunpowder from chamber. —1d: small fragment, only a sliver, from one of the reinforcing rings.

Type 4. Two breechblocks, much smaller in size, constructed differently from each other but evidently intended for the same size gun—possibly for the same gun. Illustrated in Fig.

Cat. No.	Max. Length includ. Neck	Outside Diam. of Tube	Reinforcing Bands	Diam. of Bore	Ring Handles	Weight	Remarks
1301-1	37.7	14.2 across collar	1 band, resembles a collar placed *ca.* 4.3 cm. back of mouth. 2.7 thick; 3.9 wide.	4.4	Only the stub of a *verso*-type beerstein handle.	17.24 (38 lbs.)	Neck extension 4.0 long. Neck diam. 8.7 in front of collar. This breechblock seems to have been modified from a *verso*-type by adding a thick collar back of the mouth in order to make it suitable for a hooped barrel gun.
1579-A	39.2	12.25 across front reinforcement band	3 bands, one at the mouth, one at the breech, & one at the center for ring attachment.	3.12	Possibly had only a single ring, now broken off.	20.87 (46 lbs.)	Neck extension 3.2 long. Neck diam. 6.2. Good condition. —B: ring handle broken from breechblock.

TABLE 4

CHAMBERED BREECHBLOCKS (BEER STEIN STYLE) FOR *VERSOS* OR OTHER SWIVEL GUNS

Measurements in centimeters, weight in kilograms
*Indicates breechblock is illustrated in Fig. 41, identified by italicized letter under Cat. No.
**Indicates breechblock is shown in another illustration; Fig. No. given under Remarks.

Cat. No.	Material	Length (lip not includ.)	Max. Diam. Chamber Bore	Max. Out-side Diam.	Handle	Weight	Remarks

Type 1. Breechblocks of appropriate size for large *versos.*

Cat. No.	Material	Length (lip not includ.)	Max. Diam. Chamber Bore	Max. Out-side Diam.	Handle	Weight	Remarks
318-1	Wrought iron	38.5	4.5	10.5	Missing	18.60	Charged with gunpowder; fair condition.
343-1	Wrought iron	37.5	4.5	10.5	Missing	17.46	Charged with gunpowder. Wooden plug was found in mouth but was in such bad condition it could not be saved. Projection at bottom of breechblock (the lip) served as locking device when breech wedge was in place. −2: sample of gunpowder from chamber.
1463-1	Wrought iron	38.0	4.9	10.5	Missing	18.59	Charged with gunpowder; excellent condition. −2: wooden plug found in mouth. −3: black powder residue from chamber.
1466-1	Wrought iron	39.0	4.5−5.0	11.0	Broken off but stub remains	19.96	Charged with gunpowder. −2: wooden plug found in mouth. −3: mixture of calcium carbonate & black powder from chamber.
1504* B	Wrought iron	33.5	3.7	8.0	Complete	4.70	Badly corroded
1505-1	Wrought iron	35.2	5.0	8.5	Missing	9.7	Charged with gunpowder; badly corroded. −2: gunpowder or iron oxide dust from chamber. −3: small piece of lead found inside chamber.

Continued on next page.

Cat. No.	Material	Length (lip not includ.)	Max. Diam. Chamber Bore	Max. Outside Diam.	Handle	Weight	Remarks
1513-1	Wrought iron	38.5	5.0	10.0	Missing	10.6	Charged with gunpowder; badly oxidized.
							—2: wooden plug found in mouth.
							—3: twisted hemp cordage found inside chamber directly behind wooden plug.
							—4: black powder residue from chamber.

Type 2. **Breechblocks of appropriate size for small *versos*.**

Cat. No.	Material	Length (lip not includ.)	Max. Diam. Chamber Bore	Max. Outside Diam.	Handle	Weight	Remarks
1457-1b **	Wrought iron	22.1	4.6	8.8	Missing	5.345	Found in place in *verso* 1457-1a. (Illustrated with in in Fig. 38.)
							—1e: wooden plug found in mouth.
1458-1b ** D	Wrought iron	22.2	4.0	8.0	Missing	5.920	Charged with gunpowder. Found in place in *verso* 1458-1a. (Illustrated with it in Fig. 39.)
							—1e: wooden plug in place in mouth.
							—1f: black powder residue from chamber.
1468	Wrought iron	24.0	Not measured	6.6	Missing	Not weighed	Completely oxidized, partially exposed and stabilized in encrustation that also contains potsherds & impressions of wooden plank. Kept for display.
1512 * A	Wrought iron	23.5	3.5	10.2	Complete	15.87	Good condition.
1514-1	Wrought iron	20.2	5.2	8.7	Missing	3.5	Charged with gunpowder; badly corroded.
							—2: brown & gray dist from chamber.
1515-A	Wrought iron	21.2	3.5	8.2	Missing	4.4	Charged with gunpowder; badly corroded.
							—B: wooden plug found in mouth.
							—C: twisted hemp found in touchhole.
							—D: black powder residue from chamber.

Continued on next page.

Cat. No.	Material	Length (lip not includ.)	Max. Diam. Chamber Bore	Max. Out-side Diam.	Handle	Weight	Remarks
1516	Wrought iron	19.5	3.3	7.7	Missing	2.85	Deeply corroded, badly damaged, especially at the front end where it has probably lost a few cm.
1517	Wrought iron	23.5	2.5	8.3	Complete	4.6	Fairly good condition.
1518	Wrought iron	22.5	4.0	7.7	Complete, but bad condition	4.7	Very badly corroded, especially around handle.
1519-1 * C	Wrought iron	23.0	4.0	8.0	Probably incomplete	6.1	Charged with gunpowder; fair cond. −2: wooden plug found in mouth.
1611-2 **	Wrought iron	20.9	4.65	8.0	Only a por-tion remains	5.126	Found in place in *verso* 1611-1 Fig. 40 −2" wooden plug found in place in mouth.

Type 3. **Small breechblock for unknown type of swivel gun.**

1416	Brass/bronze	20.15	3.2	6.6	Complete	4.42	Probably cast. Extra projection at bottom may be alloy extruding after casting.

TABLE 5

WROUGHT IRON BREECH WEDGES

(Measurements in centimeters)
Illustrated with guns as indicated

Cat. No.	Length	Width	Thickness	Remarks
1457-1c *	13.0	5.0—2.5	2.3	Corroded, corner of head end broken. Found *in situ* in *verso* 1457-1a (Fig. 38).
1458-1c *	24.6	4.4—2.0	1.9	Good condition. Found *in situ* in *verso* 1458-1a. (Fig. 39).
1477-8	27.3	4.3—1.5	2.5	Poor condition, badly oxidized.
1503	Incomplete 32.5	4.3 at wide end 2.6 at broken tip	Not measured	Badly corroded, broken at narrow end.
1506	22.75	4.1—2.5	2.25	Badly oxidized, poor condition.
1574	31.0	5.5—2.2	2.8	Badly oxidized, poor condition.
1575	36.5	5.0—2.5	2.4	Some corrosion but original surface largely intact and in fairly good condition.
1576	29.0	3.0—1.0	2.2	Badly oxidized, broken along perforation at head end.
1611-4	23.1	4.7—2.0	2.0	Found *in situ* in *verso* cannon 1611-1 (Fig. 40).

TABLE 6

AMMUNITION

All data after processing unless otherwise noted.
*Illustrated in Fig. 42, identified by catalogue number.

Cat. No.	Diam. (cm.)	Material	Weight (grams)	Remarks
36-9	4.30	Lead-covered iron	300.2	Cannon ball, small. Surface rough and broken.
36-10	4.40	Lead-covered iron	280.4	Cannon ball, small. Large breaks in lead cover, iron core badly oxidized.
43-12	4.10	Lead-covered iron	234.0	Cannon ball, small. Iron core about 50% corroded, large breaks in lead cover.
57-6	3.90	Lead	317.0	Cannon ball, small. Surface slightly cracked but otherwise in good condition.
57-7* L	4.00	Lead	260.0	Cannon ball, small. Surface rough and cracked but otherwise in good condition.
57-8* J	3.80	Lead	300.0	Cannon ball, small. Surface unbroken, excellent condition.
57-9	3.80	Lead	309.6	Cannon ball, small. Surface unbroken, excellent condition.
57-10	4.10	Cast iron	82.8	Cannon ball, small. Badly oxidized but shape well preserved. Mold mark visible.
58-3	4.25	Lead-covered iron	318.00	Cannon ball, small. Badly cracked and corroded .
58-4	3.90	Lead	320.00	Cannon ball, small. Small surface break but otherwise in good condition.
58-5	4.00	Lead	312.0	Cannon ball, small. Surface slightly cracked but in fairly good condition.
58-6* K	3.00	Lead	143.0	Not identified, but may be extra small, oddly shaped cannon ball. Roundish, except for a flat bottom with a depressed scar in the center; good condition.
58-7	1.30	Lead	8.4	Possibly case or canister shot or shot for arquebus. Top round, bottom flat, surface smooth.
91	4.40	Lead-covered iron	268.9	Cannon ball, small. Surface rough and broken.
105-1	4.00	Cast iron	Not weighed	Cannon ball, small. Heavily oxidized, still partially encrusted, fractured.
141-2 [See 1457-1d]				
141-3	4.10	Lead-covered iron	282.0	Cannon ball, small. Surface badly cracked and iron core corroded.

Continued on next page.

173

Cat. No.	Diam. (cm.)	Material	Weight (grams)	Remarks
210-6	3.95	Cast iron	103.0	Cannon ball, small. Surface badly cracked and metal almost completely corroded.
210-7	4.05	Lead-covered iron	250.0	Cannon ball, small. Surface badly cracked and iron core corroded.
218* C	5.70	Wrought iron	500.0	Cannon ball, medium size. Surface badly oxidized.
320-5	4.60	Cast iron	144.0	Cannon ball, small. Corroded to point of disintegration, in fragments.
323-3	4.20	Lead-covered iron	254.7	Cannon ball, small. Surface rough and cracked but in fair condition.
323-4	6.00	Cast iron	693.5	Cannon ball, medium. Surface rough and pitted but in fair condition.
344 [See 1612]				
363-1* M	1.20	Lead	8.4	Possibly case or canister shot or shot for arquebus. Round, smooth surface.
579	4.00	Cast iron	190.0	Cannon ball, small. Fairly good condition, mold mark visible.
591-1	5.10	Lead-covered iron	318.4	Cannon ball, medium. Surface rough but only one small break.
604	4.00	Cast iron	Not weighed	Cannon ball, small. Only ½ of the projectile, badly oxidized.
1431	4.30	Lead-covered iron	190.0	Cannon ball, small. Iron core almost gone, surface badly cracked.
1432	4.30	Lead	313.8	Cannon ball, small. Surface rough but in good condition.
1457-1d	4.70	Cast iron	254.7	Cannon ball, small. Removed from bore of *verso* 1457-1a. Fairly good condition.
1457-2	4.30	Lead-covered iron	362.0	Cannon ball, small. A few cracks on surface but otherwise in fair condition (same as 141-2).
1458-1d	3.50 (est.)	Lead-covered iron	Not weighed	Cannon ball, small. Found in bore of *verso* 1458-1a; lead covering torn off the iron core during removal from cannon. Iron now in fragments.
1458-2	4.00	Lead-covered iron	242.0	Cannon ball, small. Surface broken, iron core corroded.
1476-2	4.00	Lead-covered	297-2	Cannon ball, small. Surface rough but only slight break.
1476-3	4.10	Cast iron	198.1	Cannon ball, small. Small hole on surface but otherwise in good condition. Mold and sprue marks visible.
1477-5	4.00	Cast iron	142.0	Cannon ball, small. Badly oxidized, disintegrated after processing, now in fragments.

Continued on next page.

Cat. No.	Diam. (cm.)	Material	Weight (grams)	Remarks
1477-6	7.50	Wrought iron	1216.0	Cannon ball, medium. Surface badly corroded and pitted.
1501* G	8.00	Cast iron	1754.6	Cannon ball, medium. Surface rough and somewhat pitted but in fair condition.
1502* I	4.20	Lead-covered iron	310.0	Cannon ball, small. Large gaps in lead covering, iron core about 10% corroded.
1546	8.00	Wrought iron	1075.5	Cannon ball, medium. Badly corroded, probably fragments have broken off.
1547* B	8.20	Wrought iron	2150.8	Cannon ball, medium. Surface badly corroded.
1548	7.10	Cast iron	1132.0	Cannon ball, medium. Surface somewhat pitted but in fairly good condition. Mold mark visible.
1549	7.40	Cast iron	1188.6	Cannon ball, medium. Surface somewhat pitted but in fair condition. Mold mark visible.
1550	7.10	Wrought iron	1065.0	Cannon ball, medium. Surface rough and pitted, much corroded.
1551	5.50	Wrought iron	388.0	Cannon ball, medium. Surface very rough and pitted, mostly oxide.
1552	7.00	Lead-covered iron	1047.1	Cannon ball, medium. Surface rough and broken.
1553* H	6.10	Lead-covered iron	962.2	Cannon ball, medium. Surface pitted and badly cracked.
1554	Was 10.30	Lead-covered	Was ca. 2390.0	Cannon ball, large. Annealed under the assumption it was solid iron. Lead covering melted; iron core originally squarish in shape, now in fragments.
1555-1	4.00	Cast iron	151.3	Cannon ball, small. Mostly oxide, but retains its shape. Mold mark visible.
1555-2* E	4.00	Cast iron	141.0	Cannon ball, small. Mostly oxide, but retains its shape. Mold and spruc marks visible.
1556	3.90	Cast iron	133.0	Cannon ball, small. Small cracks on surface but otherwise in good condition. Mold and sprue marks visible.
1557	4.20	Lead-covered iron	305.0	Cannon ball, small. Surface rough but only a slight break, in fairly good condition.
1558	4.20	Lead-covered iron	347.0	Cannon ball, small. Surface rough but only one break, in fairly good condition.
1559	4.30	Cast iron	89.2	Cannon ball, small. Mostly oxide but shape and surface well preserved.
1560	3.90	Cast iron	153.0	Cannon ball, small. Excellent condition. Mold and sprue marks visible.
1561	5.20	Cast iron	136.8	Cannon ball, medium. Surface broken, mostly oxide.

Continued on next page.

Cat. No.	Diam. (cm.)	Material	Weight (grams)	Remarks
1562* D	4.90	Wrought iron	248.0	Cannon ball, medium. Surface rough and pitted.
1563	4.10	Lead-covered iron	360.0	Cannon ball, small. Surface rough and broken, iron core badly corroded.
1564	4.30	Lead	290.7	Cannon ball, small. Surface rough with some breaks.
1565	4.30	Lead	246.9	Cannon ball, small. Surface broken, deep cleft.
1566	4.20	Lead	319.3	Cannon ball, small. Surface rough but in good condition.
1567	4.30	Lead	348.5	Cannon ball, small. Surface rough with a few breaks.
1568	4.10	Lead	242.9	Cannon ball, small. Surface rough but in good condition.
1569	4.10	Lead-covered iron	287.0	Cannon ball, small. Surface broken and rough.
1570	4.30	Lead	279.0	Cannon ball, small. Surface rough and pitted.
1571	4.20	Lead-covered iron	356.0	Cannon ball, small. Surface rough but only a few breaks in lead covering.
1572	4.30	Lead-covered iron	364.0	Cannon ball, small. Surface rough with breaks in lead covering.
1573	4.30	Cast iron	141.5	Cannon ball, small. Badly oxidized, was split in half but now glued together.
1577-9	4.20	Lead-covered iron	268.5	Cannon ball, small. Surface rough and pitted.
1611-5	4.10	Lead-covered iron	306.1	Cannon ball, small. Found *in situ* in bore of *verso* 1611-1. Surface rough, but unbroken, in good condition.
1612	9.90	Stone	1289.9	Cannon ball, large. Was broken in 2 pieces when received. Iron oxide stain on surface. Smaller piece was later separated from larger one and mistakenly catalogued 344.
1613	12.50	Stone	2608.2	Cannon ball, large. Barnacle shells adhering to surface.
1614	12.60	Stone	2693.2	Cannon ball, large. Barnacle shells adhering to surface.
1615-1* A	11.80	Stone	2239.7	Cannon ball, large. Barnacle shells adhering to surface.
1615-2	12.20	Stone	2693.2	Cannon ball, large. Barnacle shells adhering to surface.
1623-1	4.10	Cast iron	198.1	Cannon ball, small. In good condition for cast iron. Mold mark visible.
1638-1* F	6.50	Cast iron	805.6	Cannon ball, medium. In excellent condition for cast iron. Mold and sprue marks visible.

TABLE 7

SILVER BULLION

Disks, Fragments, Lumps, and Irregular Pieces
*Indicates illustrated in Fig. 49; italicized letter under Cat. No. identifies piece
**Indicates illustrated in Fig. 63
Number in parentheses indicates number of times stamp appears on piece

Cat. No.	Description	Max. Length & Width or Diam. (cm.)	Thickness (cm.)	Weight (grams)	Marks (by Chart No.)
44-2	Fragment of small disk	5.0 x 4.3	1.30	8.48	None
64-82	Small lump	3.1 x 2.9	0.90	24.60	None
64-83	Small lump	2.5 x 2.5	1.30	14.60	None
65-41	Frag. of small disk	3.1 x 2.1	0.30	8.90	Faint circle, no details
1407	Irreg. shape, frag. of small disk	24.5 x 21.0	0.90	2,859.00	No. 4 (2); No. 5 (3); one rectangle, no details.
1408	Frag. of med. disk	21.1 x 16.0	1.40	1,832.80	No. 4 (1)
1409	Small disk	Diam. 6.3	0.60	99.05	No. 4 (1)
1410** G	Small disk	Diam. 12.0	0.80	449.07	No. 3 (1); No. 4 (1); No. 9 (1)
1411	Small disk	Diam. 10.9	0.70	432.16	No. 4 (1)
1412* F	Small disk	Diam. 11.7	1.40	849.00	Two partial, circular arcs with no details—may not be stamps.
1413	Small disk	Diam. 11.6	0.70	448.65	No. 4 (1)
1414* I	Small disk	Diam. 8.8	0.50	191.50	No. 2 (1)
1415	Frag. of med. disk	25.7 x 13.2	1.10	1,587.20	No. 4 (1)
1417* A	Large disk	Diam. 39.5	1.50	12,183.50	No. 4 (2); No. 5 (1); No. 6 (1); No. 7 (1)
1418* C	Med. disk	Diam. 24.6	0.60	2,433.80	No. 2 (2), 3 rectangles on reverse; no details.
1419	Large disk	Diam. 39.5	2.00	13,131.20	No. 4 (1)
1420	Large disk	Diam. 30.4	1.50	8,366.80	No. 1 (1)
1421* L	Med. size, irreg. shape, probably broken disk	24.8 x 19.4	0.70	1,246.20	No. 4 (1)

Continued on next page.

Cat. No.	Description & Width or Diam. (cm.)	Max. Length (cm.)	Thickness	Weight (grams)	Marks (by Chart No.)
1422	Large disk	Diam. 40.5	1.50	10,061.60	No. 2 (1) and another, circular, very faint, not identified.
1423* D	Med. disk	Diam. 22.5	0.90	2,179.10	No. 4 (2); No. 8 (1)
1424** B	Large disk	Diam. 30.4	1.00	4,867.6	No. 4 (1); No. 10 (1); and two rectangles with no details.
1425* M	Frag. of large disk (No. 1494 is a piece of this disk).	30.2 x 18.5	1.40	3,169.60	None
1426-1* J	Small disk, left encrusted with coin attached, for display	Diam. 16.5	1.50	1,231.05	Not known
1427	Small disk	Diam. 17.0	1.00	1,282.40	No. 3 (2); No. 4 (1); and two rectangles with no details.
1428	Med. disk	Diam. 26.5	1.50	3,647.00	No. 4 (1)
1441	Small irreg. piece	2.95 x 2.1	0.30	12.9	No. 1 (1)
1442	Small disk	Diam. 5.2	0.20	15.30	None
1443-2	Small lump	3.1 x 1.6	0.30	10.10	No. 1 (1)
1443-3	Small lump	2.5 x 2.1	0.40	10.90	No. 1 (1)
1443-4	Frag. of small disk	3.0 x 1.7	0.30	10.70	None—just some striations
1443-5	Frag. of small disk	3.5 x 2.7	0.30	17.90	No. 1 (1)
1443-6	Frag. of small disk	3.8 x 2.1	0.40	20.00	No. 1 (1)
1451	Two frags. broken from same small disk	8.5 x 8.0 (largest one)	0.40	26.10	None
1453-1	Small irreg. piece	4.5 x 2.7	0.70	7.10	No. 1 (1)
1454	Small disk	Diam. 10.7	1.20	80.56	Remnant of circular mark, no details
1455	Small disk	Diam. 13.0	1.20	531.00	Circular mark, no details
1460	Small piece, possibly disk fragment	3.8 x 2.8	0.30	12.00	No. 4 (1)
1461	Frag. of small disk	3.9 x 2.6	0.70	31.90	No. 3 (1), very faint

Continued on next page.

Cat. No.	Description	Max. Length & Width or Diam. (cm.)	Thickness (cm.)	Weight (grams)	Marks (by Chart No.)
1482	Small, irreg. piece, probably disk frag.	9.0 x 5.2	1.80	170.00	None
1483	Frag. of small disk	2.5 x 4.9	0.20	594.30	None
1487	Frag. of small disk; appears to have thumb mark but prob. not intentional	9.6 x 8.4	1.20	270.80	None
1488-1	Frag. of small disk	3.7 x 2.6	0.70	14.70	No. 2 (1)
1488-2	Frag. of small disk	Diam. 1.6	0.25	3.05	None
1488-3	Frag. of small disk	2.3 x 2.0	0.25	10.20	None
1490	Frags. of small disk	Diam. 8.2	0.20	29.20	None
1491	Small piece of silver, possibly disk frag.	4.9 x 4.7	0.70	80.10	None
1494	Small frag. of large disk (part of 1425)	12.0 x 4.5	1.90	3,962.00	None
1499-1	Frag. of small disk	5.2 x 2.0	0.90	18.70	None
1499-2	Small irreg. piece	2.2 x 1.6	0.20	11.70	No. 4 (1), very faint
1631-27	Small piece, broken in two, possibly frags. of small disk	3.1 x 1.4	0.30	8.20	No. 2 (1), very faint
1631-155	Frag. of small disk	3.3 x 1.1	0.80	15.40	None
1639* E	Med. disk, left encrusted for display	Diam. 25.0	1.20	3,441.28 (with encrustation)	Not known

THE AUTHOR

Dorris LaVanture Olds received her B.A. and M.S. degrees in Anthropology from Florida State University at Tallahassee and joined the staff of the Texas Memorial Museum in 1963. She was assigned the task of putting in order the University of Texas at Austin's archeological collections at the Texas Archeological Research Laboratory, Balcones Research Center.

Mrs. Olds developed a special interest in the Spanish Colonial period during the writing of her thesis on the history and archeology of an ancient Spanish fort near Tallahassee. This interest and study provided a valuable background for the investigation of artifacts collected from the sunken ships off the Texas coast.

Mrs. Olds retired in 1975 and lives at Santa Rosa Beach, Florida with her husband, a retired air force officer.

Both the Texas Memorial Museum and the Texas Antiquities Committee publish other materials separately. Each provides a list of publications upon request. Write to the museum at 2400 Trinity Street, Austin, Texas 78705, and the Texas Antiquities Committee at Box 12276, Capitol Station, Austin, Texas 78711.

A previous joint publication of TMM and TAC is *Conservation of Metal Objects from Underwater Sites: A Study in Methods* by D. L. Hamilton (Miscellaneous Papers No. 4 of the TMM and Publication No. 1 of the TAC, May, 1976). Priced at $4.50 plus tax to Texans, the book is available from either agency.

Cover photo by Texas Parks and Wildlife Department
Book design and typesetting by Willena C. Adams
Drawings on pages vii and viii by Hal M. Story
Printing by the University Printing Division

BIBLIOGRAPHY

The bibliography following is by no means comprehensive but includes, along with the references cited, a number of publications that have been particularly helpful, either for information on specific subjects or for general background. For the most part it concentrates on the sixteenth century, its history and artifacts, insofar as they apply directly to the materials in this collection. A glance at the bibliographies included with many of these reference materials will give a good idea of the wealth of information available for some aspects of the collection, and the scarcity for others. A few standard references on the conservation of artifacts have been listed, but those who are especially interested in this field are urged to consult *Conservation of Metal Objects from Underwater Sites: A Study in Methods,* by D. L. Hamilton (1976), and the other specialized references on preservation.

ABELL, SIR WESTCOTT S.
1948   *The Shipwright's Trade.* Cambridge University Press.

> Excellent descriptions of shipbuilding techniques accompany line drawings illustrating details. Traces the history of shipbuilding from Maori dugouts through the age of iron, steam, and steel, but emphasis is on English ships and their makers.

ADAMS, EDGAR H. (arranger)
1929   *Catalogue of the Collection of Julius Guttag.* New York.

> Photographs and descriptions of coins from Mexico, Central and South America, and the West Indies. Mints and kinds of coinage in these areas are also discussed. One of the most comprehensive catalogues of its type, it covers a long time period as well as a wide geographic area, and appears in most bibliographies given for these coins.

AGRICOLA, GEORGIUS
1950   *De Re Metallica.* Hoover edition (edited and translated by Herbert C. and Lou H. Hoover, with annotations). New York: Dover Publications. First published in London by Mining Magazine, 1912.

> Modern reprint and translation of one of the world's great classics on European technologies of the sixteenth century, published in 1556. Copiously illustrated with reproductions of the original woodcuts.

AITCHISON, LESLIE
1960   *A History of Metals.* Two vols, Vol. 2. New York: Interscience Publishers.

> The chapter on the Spanish Century is especially valuable. A number of Agricola's woodcuts are reproduced.

AITON, ARTHUR S. and BENJAMIN W. WHEELER
1931   "The First American Mint," *Hispanic American Historical Review,* Vol. 11, No. 2 (May), pp. 198-215.

> The first thoroughgoing account written in English on the establishment and workings of the Mexico City Mint.

ANDERSON, LAWRENCE
1941   *The Art of the Silversmith in Mexico 1519-1936*. Two vols., Vol. 1. New York: Oxford University Press.

Volume 1 presents the most thorough discussion available on the various stamped markings used on silver bullion and on products of the silversmiths. It is illustrated with a number of marks of various types. Translations of the royal ordinances pertaining to assaying, smelting, taxing, and hallmarking of gold and silver are given. While the author is particularly concerned with hallmarks, the book contains a wealth of information not to be found elsewhere. Volume 2 illustrates and describes the silversmiths' craft work.

ANDERSON, R. G. W.
1972   *The Mariner's Astrolabe*. Catalogue of an exhibition at the Royal Scottish Museum, Edinburgh, 19 August to 29 September, 1972.

Photographs, data, and notes on 12 navigational astrolabes and one planispheric astrolabe are presented. These instruments were on display during the exhibit, all documented with valuable bibliographical information.

ANDERSON, ROMOLA and R. C. ANDERSON
1963   *The Sailing Ship*. New York: W. W. Norton & Co., Inc.

The most recent edition of a small classic first published in 1926 by G. G. Harrap & Co., Ltd., London, then in 1947 by R. M. McBride & Co., New York. Traces the development of European sailing ships to the nineteenth century. The 1963 edition has a few revisions from earlier publications.

ART & ARCHAEOLOGY TECHNICAL ABSTRACTS (Vols. 6-10)
1953-
present New York University for the International Institute for Conservation of Historic and Artistic Works (formerly called IIC Abstracts). London.

Useful guide to conservation techniques.

BAKEWELL, P. J.
1971   *Silver Mining and Society in Colonial Mexico: Zacatecas 1546-1700*. Cambridge Latin American Studies 15. Cambridge University Press.

Concentrates primarily on economic and social issues, but has a good, clear chapter on mining techniques, both smelting and amalgamating. Unfamiliar Spanish mining terms are translated and a helpful glossary is provided.

BARGALLÓ, MODESTO
1955   *La Minería y la Metalurgía en la America Española Durante la Epoca Colonial*. Mexico, D. F.: Fondo de Cultura Económica.

In Spanish. An excellent general survey of the subject including a description of the various mines.

BASS, GEORGE F. (editor)
1972   *A History of Seafaring Based on Underwater Archaeology.*
        London: Thames & Hudson.

        Covers shipping, ships, and archeology from the earliest sea-
        farers in the Mediterranean and the Near East to shipping in
        the Great Lakes.

BEALS, GARY
1966   *Numismatic Terms of Spain and America.* San Diego.

        Very useful in translating and understanding specialized terms;
        especially helpful for those appearing in Spanish-language pub-
        lications.

BLAIR, CLAUDE
1962   *European and American Arms.* London and New York: Bo-
        nanza Books.

        Deals with hand weapons (firearms, swords, etc.), but has a
        good chapter on the crossbow. The time span is A.D. 1100 to
        1850. Select bibliography.

BLAKE, EDITH
1972   "The Astrolabe," *Sail,* Vol. 3, No. 7 (July), pp. 64-65.

        A well illustrated popular article on ancient land astrolabes
        with brief mention of navigational astrolabes.

BRÚ, J. PELLICER I
1971   *El Medio Duro: España Provincias de America e Imperio.*
        Barcelona.

        In Spanish. The most recent general catalogue for Spanish and
        colonial coins, covering the entire period from sixteenth to
        twentieth century. Excellent illustrations. Gives monetary
        evaluations in U. S. currency. Best reference for coins other
        than Mexican.

BURZIO, H. F.
1956,
1958   *Diccionario de la Moneda Hispanoamericano.* Three vols.
        Fondo Historico y Bibliografico José Toribio Medina. Buenos
        Aires: Peuser.

        In Spanish. Comprehensive coverage with a wealth of informa-
        tion that is arranged for easy reference. Volume 3 is the Atlas
        (1956) and consists of the plates illustrating actual coins, but
        many line drawings are found in the two "dictionary" vol-
        umes. An invaluable resource.

BYRNE, RAY
1962   "Mints of the Americas," *Numismatic Scrapbook Magazine,*
        Vol. 27 (Feb.), pp. 310-313.

        The various mints, mint marks, and dates of operation
        are listed.

CASTAÑEDA, CARLOS E.
1936   "The Dominican Martyrs of Texas, 1553-1554," *Our Catholic Heritage in Texas.* Seven vols., Vol. I, Chap. V, pp. 140-156. Austin: Von Boeckmann Jones Co.

Castañeda relates the 1553 wreck story and cites original documents by Padilla, Barcia, and Torquemada on which the account was based.

CHISM, R. E.
1899   "The Mining District of Taxco, State of Guerrero, Mexico," *The Engineering and Mining Journal, Vol. LX, 197-199.*

CHRISTENSEN, B. BRORSON
1970   *The Conservation of Waterlogged Wood in the National Museum of Denmark.* The National Museum of Denmark Studies in Museum Technology, No. 1. Copenhagen.

Describes the very successful techniques used in preserving ancient wood from sunken vessels.

CIPOLLA, CARLO M.
1965   *Guns, Sails, and Empires: Technological Innovation and the Early Phases of European Expansion 1400-1700.* New York: Minerva Press.

A highly valuable resumé of the development of ships and guns and the effect on European exploration and expansion.

CLAUSEN, CARL
1975   Personal communication.

COTTERELL, HOWARD HERSCHEL
1963   *Old Pewter: Its Makers and Marks.* London. Reprint, originally published in 1929.

The authoritative work on old pewter and its makers. Includes an illustrated listing of all the known pewterers' marks dating from 1635. An extremely helpful reference.

DASÍ, TOMÁS
1950   *Estudio de los Reales de a Ocho.* Five vols., Vol. I (1475-1565). Valencia.

In Spanish. Primarily concerned with the 8-reales pieces but provides information on the Santo Domingo mint and its coins under the name *La Española.*

DESTOMBES, MARCEL
1969   "Un astrolabe nautique de la Casa de Contratación, (Séville 1563)," *Revue D'Histoire des Sciences et de leurs Applications,* T. XXII (Jan.-Mar.), pp. 34-64. Vendome: Presses Universitaires de France.

In French. A detailed description of a navigational astrolabe, dated 1563, that was discovered a few years ago in the Conservatoire National des Arts et Metiers, in France. This publication presents the author's comprehensive and scholarly research on early mariners' astrolabes and suggests certain revisions of Waters' 1966 list (below). Particularly valuable are the findings that enabled him to identify this as a Spanish, and an earlier one as a Portuguese, instrument.

1974   Personal communication (letter).

1975   Personal communication (letter).

DI PESO, CHARLES C.
1953   *The Sobaipuri Indians of the Upper San Pedro River Valley, Southeastern Arizona.* Dragoon, Arizona: The Amerind Foundation, Inc., No. 6.

Chapter 6 has excellent descriptions, photographs, and clear line drawings of a wide range of Spanish trade goods from the seventeenth and eighteenth centuries. Although late for the period in which we are interested, most of these items would not have changed much even after 200 years. Included are metals (containers, household cutlery, tools, saddle trappings, weapons, buttons, buckles, personal ornaments, religious paraphernalia, and household items), coins, perishable materials, ceramics, and glass.

DOWMAN, ELIZABETH A.
1970   *Conservation in Field Archaeology.* London: Methuen & Co., Ltd.

A very useful reference, especially for field conservation.

ELLIS, BRUCE T.
1957   "Crossbow Boltheads from Historic Pueblo Sites," *El Palacio*, Vol. 64, Nos. 7-8 (July, August), pp. 209-214.

Description and illustrations of copper crossbow boltheads recovered during archeological investigations in New Mexico.

ENCYCLOPEDIA BRITTANICA
1969

ERICKSEN, EGON, and SVEND THEGEL
1966   *Conservation of Iron Recovered from the Sea.* Tojhusmuseets Skrifter 8. Copenhagen.

While this is primarily concerned with conservation problems encountered with attempts to preserve ancient iron cannon recovered from the seas off Denmark, it is particularly useful for the excellent photographs of the guns and their wooden stocks. The annealing process that is recommended here was subsequently found to be completely unsatisfactory for the preservation of large iron objects.

FFOULKES, CHARLES
1937   *The Gun-Founders of England.* Cambridge University Press.

An important treatise by a renowned authority on the subject. He discusses the history of gun-founding from the fourteenth to the eighteenth century and gives a list of the known English and Continental makers. Of special interest to persons studying the casting of guns are the reproductions of illustrations first presented by Gaspar Monge in *L'Art de Fabriquer les Canons, 1794,* now to be found only in the rare book section of a few libraries.

1967   *The Armourer and His Craft.* New York: Benjamin Blom.

Another excellent reference work by this author. He is concerned here with armor and armorers from the eleventh to the sixteenth century in the manufacture of both plate armor and chain mail. Well illustrated.

DE FONTECHA y SÁNCHEZ, R.
1968   *La Moneda de Vellón y Cobre de la Monarquia Española (1516-1931).* Madrid.

In Spanish. A discussion of the coinage made of copper and of *vellón,* an alloy of copper and silver.

FORBES, R. J.
1956   "Metallurgy," *A History of Technology* (Singer *et al.,* eds.) Five vols., Vol. II, pp. 41-80. New York: Oxford University Press.

FOSCUE, EDWIN JAY
1947   *Taxco, Mexico's Silver City.* Dallas: University Press, Southern Methodist University, American Resort Series No. 2.

Especially written for the tourist or visitor, this small book contains much of interest about the old mining town.

GETTENS, R. J., and B. M. USILTON
1955   *Abstracts of Technical Studies in Art and Archaeology, 1943-1952.* Freer Gallery of Art Occasional Papers, Vol. 2, No. 2.

Covers the period immediately preceding publication of the Art & Archeology Technical Abstracts listed above.

GOGGIN, JOHN M.
1964   "The Spanish Olive Jar," *Indian and Spanish Selected Writings,* pp. 253-298. Coral Gables: University of Miami Press.

The definitive study of these utility vessels, the standard reference.

GRIERSON, PHILIP
1956   "Note on Stamping of Coins and Other Objects," *A History of Technology* (Singer *et al.,* eds.). Four vols., Vol. II, pp. 485-492. New York and London: Oxford Univ. Press.

A clear and readable account of various minting techniques employed in Europe during the Middle Ages. Good illustrations.

HALE, JOHN R.
1966   *Age of Exploration.* New York: Time, Inc.

Good background information, well illustrated.

HALL, A. R.
1969   "Military Technology," *A History of Technology* (Singer

et al., eds.). Vol. III, pp. 347-376 (third edition, first published in 1957). Oxford: Clarendon Press.

A short historical summary of strategy and tactics, weapons and armor, hand-firearms, cannon, fortification, and a resumé of science, technology, and war. Mainly about land warfare, but ships' guns were about the same as those used on land. Includes a helpful list of references and a bibliography for additional reading.

HALSE, EDWARD
1908   *A Dictionary of Spanish and Spanish-American Mining, Metallurgical, and Allied Terms* (to which some Portuguese and Portuguese [Brazilian] terms are added). London: Charles Griffin & Co., Ltd.

A very useful reference in translating technical terms. Includes some Mexican terms also.

HAMILTON, D. L.
1973   "Electrolytic Cleaning and Artifacts Recovered from the Sea," *Science Diving International* (N. C. Flemming, ed.). Proceedings of the 3rd Scientific Symposium of CMAS, pp. 96-104.

Describes in detail the electrolytic cleaning methods employed by the Texas Archeological Research Laboratory, written by the Conservator.

1975   Personal communication.

1976   *Conservation of Metal from Underwater Sites: A Study in Methods.* Texas Memorial Museum Miscellaneous Papers No. 4 & Texas Antiquities Committee Publication No. 1, Austin.

Comprises not only the electrolytic cleaning techniques but others as well. Based on modern, up-to-date technology and laboratory research, this is a very important contribution to conservation studies.

HAMILTON, EARL J.
1929a   "Imports of Gold and Silver into Spain," *Quarterly Journal of Economics.* Vol. XLIII (May), pp. 436-472.

1929b   "Wages and Subsistence on Spanish Treasure Ships, 1503-1660," *The Journal of Political Economy,* Vol. XXXVII, pp. 430-450.

1934   *American Treasure and the Price Revolution in Spain, 1501-1650.* Harvard Economic Studies, Vol. XLIII, May.

Three important articles giving background information on the economics of Spanish treasure shipments.

HARING, CLARENCE HENRY
1964   *Trade and Navigation between Spain and the Indies in the Time of the Hapsburgs.* Second edition. Gloucester, Mass.: Peter Smith. First published in 1918 by Harvard University Press.

A comprehensive and authoritative work, a major reference classic. Well documented and indexed. Should be required reading on this period and subject.

HAYSEED, HENRY
1920   "Early Breech-Loading Guns," *The Mariner's Mirror,* Vol. 6, No. 1 (Jan.), pp. 120-121.

Brief notes on the history of breechloading guns with additional comments on the Bridlington gun (see Robinson, G., 1920). The author believes the gun was a "Portugel Base," a light breechloading gun of the long "culverin" type of about 36 to 50 calibers.

HEISS, ALOÏSS
1962   *Descripción General de las Monedas Hispano-Cristianas (Desde la Invasion de los Arabes).* Three vols., Vol. 1 *(Tomo Primero).* Zaragoza. Luis Marquina y Marin, ed.

In Spanish. Another comprehensive reference work on Spanish and Spanish-Colonial coins.

HELD, ROBERT
1957   *The Age of Firearms: A Pictorial History.* New York: Harper & Brothers.

A comprehensive treatise on firearms, mainly hand guns. It covers their development from the first appearance in mid-thirteenth century to the last quarter of the nineteenth. Profusely illustrated by photographs, line drawings, and reproductions of old woodcuts. A valuable resource book.

HERRERA, ADOLFO
1914   *El Duro.* Two vols., Vol. I. Real Academia de la Historia. Madrid.

In Spanish. A classic reference on coins of Spain and the Spanish Empire in Europe and the New World. Focuses for the most part on the 8-reales denomination and coins of equal value but discusses the lesser coins as well.

HIME, HENRY W. L.
1915   *The Origin of Artillery.* London: Longmans, Green and Co.

Especially valuable for the history and evolution of gunpowder, on which the author is a widely recognized authority.

HISTORY NEWS (no editor given)
1952-
present American Association for State and Local History Technical Leaflets. Nashville, Tenn.

A series of short articles on various aspects of conservation and preservation, written by specialists in the different subjects.

HODGES, HENRY
1964   *Artifacts: An Introduction to Primitive Technology.* New York: Frederick A. Praeger.

This covers the whole range of materials that were used, but the chapters on the working of metals and the examination of metal objects are particularly helpful in studying historic artifacts.

HORNER, DAVID
1971   *The Treasure Galleons: Clues to Millions in Sunken Gold and Silver.* New York: Dodd, Mead & Co.

A book for treasure hunters, but much information is offered on the ships and cargoes of the Spanish Treasure fleets. The author made an extensive study of Spanish archival records.

HOSMER, GEORGE L.
1928   *Navigation Then and Now.* Chicago: The American Library Association.

A reading course published for The American Marine Library Association. Pages 10-13 contain a brief explanation of the use of the cross-staff and the mariner's astrolabe.

HUBBARD, CLYDE
1971   Personal communication (letter).

INGERSON, DR. EARL
1971   Personal communication.

LAMB, URSULA
1969   "Science by Litigation: A Cosmographic Feud," *Terrae Incognitae* (The Annals of the Society for the History of Discoveries), Vol. 1, pp. 40-57. N. Israel and Amsterdam.

The fascinating account of litigation that took place in 1544-1555 concerning the nature and control of scientific thought.

LANDSTRÖM, BJÖRN
1961   *The Ship.* London: Allen & Unwin.

Handsome book lavishly illustrating the history of the ship with drawings and paintings, many in color. Covers the period from floating logs to ships of the nuclear age.

1969   *Sailing Ships.* Garden City, N. Y.: Doubleday & Co., Inc.

Another excellent reference work, but restricted to sailing ships.

LAUGHTON, L. G. CARR
1928   "Gunnery, Frigates and the Line of Battle," *The Mariner's Mirror,* Vol. XIV, No. 4 (Oct.), pp. 339-363.

A discussion of the changeover in naval gunnery tactics from boarding and hand-to-hand fighting, using light breechloading guns, to heavy cast iron muzzle-loaders that could sink a ship from afar.

LEVER, DARCY
1955   *The Young Sea Officer's Sheet Anchor or a Key to the Leading of Rigging and to Practical Seamanship.* New York:

Edward W. Sweetman. Reprint of the second edition, London, 1819.

Meticulously detailed descriptions and illustrations of ship rigging and handling. Major reference.

LEWIS, MICHAEL
1936   "The Guns of the *Jesus of Lubeck*," *The Mariner's Mirror*, Vol. XXII, No. 3 (July), pp. 324-325.

Professor Lewis gives an interesting analysis of guns captured by the Spaniards from John Hawkins during a battle near Vera Cruz on September 23, 1568. They include a number of brass and iron pieces typical of the period.

1961   *Armada Guns.* London: George Allen & Unwin Ltd.

The definitive work on English and Spanish armament and tactics during the Armada engagement, noted as a major reference source in almost all bibliographies dealing with sixteenth century armaments. It does not, however, treat of the smaller ships' guns of the *Verso* and *Bombardeta* class.

LINDSAY, MERRILL K.
1968   "Breech Loading Firearms," *The Gun Digest*, 22nd edition, pp. 4-16.

Gives a brief history of the development of breechloading from the mid-thirteenth century small cannons to the 1903 Mauser. Although mainly concerned with hand-held weapons, it has information on the ancient swivel guns as well.

MAHAN, WILLIAM
1967   *Padre Island:Treasure Kingdom of the World.* Waco: Texian Press.

The title indicates the special interest of the author who is a longtime treasure hunter. He traces the adventures of early explorers and publishes the Spanish version (with translation) of the 1553 wreck story as told by one of the survivors to the priest, Padilla.

MANUCY, ALBERT
1949   *Artillery Through The Ages: A Short Illustrated History of Cannon, Emphasizing Types Used in America.* National Park Service Interpretive Series History, No. 3. Washington, D. C., U. S. Government Printing Office.

This is a brief history of cannons and other war machines from the Middle Ages through the nineteenth century. Gunpowder, different types of cannon, projectiles, tools, and the practice of gunnery are discussed and a glossary and selected bibliography are provided. Important reference source.

MARX, ROBERT F.
1968   *The Treasure Fleets of the Spanish Main.* Cleveland: World Publishing Co.

A readable and entertaining description of the rise and decline of Spain's flota system, with emphasis on the round-trip voyage of the *San Francisco* in 1590. The book is well illustrated and includes interesting information on the major ports of the New World. There is no bibliography and the quoted sources are not documented.

1971   *Shipwrecks of the Western Hemisphere 1492-1825.* New York: World Publishing Co.

In addition to a listing of known shipwrecks, the author provides information on the location, identification, and dating of the wrecks and their cargoes along with a selected bibliography. Other sources have better data on the conservation of materials.

MATEU y LLOPIS, FELIPE
1958   *Bibliografía de la Historia Monetaria de España con Suplementos Referentes a los Paises con ella más Relacionados.* Madrid: Fábrica National de Moneda y Timbre.

In Spanish. This compendium is a very valuable research tool on Spanish and Colonial coins because it covers a wide range of information including technology and history of minting in addition to coinage. It lists many articles scattered through little known but world-wide publications. There are some inaccuracies in details, however, so it should be used with care.

MCKEE, ALEXANDER
1969   *History under the Sea.* New York: E. P. Dutton & Co., Inc.

The history and development of underwater archeology, covering activities in England, Europe, the Mediterranean, and the New World. Of special interest is the account of the location and salvage of materials from Henry VIII's ships *Mary Rose* and *Royal George.*

1973   "The Search for King Henry VIII's 'Mary Rose'," *Marine Archaeology* (D. J. Blackman, ed.) pp. 185-198. London: Butterworths.

1974.   *Henry VIII's "Mary Rose."* New York: Stein and Day.

MCNICKLE, A. J. S.
1953   *The Lost Treasure of King Philip IV.* Nassau, Bahamas: The Development Board.

Describes, illustrates, and identifies the marks on a 72-lb. silver bar that was recovered from the sea off the Bahamas in 1950. The author traces the history of the bar's discovery and its origin.

1962   *Spanish Colonial Coins of North America, Mexico Mint: Variations in the Coat-of-Arms as an Aid to Identification.* Sociedad Numismática de México.

Enlarged line drawings of details and variations are helpful for identification, and explanation of symbols used on the coins is very informative. Most useful for coins of the period following the Carlos and Johanna pieces.

MEDINA, JOSÉ TORIBIO
1919   *Las Monedas Coloniales Hispano-Americana.* Santiago de Chile.

This is an early standard reference work by a well known and respected authority, especially helpful because of the section on Santo Domingo coins. Many later writers have republished the illustrations from this book.

MERCER, HENRY C.
1960   *Ancient Carpenter's Tools.* Second edition, first printed in 1929. Doylestown, Pa.: The Bucks County Historical Society.

Excellent illustrations and explanations of the tools of lumbermen, joiners, and cabinetmakers up to the eighteenth century. Because a large proportion of such tools have not changed since Roman times this is a good source of information.

MONGE, G.
1794   *Description de l'art de Fabriquer les Canons.* Paris.

In French. A rare book, listed here as a source that should be checked if available; there is a copy in the Rare Book Section of the Library of Congress. Basically concerned with the casting of cannons, there is said to be also some information about construction of hooped-barrel pieces. Illustrations of casting techniques, as reproduced in other publications, are excellent.

MOODY, J. D.
1952   "Old Naval Gun Carriages," *The Mariner's Mirror,* Vol. 38, No. 4 (Nov.), pp. 301-311.

On the evolution of stages in the growth of naval mountings between the sixteenth and nineteenth centuries, illustrated by line drawings. Brief but useful and detailed article on a seldom recorded subject.

MORISON, SAMUEL ELIOT
1962   *Admiral of the Ocean Sea, a Life of Christopher Columbus.* Two vols., Vol. 1. New York: Time Inc. Reprinted from 1942 edition, Little, Brown & Co.

In this definitive biography the author gives an excellent chapter on navigation practices in Columbus's time.

1971   *The European Discovery of America: The Northern Voyages, A.D. 500-1600.* New York: Oxford University Press.

Although primarily concerned with English and Western European exploration, the noted historian presents valuable information on the development of the ships, techniques, and equipment that made these voyages possible. Especially helpful is the section on navigation.

1974   *The European Discovery of America: The Southern Voyages, A.D. 1492-1616.* New York: Oxford University Press.

Thoroughly researched and entertaining. Describes the voyages of Columbus, Vespucci, Solis, Magellan, Cabot, Drake, and others.

MOTTEN, CLEMENT G.
1950   *Mexican Silver and the Enlightenment.* Philadelphia: University of Pennsylvania Press.

Interesting background history on the role of silver in the establishment of colleges and other centers of cultural activity in New Spain.

MUSEO DEL EJÉRCITO, MADRID, SPAIN
1956   *Catálogo del Museo de Artillería*

In Spanish. A comprehensive listing of the collections in this large army museum.

1968   *Museo del Ejército*

Guide book for the collections in the Army Museum; a small, illustrated publication.

NAISH, G. P. B.
1969   "Ships and Shipbuilding," *A History of Technology* (Singer et al., eds.). Five vols., Vol. 3, third edition, pp. 471-500. Oxford: The Clarendon Press.

A very good, well documented article on the history of shipbuilding.

NESMITH, ROBERT I.
1944   "The Coinage of Charles and Johanna for Spanish Colonial America, 1536-1556," *The Coin Collector's Journal,* Vol. 11, No. 4, pp. 95-98.

A short but valuable article on "The So-called Silver Coins of Santo Domingo." Illustrates and describes the pieces that had been identified at the time written, and discusses some of the problems concerning the mint.

1955   *The Coinage of the First Mint of the Americas at Mexico City 1536-1572.* The American Numismatic Society, Numismatic Notes and Monographs No. 131. New York.

This is the authoritative reference for the Carlos and Johanna coins of Mexico City, the product of Nesmith's 15 years of research. Details of the coins were studied by enlarging photographs 15 times, tracing them, then reducing to actual size for illustration. Highly recommended as the basic source for this coinage.

NEWCOMB, W. W.
1969   "Yo Ho Ho and . . .," *The Mustang,* Newsletter of the Texas Memorial Museum, The University of Texas at Austin, Vol. 11, No. 4 (Aug.-Sept.). Also issued as *Mimeographed Papers* No. 13.

An excellent short compilation of the available information on what was known as the 1553 wreck off Padre Island.

NIELSEN, V.
1941   "Det andet Anholtfund" [The second Anholt find], *Vaaben-historiske aarboger*, Vol. 3b. København: Vaabenhistorisk selskab.

In Danish, with summary in English. Description of five ancient breechloading, wrought iron swivel guns, plus one of cast iron, that were found offshore of Denmark in 1937, along with their stocks and breechblocks. Illustrated.

NORTH, D. J.
1974   "The Astrolabe," *Scientific American*, Vol. 230, No. 1 (Jan.), pp. 96-106.

A beautifully illustrated, detailed description and explanation of the history and usage of the astronomical astrolabe. Includes mention and illustration of the mariner's astrolabe also.

OMAN, CHARLES
1968   *The Golden Age of Hispanic Silver 1400-1665.* London: Her Majesty's Stationery Office. Victoria & Albert Museum.

Illustrates and describes silver art pieces but also reproduces some hallmarks.

PARRY, J. H.
1967   "Transport and Trade Routes," *The Economy of Expanding Europe in the Sixteenth and Seventeenth Centuries.* The Cambridge Economic History of Europe, Vol. IV, pp. 155-219.

The article is concerned with what the Europeans traded back and forth among themselves during this period and of what was sent to and from the American colonies.

1969   *The Age of Reconnaissance: Discovery, Exploration and Settlement 1450-1650.* New York: Praeger Publishers. First published in 1963 by World Pub. Co. and the New American Library Inc., New York, and by J. H. Parry, London.

Highly recommended as a basic reference work. It has an excellent chapter on navigation and its development.

PATTEN, ROD
1974   Personal communication (letter).

PAYNE-GALLWEY, SIR RALPH, Bt.
1958   *The Crossbow: Mediaeval and Modern, Military and Sporting, its Construction, History & Management.* New York: Bramwell House.

The best, most comprehensive volume on the crossbow that is available in English. There is included a "treatise on the balista and catapult of the ancients" and an appendix on the catapult balista, and the Turkish bow.

PEARSON, C.
1972a   "The Preservation of Iron Cannon after 200 Years under the Sea," *Studies in Conservation*, Vol. 17:3, pp. 91-110.

Describes the techniques used in treating the cannons that

Captain Cook jettisoned in 1770 on the Great Barrier Reef off Northwestern Australia.

1972b   *Restoration of Cannon and Other Relics from H.M.B. "Endeavor."* Department of Supply, Australian Defence Scientific Service, Defence Standards Laboratories, Report 508. Australia.

PETERSON, HAROLD L.
1956   *Arms and Armor in Colonial America, 1526-1783.* Harrisburg: The Stackpole Company.

A noted expert presents a general survey of all types of arms and armor for this period excepting heavy ordnance. Book I, The Age of Colonization and Exploration, treats of firearms, ammunition, and equipment, edged weapons, and armor of 1526 to 1688.

1969   *Round Shot and Rammers.* Harrisburg: Stackpole Books.

Deals primarily with artillery and ammunition used by land forces during the seventeenth and eighteenth centuries in the American colonies. The descriptions and numerous line drawings are useful for identification of various weapons and their accessories.

PETERSON, MENDEL L.
1961   "Ordnance Material Recovered from an Early Seventeenth Century Wreck Site," *The Military Collector and Historian,* (Journal of the Company of Military Collectors and Historians), Vol. XIII, No. 3 (Fall), pp. 69-82.

1963   "Additional Notes on Ordnance Materials Recovered from an Early Seventeenth Century Shipwreck Site," *The Military Collector and Historian,* Vol. XV, No. 3 (Fall), pp. 89-90.

Valuable for the excellent photographs and descriptions of *Verso* swivel gun, breechblocks, wedge, and various types of projectiles, iron ring gauges, grenades, and gunstocks. Materials may have come from a Spanish vessel, the *San Pedro,* sunk in 1594.

1967   "Ordnance Materials Recovered from a Late Sixteenth Century Wreck Site in Bermuda," *The Military Collector and Historian,* Vol. XIX, No. 1 (Spring), pp. 1-8.

1969   *History under the Sea: A Handbook for Underwater Exploration.* City of Washington: Smithsonian Institution Press.

Instructions on how to locate and survey sites, excavate and recover materials, preserve recovered artifacts, and identify shipwreck sites. Sections on the condition of materials recovered from the sea and identification of shipwrecks by means of the artifacts are particularly useful. More detailed and up-to-date works are available on excavation and preservation techniques. A helpful selected bibliography is included, and the photographs and drawings are excellent.

1972   "Traders and Privateers across the Atlantic: 1492-1733," *A*

History of Seafaring (George F. Bass, ed.), pp. 256-264.

Describes several wrecks that have recently been salvaged by treasure hunters; these include Spanish and English ships of the late sixteenth to the eighteenth century.

1974   "Exploration of a 16th-century Bahaman Shipwreck," *National Geographic Society Research Reports, 1967 Project*, pp. 231-242. Washington, D. C.

Various wrought iron objects recovered are described and illustrated. They include an anchor, harpoon, keyed-bolt, eyed-bolt, anchor shank, three hooped-barrel guns, and a breech-block of the same type, a swivel gun with breechblock and broken swivel yoke for a gun of the same type. Sketches show artist's reconstruction of ship timbers.

PLENDERLEITH, J. J, and A. E. A. WERNER
1971   *The Conservation of Antiquities and Works of Art: Treatment, Repair, and Restoration.* Second edition, first published in 1956. London: Oxford University.

A recently revised edition of the basic standard reference work on conservation that is found in almost every conservation laboratory.

POLLARD, MAJOR H. B. C.
1930   *A History of Firearms.* Reprint of 1926 edition. London: Geoffrey Bles.

Especially helpful for early hand firearms dating from the latter half of the sixteenth century.

PORTEOUS, JOHN
1973   *Coins.* London: Octobus Books Limited.

A small book that skims the history of coinage from ancient Greek to modern time, using handsome color and black and white photographs. Various aspects of coining are shown in reproductions of early paintings and woodcuts.

POTTER, JOHN S. JR.
1960   *The Treasure Diver's Guide.* Garden City, New York: Doubleday & Co., Inc.

Good tips on locating and identifying wrecks; provides an index of alleged treasure ships, identifying them by name if possible, by nationality and class, and giving the location where wrecked. Some details on gun identification are given but no sources are provided. Matching the gun illustrations with descriptions is awkward for the reader. Useful notes on what to look for in ship identification are included.

PRADEAU, ALBERTO FRANCISCO
1938   *Numismatic History of Mexico from the Pre-Columbian Epoch to 1823.* Los Angeles.

A standard reference work on the coins of Mexico by a recognized authority. Superseded only by a later research by R. L.

Nesmith on the Carlos and Johanna coins of 1536–1572, but of course, covers a much longer period of time.

1972   Personal communication (letter).

PRICE, DEREK J.
1957a   "Precision Instruments: to 1550," *A History of Technology,* (Singer et al., eds.), Vol. III, pp. 583-619. Oxford: The Clarendon Press.

1957b   "The Manufacture of Scientific Instruments," *A History of Technology,* Vol. III, pp. 620-647.

These two articles present a scholarly history of the development of scientific instruments.

PRIETO, CARLOS
1973   *Mining in the New World.* New York: McGraw-Hill Book Co. Earlier edition published in 1969 under the title *La Mineria en el Nuevo Mundo,* by Revista de Occidente. Madrid.

One of the few English-language books on New World mining. A section entitled "Chronological Table of Discovery and the Development of Mining in the New World" is particularly helpful. An extensive bibliography provides a broad spectrum of works that include the history of mining and general studies of Latin American history indicating the influence of mining and the roles of Spain and Portugal in the life and culture of their New World colonies.

PROBERT, ALAN
1969   "Bartolomé de Medina: the Patio Process and the Sixteenth Century Silver Crisis," *Journal of the West,* Vol. VIII, No. 1, (Jan).

Interesting account of the introduction of the patio process that revolutionized silver mining in New Spain and Peru.

RAWLINS, F. I. G., and GARRY THOMSON (editors)
1952-
1967   *Studies in Conservation: Cumulative Index.* The Journal of the International Institute for Conservation of Historic and Artistic Works.

A quick way to locate special articles on conservation techniques. Later abstracts may be found in *Art & Archaeology Technical Abstracts,* cited above.

RAYMOND, WAYTE
1942   "The Coins of the West Indies, Silver and Copper, including the Cut and Counter-stamped Pieces," *Coin Collector,* Vol. 10, p. 1085.

REINFIELD, FRED
1963   *A Catalogue of the World's Most Popular Coins.* Revised edition. New York: Sterling Publishing Company.

Covers a number of kinds of coins, thus helpful in preliminary identification. Gives monetary evaluations.

REVELLO, JOSÉ TORRES
1943   "Merchandise Shipped by the Spaniards to America (1534-1586)," *Hispanic-American Historical Review*, Vol. 23, pp. 773-781.

A detailed account of what was brought over as cargo. Might be useful in ship identification.

REYNIERS, M. Le COLONEL
1956   "Armes Anciennes Découvertes en 1945 dans la Charante," *Mémorial de l'Artillerie Française*, Part 2, pp. 518-545. Paris: Imprimerie National.

In French. A detailed description of two ancient swivel guns found in the River Charente that dated to about 1420. The paper includes notes on the history of breechloading. Illustrated.

ROBINSON, GREGORY
1920   "The Ancient Breech-Loading Gun," *The Mariner's Mirror*, Vol. 6, No. 1 (Jan.), pp. 10-14.

The author describes a wrought iron swivel gun (although with a very short tiller) that was brought up in a net by a fisherman. Labeled a *perrier*, 1550-60, where it was displayed at Bridlington, Robinson believed this to be in error and that the gun could have been considerably older. See also Henry Hayseed's notes, previously cited for the same issue.

SADLER, JERRY
1967   *Treasure Tempest in Texas.* Austin: Texas General Land Office.

The former Texas Land Commissioner's account of events surrounding Platoro's recovery of the Spanish ship wreckage in 1967 and the subsequent activities resulting in the return of the collection to Austin.

SCAIFE, J. VERNER, JR.
1950   "Early Mints of the New World," *The Numismatist*, Vol. LXIII, No. 5, pp. 243-253.

A listing of the mints with dates of operation.

SENTENACH, N.
1905-6 *Revista de Archivas, Bibliotecas y Museos,* Third Series, Vol. XII, pp. 195-220, Vol. XIII, pp. 150-199; Vol. XIV, pp. 329-345.

In Spanish. Articles on Spanish coinage.

SHAW, PHIL
1970   Personal communication.

SINGER, CHARLES, and E. J. HOLMYARD, A. R. HALL, TREVOR WILLIAMS, editors, assisted by Y. PEEL and J. R. PETTY
1954-8 (Vol. III reprinted in 1964, 1969). *A History of Technology.* Five vols. Oxford: Clarendon Press.

This huge compendium contains a treasure house of information on all sorts of matters, contributed by experts from all over the world. A basic reference.

STÉNUIT, ROBERT
1973   *Treasures of the Armada.* New York: E. P. Dutton & Co., Inc.

A popular account of the 1967-1969 excavation of the Spanish Armada ship *Gerona.* Descriptions of the artifacts recovered, among which were two navigational astrolabes, five nautical dividers, three sounding leads, and two possible fragments of hourglasses.

1974   "Early Relics of the VOC Trade from Scotland: The Wreck of the Flute *Lastdragger* lost off Yell, 1653," *The International Journal of Nautical Archaeology and Underwater Exploration,* Vol. 3, No. 2, pp. 213-256.

Describes and illustrates items from the ship's inventory and stores, armament, ammunition, small arms ammunition, navigational instruments, cargo, coins, small change, quicksilver, personal belongings. Scale drawings, photographs, and tables make the article especially useful for artifact identification. The ship was Dutch.

STONE, GEORGE CAMERON
1961   *A Glossary of the Construction, Decoration and Use of Arms and Armor: in All Countries and in All Times together with Some Closely Related Subjects.* New York: Jack Brussel. Second edition, first published in 1934 by Southworth Press.

Brief descriptions, many illustrations, and a comprehensive bibliography in a 694-page tome. Arranged for quick reference.

TAYLOR, E. G. R.
1957a   *The Haven-Finding Art: A History of Navigation from Odysseus to Capt. Cook.* New York: Abelard-Schuman Ltd.

One of the best books available on the subject; interesting and lively reading. Taylor is widely acclaimed as an authority on navigation.

1957b   "Cartography, Survey, and Navigation 1400-1750," *A History of Technology* (Singer et al., eds.), Vol. II, pp. 546-625. Oxof Technology (Singer et al., eds.) Vol. II, pp. 546-625. Oxford: The Clarendon Press.

An excellent presentation of the subject in concise form.

——————, and M. W. RICKEY
1962   *The Geometrical Seaman.* London: Hollis & Carter (for the Institute of Navigation.

An important contribution, concentrated on later periods than the sixteenth century.

THOMSON, G. (ed.)
1963   *Recent Advances in Conservation.* Contributions to the IIC Rome Conference, 1963. London: Butterworths.

Brings the reader up to date as of the time of publication.

TINNISWOOD, J. T.
1945   "Anchors and Accessories 1340-1640," *The Mariner's Mirror*, Vol. 3, No. 2 (April), pp. 84-105.

Useful description of styles of anchors through the centuries.

TRYCKARE, TRE
1963   *The Lore of Ships*. New York: Holt, Rinehart, & Winston.

In this large picture book the elements of ship construction and rigging, equipment, armament, and handling are illustrated. Many color plates; color is used to emphasize specific parts under consideration in separate sections. Descriptions are good and line drawings are unusually clear and easy to follow. Text traces the development of ship construction from ninth century Viking examples to modern steamships and includes sections on navigation and ornamentation as well. Highly recommended reading and studying.

UNESCO (no editor given)
1968   *The Conservation of Cultural Property: with Special Reference to Tropical Conditions*. UNESCO Museum and Monuments Series CI.

An excellent compilation on the subject. Articles are written by specialists; highly recommended as a general reference.

USHER, ABBOT PAYSON
1932   "Spanish Ships and Shipping in the Sixteenth and Seventeenth Centuries," *Facts and Factors in Economic History*, pp. 189 213. Cambridge: Harvard University Press.

In a volume of articles by former students of Edwin Francis Gay is this useful article on the development of Spanish shipbuilding, well documented.

UTBERG, NEIL S.
n.d.   *The Coins of Mexico 1536-1963*. Privately printed.

For the collector rather than the historian or researcher, but the book has good photographs and includes monetary evaluations.

UTRERA, Fr. CIPRIANO DE
1951   *La Moneda Provincial de la Isla Española*. Ciudad Trujillo.

In Spanish. Presents documents concerning the establishment of a mint in Santo Domingo, with a historical introduction and notes by de Utrera.

VAN NOUHEYS, J. W.
1951   "The Anchor," *The Mariner's Mirror*, Vol. XXXVII, Maritime Miscellany Series No. 3, pp. 17-47.

On the very early development of the anchor, illustrated with line drawings.

VIGON, JORGE

1947   *Historia de la Artillería Española.* Three vols., Vol. 1 *(Tomo I)* Consejo Superior de Investigaciones Cientificas, Instituto Jeronimo Zurita, Madrid.

In Spanish. A comprehensive publication on the history of Spanish artillery, based on the collections of the Spanish Army Museum (the Museo del Ejército) in Madrid. Vol. I comprises the earliest armament examples.

VIVES y ESCUDERO, ANTONIO

1899   "Numismática Americana: La Çeca de Santo Domingo," *Revista de Archivos, Bibliotecas y Museos.* Tercera Época, Vol. 3 *(Tomo III)*, pp. 671-675. Madrid.

These are notes and documents concerning the Santo Domingo mint with illustrations of the coins.

VLASOFF, VINCE

1969   *In Search of a Cannon: Aftermath of Capt. Cook's Epic Voyage.* Cairns [Australia] : G. K. Bolton.

Pictorial story of how all six of Captain Cook's cannons were found. They were jettisoned off Northwest Australia when *The Endeavor* struck a reef in 1770. Profusely illustrated with color and black and white photographs and line drawings. The cannons were recovered in 1969 by members of an expedition from the Philadelphia Academy of Natural Sciences.

WATERS, DAVID W.

1958   *The Art of Navigation in England in Elizabethan and Early Stuart Times.* London: Hollis and Carter.

This masterwork details the history of navigation between the fifteenth and eighteenth centuries. Although the major focus in on England and its contribution to the knowledge accumulated by the early Portuguese and Spanish, it traces the progress made by all the Europeans in the application of astronomical theory and instruments to the practical needs of seamen during this period. Generously illustrated with excellent photographs and line drawings. Thirty-two appendices augment the text with original documents and explanatory notes along with an extensive bibliography. One of the most valuable sources for understanding the navigational practices and the instruments used during these centuries of exploration. Fully indexed.

1966   *The Sea-or Mariner's Astrolabe.* Agrupamento de Estudos de Cartografia Antiga, Vol. XV. Seccão de Coimbra. Junta de Investigaçães do Ultramar. Coimbra.

Full descriptions of 19 astrolabes, all of this type that were known at the time of publication. Illustrated by line drawings. The four specific types that the author distinguished have been accepted by all subsequent writers on the subject, although discoveries of additional instruments since then, and further research, have modified the original list to some extent. Much background information and many interesting illustrations. Important reading for those interested in sea-astrolabes.

WEBSTER, Mr. and Mrs. RODERICK S.
1971   Personal communication.

WIGNALL, SIDNEY
1973   "The Armada Shot Controversy," *Marine Archaeology* (D. J. Blackman, ed.), pp. 463-477. London: Butterworths.

The author presents his argument that Spanish ammunition, poorly made and faulty, contributed considerably to the defeat of the Spanish Armada, a contention with which others disagree.

1971-4 Personal communication.

WILLIAMS, LEONARD
1907   *The Arts and Crafts of Older Spain.* Three vols., Vol. 3. London: T. N. Fouhs.

Describes and illustrates a wide variety of Spanish materials from Gothic to Renaissance times, including much detail. Armorer's marks are illustrated dating from fifteenth century.

WOOD, HOWLAND
1914   "The Coinage of the West Indies and the Sou Marque," *American Numismatic Society*, Vol. XLVIII, pp. 89-136.
A useful reference although mostly concerned with coinage later than the sixteenth century.